Digitalization and Asia-Pacific Business Models

Owing to the convergence of multiple cultures coupled with the unprecedented rapid development in the decades since the late 1990s, the value creation and innovation logic of Asia-Pacific business models (BMs) has been constantly altered by cultural heterogeneity. As a result, a more complex and diverse landscape relative to Western developed economy BMs evolved. Moreover, the digitalization has fundamentally changed the way people do business, which has promoted a new wave of BM evolution. Unlike a typical linear mode of innovation driven by market demands in many Western cultures, a large number of entrepreneurial enterprises from the Asia-Pacific with eastern religions and philosophies have tended to adopt unconventional, culturally grounded strategies of value creation and innovation in their BMs. However, it is difficult to find a Western equivalent to the value-creating route that embodies the humanitarian spirit of Confucianism accommodating simultaneously social and economic values to accelerate innovation during internationalization in existing literatures. This book offers a more holistic picture and contemporary interpretation for identifying and characterizing the unorthodox innovation patterns and the perplexing value-creating logic of Asia-Pacific BMs at the crossroads of diverse cultures. It was originally published as a special issue of the *Asia Pacific Business Review.*

This book is supported by the National Natural Science Foundation of China (No. 72272136; 71988101).

Tachia Chin, PhD, is Professor at the School of Management at the Zhejiang University of Technology, Hangzhou, China. Before starting her academic career, she spent more than 12 years working in Singapore and China. She has published more than 100 articles in top English and Chinese journals and has served as leading Guest Editor for several top-tier journals such as *Journal of Knowledge Management*, *Career Development International*, and *Asia Pacific Business Review.*

Chris Rowley is Visiting Fellow at Kellogg College at the University of Oxford, UK, and Visiting Professor at the Graduate School of Education at Tohoku University, Japan, and at the University of Business and International Studies, Switzerland. He is Professor Emeritus at Bayes Business School at the City, University of London, UK. He has over 30 years' experience in university systems in the UK, Europe, and Asia and has won several international grants. He is Editor of the important SCI-rated journal *Asia Pacific Business Review* and has published over 700 articles, books, chapters, and practitioner pieces. He regularly provides interviews, expert comments, and opinion pieces to the international media, including news services, TV, radio, and practitioner outlets.

Shouyang Wang, PhD, is Chair Professor at the School of Economics and Management at the University of the Chinese Academy of Sciences, China. He has published over 40 books and over 450 papers in leading journals. He is Editor of Taylor & Francis book series *Advances in Risk Management* and is/was Editor-in-Chief and Department Editor of over 10 journals including *Information and Management* and Guest Editor for a special issue of the *Asia Pacific Business Review.*

Digitalization and Asia-Pacific Business Models

At the Crossroads of Multiple Cultures, Innovation and Value Creation

Edited by
Tachia Chin, Chris Rowley and Shouyang Wang

Routledge
Taylor & Francis Group
LONDON AND NEW YORK

First published 2023
by Routledge
4 Park Square, Milton Park, Abingdon, Oxon, OX14 4RN

and by Routledge
605 Third Avenue, New York, NY 10158

Routledge is an imprint of the Taylor & Francis Group, an informa business

British Library Cataloguing-in-Publication Data
A catalogue record for this book is available from the British Library

ISBN13: 978-1-032-41633-5 (hbk)
ISBN13: 978-1-032-41634-2 (pbk)
ISBN13: 978-1-003-35901-2 (ebk)

DOI: 10.4324/9781003359012

Typeset in Myriad Pro
by codeMantra

Publisher's Note
The publisher accepts responsibility for any inconsistencies that may have arisen during the conversion of this book from journal articles to book chapters, namely the inclusion of journal terminology.

Contents

Citation Information

The chapters in this book were originally published in the journal *Asia Pacific Business Review*, volume 27, issue 3 (2021). When citing this material, please use the original page numbering for each article, as follows:

Chapter 1
Business models in the Asia-Pacific: dynamic balancing of multiple cultures, innovation and value creation
Tachia Chin, Qianqian Hu, Chris Rowley and Shouyang Wang
Asia Pacific Business Review, volume 27, issue 3 (2021) pp. 331–341

Chapter 2
Confucian business model canvas in the Asia Pacific: a Yin-Yang harmony cognition to value creation and innovation
Tachia Chin, Yi Shi, Chris Rowley and Jianwei Meng
Asia Pacific Business Review, volume 27, issue 3 (2021) pp. 342–358

Chapter 3
User-driven business model innovation: an ethnographic inquiry into Toutiao in the Chinese context
Li-Chung Chang, Xin Wang, Su-Qun Zhang, Chang-Bin Chen, Zhi-Hong Yuan, Xian-Ju Zeng, Jian-Qi Chu and San-Bing Tsai
Asia Pacific Business Review, volume 27, issue 3 (2021) pp. 359–377

Chapter 4
How business model innovation overcomes barriers during manufacturers' servitization transformation: a case study of two top piano manufacturers in China
Qiang Xu, Jinghui Yu, Jianxin Xu, Guangxi Zhang and Canying Liang
Asia Pacific Business Review, volume 27, issue 3 (2021) pp. 378–404

Chapter 5
'It's not like we can charge for everything': revenue models to capture value from smart services in Pacific Asia
Moritz Classen and Thomas Friedli
Asia Pacific Business Review, volume 27, issue 3 (2021) pp. 405–430

Chapter 6

New business models and government features: an example from China
Haixu Bao, Xiao Hu and Lijuan Si
Asia Pacific Business Review, volume 27, issue 3 (2021) pp. 431–443

Chapter 7

The business model and innovation mix in the transition of contract manufacturers in the greater China region
Tung-Fei Tsai-Lin, Hui-Ru Chi and Yuan-Chieh Chang
Asia Pacific Business Review, volume 27, issue 3 (2021) pp. 444–469

Chapter 8

Influencing mechanism of strategic flexibility on corporate performance: the mediating role of business model innovation
Hongjun Xiao, Zhen Yang and Yelin Hu
Asia Pacific Business Review, volume 27, issue 3 (2021) pp. 470–492

Notes on Contributors

Haixu Bao is Associate Professor of Government Governance at the School of Management at Lanzhou University, China. He received his PhD from Lanzhou University, China. His current research focuses on the policy performance.

Li-Chung Chang is Associate Professor at the Department of Management at the University of Electronic Science and Technology of China (UESTC), Zhongshan Institute, Chengdu, China. He is also Academic Leader and Director of the Institute of Contemporary Service Management. He was director and research fellow at Topology Technology, Associate Research Fellow at TIER (Taiwan Institute of Economic Research), and Analyst at TECO Group and OSE (Orient Semiconductor Electronics).

Yuan-Chieh Chang is Professor at the Institute of Technology Management at National Tsing Hua University, Taiwan. Dr Chang serves as Editorial Advisory Board for the journals *Technovation* and *R&D Management* and as Managing Editor of the *Journal of Technology Management* (in Chinese), Taiwan. His current research interests include technology–service convergence, R&D internationalization, service innovation, and academic entrepreneurship.

Chang-Bin Chen is Professor at the Department of Management at the University of Electronic Science and Technology of China (UESTC), Zhongshan Institute, Chengdu, China.

Hui-Ru Chi is Assistant Professor at the Department of Business Management at National United University, Taiwan. Her research interests are organizational innovation, innovation capability, strategy management, and human resource management.

Tachia Chin, PhD, is Professor at the School of Management at the Zhejiang University of Technology, Hangzhou, China. Before starting her academic career, she spent more than 12 years working in Singapore and China. She has published more than 100 articles in top English and Chinese journals and has served as leading Guest Editor for several top-tier journals such as *Journal of Knowledge Management, Career Development International*, and *Asia Pacific Business Review.*

Jian-Qi Chu is Professor at the School of Business and Law at Foshan University, China. He received his PhD from National Sun Yat-sen University, Kaohsiung, Taiwan.

Moritz Classen is Research Associate and Doctoral Candidate at the Institute of Technology Management at the University of St. Gallen, Switzerland, where he leads the Competence Center for Smart Services. His research interests include industrial service strategy, marketing, pricing, and sales.

Thomas Friedli is Professor of Production Management at the University of St. Gallen, Switzerland. His main research interests are in the fields of managing operational excellence, global production networks, and industrial services.

Qianqian Hu is PhD Student at the School of Management at the Zhejiang University of Technology (ZJUT), Hangzhou, China. She focuses on the research of corporate innovation and corporate strategy.

Xiao Hu is PhD Candidate of Cultural Anthropology at the School of Social Sciences at Tsinghua University, Beijing, China.

Yelin Hu is PhD Candidate at the Graduate School at the University of Chinese Academy of Social Sciences, China.

Canying Liang is Postgraduate Student at the School of Management at the Zhejiang University of Technology, Hangzhou, China. Her research interests include strategy management and business model innovation.

Jianwei Meng, PhD, is Professor at the School of Humanities at the University of Chinese Academy of Sciences, China. His research interests include philosophy of science, philosophy of culture, and scientific research management. His recent studies have been published in journals including *Journal of Dialectics of Nature*, *Educational Research*, *Social Science Front*, *Philosophical Trends*, and *Journal of Renmin University of China*.

Chris Rowley is Visiting Fellow at Kellogg College at the University of Oxford, UK, and Visiting Professor at the Graduate School of Education at Tohoku University, Japan, and at the University of Business and International Studies, Switzerland. He is Professor Emeritus at Bayes Business School at the City, University of London, UK. He has over 30 years' experience in university systems in the UK, Europe, and Asia and has won several international grants. He is Editor of the important SCI-rated journal *Asia Pacific Business Review* and has published over 700 articles, books, chapters, and practitioner pieces. He regularly provides interviews, expert comments, and opinion pieces to the international media, including news services, TV, radio, and practitioner outlets.

Yi Shi is PhD Student at the School of Management at Zhejiang University of Technology, Hangzhou, China. Her research interests include strategy management and cross-culture management.

Lijuan Si is Professor at the School of Economics at Lanzhou University, China, and Associate Dean of the Institute of Green Finance at Lanzhou University, China. Her research interests include urban and regional development, resources and environment, and sustainable development.

San-Bing Tsai is Researcher at Regional Green Economy Development Research Center at the School of Business at Wuyi University, Jiangmen, China.

Tung-Fei Tsai-Lin is Assistant Professor at the Department of Business Management at National United University, Taiwan. His research interests cover academic entrepreneurship, innovation system, open innovation, and business strategy and innovation.

Shouyang Wang, PhD, is Chair Professor at the School of Economics and Management at the University of the Chinese Academy of Sciences, China. He has published over 40 books and over 450 papers in leading journals. He is Editor of Taylor & Francis book series *Advances in Risk Management* and is/was Editor-in-Chief and Department Editor of over 10 journals including *Information and Management* and Guest Editor for a special issue of the *Asia Pacific Business Review*.

Xin Wang is Associate Professor at the Institute of Industrial Economics at the Chinese Academy of Social Sciences (CASS), China.

Hongjun Xiao is Professor at the Institute of Industrial Economics at the Chinese Academy of Social Sciences, China. His research interests include technological innovation and business model in digital era.

Jianxin Xu, PhD, is Associate Professor at the School of Management at Hangzhou Dianzi University, China. His research interests include corporate governance in state-owned firms in China, corporate headquarter relocation, and catch-up of high-tech firms in China.

Qiang Xu, PhD, is Professor at the School of Management at the Zhejiang University of Technology, Hangzhou, China. His research interests include strategy and innovation management and business model innovation.

Zhen Yang is PhD Candidate at the School of Economics and Management at Tsinghua University, Beijing, China. His research interests include technological innovation, business model, and corporate social responsibility.

Jinghui Yu is Postgraduate Student at the School of Management at the Zhejiang University of Technology, Hangzhou, China. Her research interests include strategy management and business model innovation.

Zhi-hong Yuan is Lecturer at the Department of Economics and Commerce at the University of Electronic Science and Technology of China (UESTC), Zhongshan Institute, Chengdu, China. He received his PhD and master's degree in Business Administration from National Sun Yat-sen University, Kaohsiung, Taiwan.

Xian-Ju Zeng is Associate Professor at the Department of Business Management at the College of Management at Shenzhen University, China. He received his PhD degree in Management from the School of Management at Xi'an Jiaotong University, China. His research interests include strategy management and corporate governance.

Guangxi Zhang, PhD, is Associate Professor at the School of Management at the Zhejiang University of Technology, Hangzhou, China. Her research interests include social network and innovation management.

Su-Qun Zhang is Research Assistant at the Institute of Contemporary Service Management at the University of Electronic Science and Technology of China (UESTC), Zhongshan Institute, Chengdu, China.

Introduction—Digital dynamics of Asia-Pacific business models: balancing cultures, innovation and value creation

Tachia Chin, Qianqian Hu, Chris Rowley and Shouyang Wang

ABSTRACT

Owing to the convergence of multiple cultures coupled with the unprecedented rapid development in the decades since the late 1990s, the value creation and innovation logic of Asia-Pacific business models (BMs) has been constantly altered by cultural heterogeneity and thus, have evolved into a more complex and diverse landscape relative to Western developed-economy BMs. Given that relevant issues remain under-researched, the main purpose of our collection is to fill this gap. We provide new insights into identifying, exploring and rationalizing the indigenous innovation ecosystems and unorthodox value-creating logic of BMs emerging from the Greater China territory. Moreover, whereas the COVID-19 crisis has fundamentally changed the way people do business along with the lockdowns followed by some forms of de-globalization; it is expected to see a new wave of BM evolution. We, thus, outline three promising and nascent pathways for future efforts departing from a cultural view to explore the value logic of BMs and BM innovation within the Asia-Pacific region in the post-COVID-19 era: (1) the role of culture in BM innovation; (2) new ways of creating the knowledge and managing knowledge iceberg phenomenon and (3) using the 'Bottom of Pyramid' approach to BM innovation for incorporating social goals into value creation logic.

Introduction

> The fault lines between civilizations will be battle lines of the future.
>
> –Huntington (1993)

Notwithstanding the definition of a business model (BM) remains controversial and murky (Chin, Wang, and Rowley 2020a), BM has been widely viewed as a new dimension of innovation (Massa, Tucci, and Afuah 2017), as the most critical kernel of a firm's BM is characterized by how the focal firm leverages its innovation capability to create value for all stakeholder groups, such as customers, suppliers, strategic partners and employees. In this vein, the value creation mechanism of the focal firm can be deemed as the core strategy activated by its innovation impetus for undertaking boundary-spanning activities in its BM (Foss and Saebi 2017; Amit and Zott 2012; Teece 2010). However, due to the convergence of multiple cultures coupled with the unprecedented rapid development for more than two decades since the late 1990s, the value-creating logic and its corresponding innovation practices of Asia-Pacific BMs has been constantly altered by cultural heterogeneity and, thus, have evolved into a more complex and diverse landscape relative to Western developed-economy BMs (Paulet and Rowley 2017).

More specifically, unlike a typical linear mode of innovation (technology push) driven by market demands (market pull), in many advanced economies with a capitalism culture, a large number of entrepreneurial enterprises from the Asia-Pacific with eastern religions and philosophies have tended to adopt unconventional, culturally grounded strategies of value creation and innovation, whose most prominent feature lies in seeking and complying with the ultimate guidance of their governments (Chin et al. 2020a; 2020b; Chin, Jawahar, and Li, 2021). For instance, it is difficult to find a Western equivalent to the value-creating route that embodies the humanitarian spirit of Confucianism accommodating simultaneously social and economic values to accelerate innovation during internationalization by Chinese giant multinational corporations (MNCs) such as China Railway Corporation (CRRC), Haier and Alibaba.

Echoing the foregoing arguments, evidence indicates that the rationale for stimulating context-specific innovation to create value by Asia-Pacific BMs is largely determined by the dynamic and constant interactions between the influence of local bureaucratic systems and the focal firm's entrepreneurship, which, as may easily be imagined, *must* embody indigenous cultural norms, values and beliefs (Chin et al. 2020b). Nevertheless, given the encounter of multiple cultures with plural and even conflicting norms and values, the collision of cultures has often occurred and will continue to occur even more frequently. Such cultural fault lines between countries are expected to trigger severe civilizational conflicts in the future because over 60% of the world's Muslim population now dwell in this area, who were identified as the fundamental source of East-West cultural conflicts by Huntington (1993). As a result, deeper, more comprehensive research is required to probe into how culture shapes innovation and value-creating processes of Asia-Pacific BMs for achieving unique competitive advantages and sustainability in fierce international business competitions.

Although a significant role that culture plays in forming and implementing BMs has been identified (Chin et al. 2020b), the dominant BM research agenda is still mainly driven by western and universalist assumptions, while culture-related issues have not been clearly addressed in the literature. In order to fill this knowledge void, scholars have called for the development of context-specific theories to illuminate how Oriental cultures enhance or constrain value creation and innovation in Asia-Pacific BMs, especially Chinese ones. After all, in spite of having been the world's second largest economy as well as being a vital engine for growth, trade and opportunities in the Asia-Pacific, China as a time-honoured cultural 'melting pot' remains in an initial stage of creating a friendly environment conducive to innovation and building highly sophisticated R&D facilities. It is, thus, imperative to use a more multifaceted, holistic lens to probe into the various mechanisms between cultures and BMs in China (Rowley and Oh 2020a). This explains our primary motivation for this collection with a strong emphasis on China.

It should be noted, with the Covid-19 contagion continuing to unfold onto the second wave, global growth now is projected at −4.4% in 2020 according to the June 2020 *World Economic Outlook Update*. Despite the deep and prolonged wounds to the Asia-Pacific economy caused by the pandemic-induced recession, China seems to have bucked this trend by its faster-than-expected resilience as its economic outlook has been modified to 1.9% for 2020 recently (*World Economy Outlook*, 2020). In this vein, it appears to be particularly meaningful to give our most attention to Chinese BMs for a prospected forecast during this critical period.

Objective and organization

As shown in Figure 1, from 2000 to 2019, the Asia-Pacific region has kept up the contribution about 25–31% of the world's gross domestic product (GDP) annually, of which the contribution from China has risen from 16.75% to 54.72%. It is evident that the Chinese context with its far-reaching Confucianism culture, indeed, provides a fertile setting for challenging orthodoxy in the field of BMs and relevant domains. However, as described above, despite the fact that heterogeneous BMs engrained with Confucian culture emerging from China has attracted increasing attention, most of the existing studies shed light on delineating the distinct constructs of such BMs and their links to strategy, innovation, technology and entrepreneurship but the critical effects of cultural factors are still far from being fully unexplored. In this vein, we see an urgent imperative as well as substantial room for enriching the existing body of knowledge on relevant issues through a cultural lens with more diversified, cross-disciplinary perspectives. Taking to heart the aforementioned concerns, the purpose of this collection is to deepen and refine our understanding of the distinctive characteristics and dynamic nature regarding the underlying logic of value creation and the peculiar indigenous modes of innovation by domestic BMs in China beyond western logic and rationales.

With the support from Editor-in-Chief-Professor Chris Rowley, we organized a symposium to bring forth ideas, issues and concerns related to this topic. Sponsored by Zhejiang University of Technology (ZJUT), on 22 December 2019, a development workshop was hosted at School of Management of ZJUT in Hangzhou, China. From 25 initial abstract submissions, 16 that fitted well with our themes of our SI were selected to provide full papers. After being carefully reviewed, 10 revised full papers were presented at the workshop, while 28 scholars plus 19 PhD students participated in the discussion.

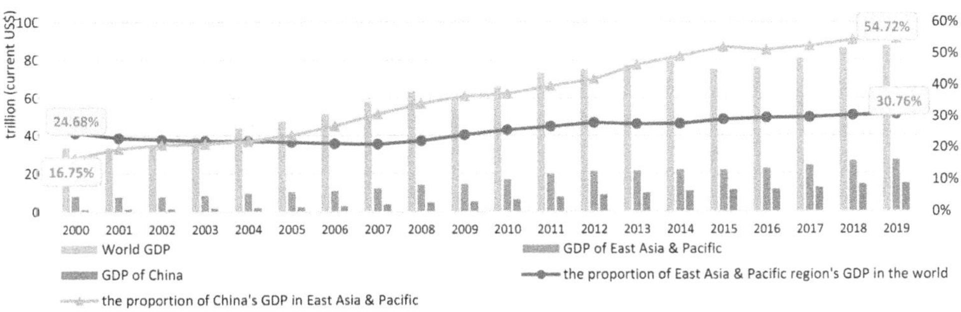

Figure 1. GDP in the world, east Asia & Pacific and China 1.

After a rigorous double-blind peer-review process, we finally selected seven of these papers included in our collection.

As guest editors, we would like to show our sincere gratitude to Professor Chris Rowley again for his marvellous guidance in leading us to complete this collection, and to the outstanding efforts of more than 20 dedicated reviewers. We also wish to thank the authors, those that were published and those submitted; without their precious contributors, this collection would not have been possible.

Overview

The foregoing discussion has elucidated why the rapidly evolving forms of Chinese BMs can be deemed as a representative phenomenon delineating a holistic picture of the dynamic interactions among multiple cultures, innovation and value creation of Asia-Pacific BMs. Following this line of thought, this collection includes seven papers that tap into the complexity and headwinds from the fast-changing government policy, distortionary innovation measures, increasing transformation stress and surging cultural conflicts facing Chinese BMs.

Echoing our themes, the first two contributions consider the contemporary digital economy as their background setting and the dominant role of government as a basic premise, integrating Western theoretical logic with Chinese cultural characteristics to illustrate the distinct value-creating and innovation paths adopted by BMs in China. The first contribution refers to the theoretical reasoning that deems the Oriental Yin-Yang harmony philosophy embodying the core spirit of Confucianism as the counterpart of Western paradox theory, whereby to expound the underlying logic for an indigenous synergistic mode of innovation with three fundamental strategic principles of Confucian cultural values. These are as follows: (1) A tendency to harmonize contradictions in all situations, (2) a preference to adopt an authority-bound, ironic approach and (3) a pursuit for 'temporarily balanced yet continuously changing' and 'morally correct' solutions. Based on this, they further look into the core content – the value creation and innovation modality – of Asia-Pacific BMs and thereby propose a Confucian BM canvas with a newly added, cognitively based building block (i.e. social legitimacy) including three new compositional elements: Institutional enabler; institutional disabler; Confucian social legitimacy, to the architecture of the original BM canvas created by Osterwalder and Pigneur (2010). The idiosyncratic contribution of their work is to manifest and characterize how the intricate, yet relatively abstract, interactions of critical institutional rationalities underpinned by Confucian norms enable or disable the value creation and innovation behaviour of the BM's focal firm.

The second contribution demonstrates how the government as the main actor of innovation propels the speed of BM innovation in China's infrastructure service sector, in which the region of mayor's birth was posited as a manifestation of the socialization experience and native cultural identity of the municipal leader. Using the open data offered by GoFun, a well-known car-sharing company in China, they discovered the mediating effect of local government' service quality between the region of mayor's birth and BM innovation velocity in the car-sharing industry. In addition to providing evidence about the leading role of government in establishing BMs in China, the points of view also imply the Confucian doctrine of patriotism about serving one's hometown, thus adding value to the interdisciplinary research between culture and BMs.

China has held the position of a global production powerhouse for decades and announced a new round of industrial transformation towards 'Made in China 2025', facing the new digital age where the rapid advancement of artificial intelligence (AI) and internet technologies has largely changed the BM landscape in manufacturing industry (Chin and Rowley 2018; Chin et al. 2018). However, China's export manufacturing has experienced a pronounced decline since late 2018 (Chin, Jiao and Jawahar, 2019; Chen, Wang, and Huang, 2019), which is partly attributed to the rising US–China trade war that significantly relates to cross-cultural collisions. It is forecast that manufacturing firms in Greater China will need to devise new BMs or conduct radical BM innovation to tackle forthcoming grand challenges. In consideration of the aforementioned imminent problems necessitating a more comprehensive understanding, we next present three contributions below that investigated in-depth BM-associated issues in the Asia-Pacific manufacturing sector from a synthesizing angle of diverse geographical cultures and different ownership structures, as their sample firms cover the manufacturers registered in Taiwan, China, foreign-invested manufacturers in Great China, Singapore and Korea and domestic Chinese manufacturers, respectively).

First, we present research that involves a long-lasting debate about a frequently used upgrading strategy by traditional manufacturing firms in the Asia-Pacific, namely to transform along the global value chain (GVC) from original equipment manufacturing (OEM) to original design manufacturing (ODM) and ultimately to original brand manufacturing (OBM). Using manufacturers in Taiwan as samples, they adopt a perspective of BM innovation with much emphasis on repositioning the value proposition to delineate how OEM firms reconfigured business activities of their GVCs to complete the BM transition and eventually achieve the OBM status for more economic returns. Their findings shed light on the importance of contract manufacturers to interconnect with a mix of innovative practices encompassing a wide range of production and organizational works to realize new value propositions.

The other two studies focus on discussing a state-of-the-art yet relatively complex approach of BM innovation among manufacturers- The servitization of manufacturing that enables the increase of profits through providing (additional) smart services underpinned by digital technologies to customers rather than increasing sales of main products. Xu et al. (2021) depict the evolutionary trajectories of two Chinese piano manufacturers that relied on key dynamic capabilities to overcome servitization barriers with an ambidexterity strategy balancing innovation and efficiency to fulfil BM innovation. To a certain extent, this research reveals a typical, domestic way Chinese traditional manufacturers chose to contextualize their BMs in adaptation to the new normal of economic growth. Classen and Friedli (2021) used a multiple case study articulating the influence of the oriental cultural values on BM innovation by western Europe-invested manufacturers operating in China (including the Hong Kong region), Japan, Singapore and Korea. More specifically, they address how six western European manufacturers headquartered in Switzerland and Germany took into account local cultural values to formulate non-western, distinct smart service BMs capturing value from customers in different Asia-Pacific countries. Implicitness in this research also indicates the subtle impact of subcultures on the value creation and innovation mechanisms of BMs in this context.

While these three contributions above depart from a cultural perspective linking indigenous value-creating patterns engrained with the Confucian ideology to BM innovation, thus offering fruitful practical implications to the huge number of manufacturing firms in Greater China, the last two contributions enrich the existing knowledge of BM innovation in non-Western contexts from a more strategic view. The first provides empirical evidence examining the mediating effect of BM innovation on the relationship between strategic flexibility and firm performance in the fast-changing digital age riddled with uncertainties, while the next uses an ethnographic method to explore the Toutiao case, discovering several culturally grounded strategic features, particularly the concept of '*Quanzi*' (圈子), in the forming process of a unique user-driven BM innovation in China.

Future research agenda

Overall, the final seven studies in our collection include one conceptual, three empirical and three multiple-case studies. These shed much light on identifying, exploring and rationalizing the indigenous innovation ecosystems and the unorthodox value-creating logic of BMs emerging from the Greater China territory. Although our idea was originally positioned to catalyse BM research in the whole Asia-Pacific, the submissions were mainly from Greater China. Fortunately, this region represents the fastest-growing economic area of Confucian Asia and features several of the world's most astonishing economic booms, beginning from Japan's economic miracle (1950–1990) and South Korea's Han River miracle (1961–1996) and to China's extraordinarily rapid prosperity over the last two decades (about 1994–2013). More specifically, it is not synonymous with, but, instead, can be seen as the heartland of the Asia-Pacific area. As a result, the most remarkable contribution of our collection lies in offering a more holistic picture and fresh interpretations characterizing the perplexing nature of the value creation and innovation logic for BMs immersed in the Confucian business thought.

However, in spite of some insightful theoretical and practical implications, we acknowledge that our collection does not respond to all the grand challenges Asia-Pacific BMs encounter, but only sows the seeds for generating more significant BM research across cultures and disciplines in the Asia-Pacific. As mentioned at the outset, COVID-19 has not only threatened human health and the US economic recovery that is critical to the Asia-Pacific economy but has also fundamentally changed the way people do business along with the lockdowns followed by a trend of some de-globalization in some dimensions (such as people and product but not necessary information and ideas); it is expected to see a new wave of BM evolution in the near future. As such, further investigations are definitely warranted to gain a more comprehensive and profound understanding of the subtle, dynamic balancing of culture, value creation and innovation by Asia-Pacific BMs. Given there exist manifold new research opportunities, below we outline at least three promising and nascent pathways for future efforts departing from a cultural view to explore the value logic of BMs and BM innovation within the Asia-Pacific region in the post-COVID-19 era.

The role of culture in BM innovation: a contingent variable or a driver?

According to the prior literature on BMs, globalization and deregulation coupled with the rapid development of information technologies that facilitates the development of the value-creating logic transcending borders, are the main driving engines for BM innovation (Massa, Tucci, and Afuah 2017; Zott, Amit, and Massa 2011; Fjeldstad and Snow 2018), while the role of culture has not received much attention (Chin et al. 2020a). Nevertheless, since the outbreak of COVID-19, the responses of individuals, organisations and especially the governments have presented salient cultural differences. Such cross-cultural variances in cognition have led to a variety of collisions among countries at an unprecedented grand scale and high speed during the pandemic; the continuously deteriorating China–US political and trade conflict is deemed as one of the most severe events.

Given that multiple cultures converge in the Asia-Pacific region, it was already difficult for BMs to create value in such a context of institutional complexity where the differences in cultural values serve as an invisible substratum justifying the interactions of different institutional and social norms underlying the formation of BMs (Chin et al., 2020b). The COVID-19 pandemic has exacerbated cross-cultural tensions due to different systems of value and ethics in countries. As such, we argue that facing a different context in the world economy, culture may not just play a moderating role in affecting the value logic of BMs as a contingent variable, but a more proactive role as a driving force in propelling BM innovation. Relevant topics at the intersection between cultures and BMs necessitate the use of phenomena-based, cross-disciplinary and more contemporary perspectives, as well as the conduct of a more broadly conceived analysis with consideration of geo-cultural diversity in the future.

New ways of creating knowledge by BMs: managing knowledge iceberg phenomenon

From the knowledge-based view (Kogut and Zander 1992), the focal firm of BMs across cultures can be regarded as an arbitrageur of overarching knowledge sourced in different cultural territories. However, COVID-19 broke the existing context-specific knowledge boundaries for BMs by creating new forms of social networking and connectivity via the Internet among individuals and organisations during the global lockdown – a dimension of enhanced globalisation – which further surfaced some originally hidden yet substantially existent problems based on ethnocentric assumptions. For example, collective cultures make it easier for people to accept compulsory rules enacted by government on wearing face masks and collecting personal data for health codes than those with individualistic cultures; Chinese and Japanese people seemed to feel more comfortable with social distancing than Australians. Due to prominent cognitive variances embedded in people's values, it is not surprising that COVID-19 as a global health emergency appeared to have stimulated a surge of the knowledge iceberg phenomenon that embodies how individuals' cognitive differences perplex the creation of knowledge in cross-cultural contexts (Wang and Chin 2020).

Considering the discussion above, we thus argue that it is imperative to take new, more holistic and sophisticated ways or modes of thinking to make *culture* work for knowledge management (KM) practices in Asia-Pacific BMs, especially when civilizations- defined as the broadest sense of cultural identity by Huntington (1993) – were found to more frequently collide amid the COVID-19 pandemic. Moreover, through the lens of KM, this ongoing pandemic has accelerated the investment in and the building of a modern digital infrastructure, thus promoting the fundamental restructuring and adjustment of KM systems on a large, multi-level scale, ranging from knowledge sharing, transfer, combination to integration, among the focal firms of a BM and its international stakeholders. For instance, given that quite a few Asia-Pacific countries have embraced advanced computer technologies, KM on virtual reality that refers to immersing users in an artificial digital environment is believed to have become a hot topic related to the new round of BM evolution in the Asia-Pacific.

The 'Bottom of Pyramid' approach to BM innovation: incorporating social goals into value creation logic

Related to the two points above, COVID-19 has also brought forth another big question arising from the widening polarization of wealth and (medical) resources between low-income developing countries (e.g. Cambodia and Laos) and high-income economies (e.g. Japan and Singapore) in the Asia-Pacific as well as the world. More specifically, the poor and the middle-class populations of developing nations with institutional and market imperfections are very likely to suffer the most and will thus fall into an acute lack of many valuable resources, particularly medical resources. In this vein, MNCs in wealthy countries can adopt the 'Bottom of Pyramid' (BoP) approach (Ansari, Munir, and Gregg 2012) to earn more profits by providing social goods and services with affordable prices to the customers in the low-income regions who are hungry for basic resources regarding bare necessities of life.

Although the BoP approach seemed to provide market-based solutions to alleviate persistent poverty, scholars have questioned its actual effectiveness (Ansari, Munir, and Gregg 2012). It is because marketing social welfare similar to a utilitarian effort may mainly stimulate non-essential desires of customers rather than meeting primary human needs for well-being, which neither enables the formation of a sustainable BM nor enhances prosperity for the poor (Davidson 2009). The increase in income or consumption should be seen as the means instead of the ends of human flourishing. Implicit in these arguments, therefore, indicates the vital need to advance research towards undertaking BM innovation through the lens of BoP – the focal firm could incorporate social goals of cultivating the capabilities of individuals and organizations from impoverished countries into the value-creating logic of BMs by treating them as business cooperators or strategic partners. Although, COVID-19 may probably exacerbate the humanitarian crisis in the BoP communities, relevant challenges merit more academic attention and should be given their own identity.

Conclusion

While the developed countries have been suffering a structurally weak growth of about 2% since the 2008–2009 global financial crisis, the Asia-Pacific emerging countries, notably, China, India and Vietnam relied on their export-led manufacturing to maintain strong momentum in growth. However, the growing speed has started to soften to about 5% after mid-2019 because of the deepening US–China trade and political tensions. Worse than all, in the first half of 2020, the COVID-19 pandemic further plunged the Asia-

Pacific region into a prolonged recession. Despite the dark cloud, the recent establishment of the Regional Comprehensive Economic Partnership including many Asia-Pacific countries, such as Cambodia, Indonesia, Laos, China, Japan and Singapore, seems to signify a silver lining facilitating more BMs developed in this context.

In summary, the Asia-Pacific region, which can be taken to encompass many countries, has been identified as a critical crossing-point of Eastern and Western cultures, philosophies and religions, the extended uncertainty is likely to trigger egregious civilizational frictions and conflicts in the future. This may further perplex the dynamic balancing of culture, innovation and value creation of BMs, and thereby raise even greater puzzles for scholars, practitioners and policymakers to resolve.

Disclosure statement

No potential conflict of interest was reported by the authors.

Funding

This research was supported by the National Natural Science Foundation of China [No.72032008, No.71772165, No.71988101] and the National Social Science Fund of China (NSFC) [No.19BZX026].

References

Amit, R., and C. Zott. 2012. "Creating Value through Business Model Innovation." *MIT Sloan Management Review* 53 (3): 41–49.

Ansari, S., K. Munir, and T. Gregg. 2012. "Impact at the 'Bottom of the Pyramid': The Role of Social Capital in Capability Development and Community." *Journal of Management Studies* 49 (4): 813–842. doi:10.1111/j.1467-6486.2012.01042.x.

Chen, Q., C. H. Wang, and S. Z. Huang. 2019. "Effects of Organizational Innovation and Technological Innovation Capabilities on Firm Performance: Evidence from Firms in China's Pearl River Delta." *Asia Pacific Business Review* 1–25. doi:10.1080/13602381.2019.1592339.

Chin, T., I. M. Jawahar, and G. Li. 2021. "Development and Validation of a Career Sustainability Scale." *Journal of Career Development* (February). doi:10.1177/0894845321993234.

Chin, T., and C. Rowley. 2018. *The Future of Chinese Manufacturing*. UK: Elsevier.

Chin, T., C. Rowley, G. Redding, and S. Wang. 2018. "Chinese Strategic Thinking on Competitive Conflict: Insights from Yin-Yang Harmony Cognition." *International Journal of Conflict Management* 29 (5): 683–704. doi:10.1108/IJCMA-09-2017-0101.

Chin, T., H. Jiao, and I. M. Jawahar. 2019. "Sustainable Careers and Innovation in Digital Manufacturing." *Career Development International* 24 (5): 397–403. doi:10.1108/CDI-09-2019-331.

Chin, T., S. Wang, and C. Rowley. 2020a. "Polychronic Knowledge Creation in Cross-Border Business Models: A Sea-Like Heuristic Metaphor." *Journal of Knowledge Management* 25: 1–22. ahead-of-print. doi:10.1108/JKM-04-2020-0244.

Chin, T., Shi, Y., Rowley, C., and Meng, J. 2020b. "A Confucian Business Model Canvas in the Asia Pacific: A Yin-Yang Harmony Cognition to Value Creation and Innovation." *Asia Pacific Business Review* 3: 1–17. doi:10.1080/13602381.2020.1795481.

Classen, M., and Friedli, T. 2021. "'It's Not Like We Can Charge for Everything': Revenue Models for Capturing Value from Smart Services in Pacific Asia." *Asia Pacific Business Review*. doi:10.1080/13602381.2021.1894770

Davidson, D. 2009. "Ethical Concerns at the Bottom of the Pyramid: Where CSR Meets BOP." *Journal of International Business Ethics* 2 (1): 22–32.

Fjeldstad, Q. D., and C. C. Snow. 2018. "Business Models and Organization Design." *Long Range Planning* 51: 32–39. doi:10.1016/j.lrp.2017.07.008.

Foss, N. J., and T. Saebi. 2017. "Fifteen Years of Research on Business Model Innovation." *Journal of Management* 43 (1): 200–227. doi:10.1177/0149206316675927.

Huntington, S. 1993. "The Clash of Civilizations?" *Foreign Affairs* 72: 22–49. Summer. doi:10.2307/20045621.

Kogut, B., and U. Zander. 1992. "Knowledge of the Firm, Combinative Capabilities, and the Replication of Technology." *Organization Ence* 3 (3): 383–397. doi:10.1287/orsc.3.3.383.

Massa, L., C. Tucci, and A. Afuah. 2017. "A Critical Assessment of Business Model Research." *Academy of Management Annals* 11 (1): 73–104. doi:10.5465/annals.2014.0072.

Osterwalder, A., and Y. Pigneur. 2010. *Business Model Generation: A Handbook for Visionaries, Game Changers and Challenges*. Hoboken, NJ: John Wiley and Sons.

Paulet, E., and C. Rowley. 2017. *The China Business Model: Originality and Limits*. Chandos Publishing. ISBN-13: 978-0081007501.

Rowley, C., and I. Oh. 2017. *Business Ethics in Asia: Examples in Historical Context*. Abingdon: Routledge.

Rowley, C., and I. Oh. 2020a. *Leadership in East Asia: Globalization, Innovation and Creativity*. Abingdon: Routledge.

Rowley, C., and I. Oh. 2020b. "Trends in Chinese Management and Business: Change, Confucianism, Leadership, and Knowledge & Innovation." *Asia Pacific Business Review* 26 (1): 1–8. doi:10.1080/13602381.2019.1698707.

Teece, D. J. 2010. "Business Models, Business Strategy and Innovation." *Long Range Planning* 43: 172–194. doi:10.1016/j.lrp.2009.07.003.

Wang, S., and T. Chin. 2020. "A Stratified System of Knowledge and Knowledge Icebergs in Cross-cultural Business Models: Synthesizing Ontological and Epistemological Views." *Journal of Intellectual Capital* 26: 4. doi:10.1016/j.intman.2020.100780.

Xu, Q., J. Yu, J. Xu, G. Zhang, and C. Liang. 2021. "How Business Model Innovation Overcomes Barriers during Manufacturers' Servitization Transformation: A Case Study on Two Top Piano Manufacturers in China." *Asia Pacific Business Review*. doi:10.1080/13602381.2021.1894722

Zott, C., R. Amit, and L. Massa. 2011. "The Business Model: Recent Developments and Future Research." *Journal of Management* 37 (4): 1019–1042. doi:10.2139/ssrn.1674384.

Confucian business model canvas in the Asia Pacific: a Yin-Yang harmony cognition

Tachia Chin, Yi Shi, Chris Rowley and Jianwei Meng

ABSTRACT

From an integrative view of paradox and culture, this research aims to elucidate the impact of cultural heterogeneity on the compositional structure of business models (BMs) in the Asia Pacific by focusing on the core BM content about the mechanisms of value creation and innovation. After a systematic review addressing the knowledge void, we refine the widely accepted, renowned model of a BM canvas to propose a new, indigenous *Confucian BM canvas* using the *Yin-Yang harmony cognition* as the underlying rationale for identifying the peculiar, innovative value-creating patterns of BMs in Confucian Asia. Our canvas encompasses three new building blocks: Social Legitimacy, Institutional Enabler, Institutional Disabler, that reflects the idiosyncratic Confucian cultural values and, thereby, can serve as a vital strategic map. Based on the insights distilled from this new canvas, we further suggest a novel 'networked synergistic mode of innovation for value creation' with an example of the electric motor industry in the Asia Pacific region. Theoretical, practical and policy implications are also discussed.

Introduction

The concept of business models (BMs) – which describes and specifies how firms match their product/service offering to a set of existing or potential customers has drawn much attention and caused a variety of debates on its definitions, classifications and archetypes (Fjeldstad and Snow 2018; Paulet and Rowley 2017; Shi, Bigdeli, and Li 2015; Amit and Zott 2012). There is no complete consensus and clarity on BM conceptualization in the literature (Foss and Saebi 2016; Wirtz et al. 2016). At the most general, relatively intuitive level, the mainstream studies follow Drucker's (1954) theory of business that the primary objective of BMs is to create 'value' to demand-side customers or users for economic returns (Zott, Amit, and Massa 2011; Chesbrough 2010; Teece 2010). The core content of a BM, therefore, lies in its unique modes of value creation and innovation led by its focal organization (Massa, Tucci, and Afuah 2017).

Google, Apple, and Amazon, as the renowned giants of information and communication technologies (ICTs) and the internet from the West, are often cited as contemporary emblematic BM, given they, as focal firms, ushered in the new trend of radical innovation in ICT-related industries. However, in recent years, more and more entrepreneurial companies, particularly from the Asian Pacific region, have displayed novel, context-specific patterns of value creation and innovation, in which the lead organization to innovate was the government instead of an enterprise, while the economic revenue was not the main goal of value creation (Paulet and Rowley 2017; Chin et al. 2018, 2019a, 2019b). For instance, with the thriving sales of electric motor scooters in several populous countries like Vietnam, India and China, new business models related to its by-products and spin-offs, such as battery rental/charger services and bike sharing, also quickly flooded their domestic markets (Rowley 2019). This is mainly because their governments enacted policies and provided subsidies to promote the innovative development of the electric motor industrial chain in view of its benefit to energy conservation and environmental protection.

In other words, unlike typical Western/American BMs led by for-profit firms, the underlying logic of value creation in some Asian Pacific BMs led by the government may not be dominated by the commercial market logic about achieving higher financial returns for stakeholders, but by the ultimate vision to fulfil both social and commercial missions. Partly, this also indicates the birth of a new breed of *networked synergistic innovation* in non-Western market economies, which may be first initiated by one or several core giant enterprises under the guidance and patronage of governments, then followed by these firms' further engagement with and spread to various stakeholders through their value chain networks.

Scholars claim that the institutional logic justifying the emergence of the above-mentioned Asian Pacific BMs is actually underpinned by the deep cultural meaning that reflects the mental programming and shared values among people and thereby makes sense of the strategic actions of their organizations in that context (Hofstede and Minkov 2010; Redding 2017; Chin et al. 2018). Evidence also shows that the cultural differences between Eastern and Western thinking often lead to the presence of cognitive paradoxes, which makes Western theory inappropriate to fully explain the indigenous modality of value creation and innovation in non-western BMs (Barkema et al. 2015; Cappelli 2009). Nevertheless, despite the importance of *cultural heterogeneity* being identified and scrutable, its effects on BMs have been under-investigated in the literature, as elaborated by our systematic review below. To fill this knowledge void it seems imperative to employ an integrative view of paradox and culture to gain a deeper, richer understanding of relevant issues.

Confucianism, as emblematic of the oriental culture and Eastern philosophy is believed to exert major influence over individuals' values as well as to underlie the legitimate rationale for BMs to create value in almost every country within the Asian Pacific region (Rowley and Oh 2020, 2016; Meng 2012, 2017). Following on the previous point of view, we, thus, decided to adopt a Yin-Yang harmony cognitive perspective (Chin et al. 2018) that not only characterized the core spirit of Confucian cultural values, but also acts as the counterpart of Western paradox theory (Chin et al. 2018), as our theoretical foundation here.

It should be noted that the BM concept is deemed as a cognitive instrument for actors inside and outside a focal organization (Martins, Rindova., and Greenbaum 2015; Baden-Fuller and Haefliger 2013), whose cognitive structure embodying its key actors' cultural cognition and its leader's mental schema, serves as the primary platform for participants to creating value and innovation. This cognitive structure can be characterized and visualized by its compositional framework (Spieth et al. 2018; Bidmon and Knab 2018;

Osterwalder and Pigneur 2010). We, therefore, focus on exploring the distinct compositional elements or constructs of BMs in the Asia Pacific in this research.

Overall, this research suggests a nuanced interdisciplinary lens to grasping the peculiar, complex nature of value creation and innovation of BMs in the Confucian context. Our main contribution to the literature is to connect the impact of culture into constructing the frame of BMs in the Asia Pacific by proposing a new architecture for a Confucianism business model canvas based on a culturally-grounded paradoxical angle.

Theoretical foundation

Value creation and innovation as core themes of business models

The business model literature has been surging since the early 21st century when the rapid advance and breakthrough of the ICT started to encourage the emergence of new types of e-business ventures and the forming of a novel, internet-based platform economy (Nambisan, Zahra., and Luo 2019; Schaltegger, Ludeke-Freund., and Hansen 2016; Tongur and Engwall 2014; Zott, Amit., and Massa 2011; Chesbrough 2007; Magretta 2002). For instance, we found more than 10,000 publications on the 'business model' topic during 2000 to 2019 when roughly searching famous online databases with the key word of 'business model'. In the same period, the numbers of special issues, edited volumes, and conference sessions dedicated to the topics regarding BMs were also fast growing. This signifies a crucial fact that ICTs have radically reshaped the global business ecosystem via expediting the intangible flows of data, information and knowledge, which enabled the instant worldwide access to more variety of open resources across cultures. In this vein, the scale and scope of the value creation and innovation in BMs requires a fundamental re-thinking transcending traditional borders and sectors in the contemporary digital era.

It should be highlighted that in earlier academic works the lack of conceptual clarity of BMs was a critical challenge as the literature spanned numerous domains, including ICT, innovation, strategy, entrepreneurship and sustainability, resulting in diversified foci and levels, ranging from a very detailed product, business unit, firm to the very aggregated industry level (Bohnsack, Pinkse and Kolk 2014; Osiyevskyy and Dewald 2015; Wirtz et al. 2016; Kajanus et al. 2018).

A lot of idiosyncratic definitions have been adopted by scholars in favour of the purposes of their own studies. However, fortunately, following the new trend to re-evaluate the patterns of value creation and innovation in ICT-driven platforms as well as the corresponding complex, multi-lateral e-markets, researchers have gradually constituted a common ground about the conceptualization of BMs in recent years (Massa, Tucci, and Afuah 2017). More specifically, this consensus mainly resonates with the spirit of Amit and Zott (2001) seminal work that draws on a systematic perspective with particular emphasis on e-business models and innovation; the value logic of BMs mirrored by the above-mentioned systematic view can be articulated by Osterwalder and Pigneur's (2010) BM canvas. We detail the main points below:

(1) The BM indicates a systematic, holistic approach visualizing how an organization collaborating its external partners 'does business' and 'make innovation', and thus has far wider boundaries than those of that of focal organizations;
(2) The *value logic* as the core content of BMs is characterized by the organic combination of the value proposition, creation, delivery and capture mechanisms manifested by the key activities of a focal organization cooperating and transacting with its stakeholders in which value creation comes first;
(3) The BM is a novel, comprehensive, yet abstract, representation as it derives from the cognitive interpretation of the focal organization's top leaders to achieve collective *cognitive understanding* of its stakeholders.

Following the foregoing line of thought, we further argue that the core constituents of BMs lie in the boundary-spanning *value creation* and *innovation* mechanism which differs from that of strategy whose major emphases are the innovations and competitions made against rivals for maximizing *value capture (monetization).*

A systematic review on value creation, innovation, business models, and culture

In the introduction section, the knowledge gap about the influence of culture on the value creation and innovation of BMs has been identified. To more comprehensively clarify this research gap, we decided to carry out a systematic literature review methodology next (Rosado-Serrano, Paul, and Dikova 2018). As noted above, although we limited the search to articles published after 2000 when the concept of BMs created momentum for the first time, there still exists more than 10,000 counts when searching articles and books published with the key words 'business model' in major publisher databases – Emerald Insight, Springer Link, Science Direct, Scopus – and online databases – ISI Web of Science and Google Scholar. However, the number of articles dropped to 304 when searching for 'business model' plus another two key words of 'innovation' and 'value creation'. To ensure the quality of our selection, we further implemented a deliberate filtration process to refine the dataset that constrained the papers to those published in the peer-reviewed journals closely related to the fields of management and economics and included in the approved list of the Social Sciences Citation Index (SSCI). As a result, 176 articles were left. We conducted the final selection process by adding the key word 'culture' and only 2 articles – published in 2017 and 2018 – were identified.

After carefully reading the two articles we found that they both did not discuss the impact of national culture that embodies the differences in mental programming and cognitive thinking of people with different ethnical roots (Redding 2005), but briefly mentioned the influence of an organizational culture that mainly reflects employees' work values (Hofstede and Minkov 2010) in respect to knowledge and strategy management in BM innovation. Larissa, Al-Htaybat., and Hutaibat (2017) outlines a unique BM characterized by disruptive technologies through a single case study of the global logistics company Aramex. Their findings showed that Aramex's organizational culture was deeply penetrated with its new BM design of disruptive technological innovation, thus allowing for a knowledge fusion between old and new technology knowledge. Bashir and Verma (2018) suggested that organizational culture as an important antecedent of BM innovation may indirectly enhance the competitiveness and strategic flexibility of a firm. As a result, the two articles did not fit well with our research focus regarding the heterogeneity of cultural contexts. Considering the recent publication dates and a trivial number of publications including all three key words (culture, value creation, innovation), seems to indicate the prominent knowledge void about overlooking the impact of culture on value creation and innovation of BMs.

Understanding BMs in the Asia Pacific: culture does matter

It has been acknowledged that the natural sciences are deemed as being concerned with the study of external processes, while the cultural and social sciences pertain to the internal and intangible processes of human kind (Burrell and Morgan 1979). Explanations of social affairs, thus, must consider the way in which individuals attach their subjective meaning to situations and to orient their behaviours in concert with their perceptions and cognition of those situations conditioned by their cultural backgrounds. In other words, *culture* encompassing norms, values and socially-constructed realities serves as the underlying basis for rationalizing all humanly-devised constraints, activities and actions, whereby individuals and organizations interpret their surrounding environment and make social interactions so as to gain social identify and legitimacy in a particular context (Redding 2017; Rowley and Oh 2020).

As per Weber's (1964) theory of social action, the institutional fabric within a specific society where BMs emerge and evolve is shaped by the interdependence of the material and ideational components and of their combined role, in which culture serves as an invisible substratum explaining the formation of material wants, the forming of ideational meanings and the interactions of material and ideational logics. Based on this Weberian view, Redding (2005) proposed a business system model, further highlighting how the rationale within culture addresses the economic exchanges and behaviours by organizations in a society. His model consists of three layers: At the top is the realm of the business system with three determinants, ownership, networks and management, which analyses the structures and types of organisations, as well as their co-ordinating activities. The middle realm of institutional order that expresses the formal rules and informal constraints regarding capital allocation, knowledge creation and interpersonal trust includes three determinants, namely, capital, human capital and social capital. At the base is the underlying realm of culture including three determinants, namely, rationale, identity and authority, which provides meanings to all social and economic exchanges happening in the upper layers.

Referring to Redding's (2005) model, obviously 'culture' makes sense of the term of BMs in a specific context that is featured by dynamic, idiosyncratic interplays of local institutional logic and local business/market systems. Hence, apart from engaging in material activities involving complex, synthetic exchanges of resources with strategic partners in BMs, focal firms also need to build a thorough and sophisticated cultural understanding that allows their stakeholders to more accurately interpret the institutional governance, regulations and economic structures of hoe they do business. For example: The pyramid scheme BM adopted by the US companies Amway and Avon in America and Europe sometimes may not be carried out well in a Confucian society as such a BM is deemed inappropriate in the Chinese context. This crucial fact reflects the inherent cognitive paradox embedded in Western and Eastern thinking to the meaning of value creation and innovation in BMs.

Considering the foregoing discussions, we contend that organizations must take into account the role of culture in a particular context when conceiving of BMs to compete there. In the introduction section, we suggested that *cultural heterogeneity* acts as a key source of addressing the ontological and structural discrepancies between BMs in Western market economies and the Asian Pacific region. In the section of theoretical development, after undertaking a deep introspection of BM studies, our systematic review identified the paucity of culturally-grounded literature in the spectrum of BM research. Next, with an attempt to unpack the black box about the linkage of culture with BMs, we bring our focus 'back to basics' – we adopt a culturally-grounded Yin-Yang harmony cognition, proposing a *Confucian BM canvas* that reflects the *social legitimacy* of Confucianism in the Asia Pacific because the Confucian cultural cluster dominates the Asia Pacific region (Rowley and Oh 2016, 2020). Based on the insights distilled from this new *Confucianism BM canvas*, we then identify a distinctive, indigenous value creation pattern, namely the networked synergistic innovation mode to create value for both commercial and social goals in the Asia Pacific context.

***Confucian BM canvas* in the Asia Pacific**

The Yin-Yang harmony cognition: a counterpart of western paradox theory

Analogousness in nature; differences in strategic cognition

The concept of *Yin-Yang harmony* embodies the core thought of *Yijing* that was originally written 3,000 years ago. Then, along with the increasing text annotations and interpretations added by Chinese intellectuals, it was legitimized by the Chinese emperor to be one of the Five Confucian Classics in the Western Han dynasty (202 BCE to 8 AD), whereby it gained critical political significance and has gradually become the most influential philosophical scripture in Confucian Asia (Chin et al. 2018; Lai 2008).

According to *Yijing*, every single thing – either tangible or intangible – possesses both the elements of *Yin* (symbolized by an unbroken line) and *Yang* (symbolized by a broken line) simultaneously. In general, *Yin* represents the soft power, passive energies, and feminine aspects, while *Yang* accounts for the hard strength, positive force and masculine aspects (Lai 2008; Chin 2015). *Yin* and *Yang* are aspectual and relational as correlatives of a larger whole that must be defined in terms of one another. What is *Yin* in one respect may be *Yang* in another. *Yin* will begin to reassert itself when *Yang* rises to its strongest, and *vice versa* (Lloyd 1996). Ontologically and epistemologically, the dialectic nature and philosophical essence of *Yin-Yang* is akin to the Western thinking of paradox (Redding 2017; Putnam, Fairhurst, and Banghar 2016). Both refer to a *persistent contradiction* between two interdependent elements of one thing that exists simultaneously and synergistically over time and their manifestation mode may even look ostensibly fallacious or irrational sometimes.

However, there remains certain striking differences in the strategic cognition between Eastern *Yin-Yang* harmony and Western paradox theories (Lloyd 1996). As indicated by Chin et al. (2018), notwithstanding the conceptual similarity between the term of '*Yin-Yang*' (阴阳) composed of two Chinese characters and English 'paradox', the phrase of *Yin-*

Yang harmony (阴阳和谐) constituted of four Chinese characters alludes to an underlying assumption transcending the meaning of paradox – a distinct Confucianism-oriented '*harmonious cognitive mentality*' in thrall to collective priority and correctness. To a certain extent, it reflects a salient Confucian virtue of 'tolerance' (Redding 2017) that does not equate to docility, but reveals a culturally-grounded strategic mindset to avoid all kinds of direct conflict by making best use of perceived intricate and even subtle inter-relationships and inter-dependences of actors within a system for settling competing demands in a peculiar circumstance of time and space.

Three laws of the Yin-Yang harmony cognition

Cognition refers to the conscious and unconscious activities of knowing that occurs in the context of purposeful activity (Neissuer 1976) and strategic cognition thereby usually involves specific strategic goal orientations. The *Yin-Yang* harmony cognition leads people engrained with Confucian culture to pursue the development of symbiotic co-existence or paragenetic relations with, rather than to take a contentious stance against, competitors or enemies.

In recent years, the *Yin-Yang* harmony cognition has emerged as a viable meta-theorising tool to decipher generic principles in or lay the theoretical ground for understanding varying, complex phenomena in the fields of management and organization research (Redding 2017; Chin et al. 2018). In order to facilitate the application of this Eastern cognitive framework into our study, we synthesize the foregoing discussions and advance to propose *three laws of the Yin-Yang harmony cognition* on the premise that *Yin-Yang* (阴阳) symbolises a 'permanent contradictory complementarity between interdependent and co-evolving elements in everything and can function as two separate variables or a process linkage in any open system':

(1) *Yin-Yang* harmony cognition indicates a persistent mental process to harmonizing contradictions within a specific system/context, which may be physical, abstract or virtual;
(2) Strategically, it prefers the use of nonlinear thinking style and authority-bound, irenic approaches;
(3) Ultimately, it pursues 'temporarily balanced yet continuously changing' as well as 'morally-correct' solutions.

Confucian BM canvas

In summary, the arguments above highlight a few critical points. First and foremost, the notion of BMs visualizes how the key collaborative activities conducted by an organic system consisting of a focal organization and its strategic partners realize economic and social returns where *value creation* and *innovation* come first. Second, the value creation and innovation mechanisms of BMs are deeply embodied by the objective contract relationships of organizations (e.g. strategic partners) coupled with subjective cognitive understanding of individuals working in those organizations. Third, there exist prominent structural discrepancies in BMs between the East and in the West, which may be explained by the underlying cultural cognition of people. Following these lines of logic, the BM construct that varies across cultures can also be viewed as a cognitive schema existing in the mind of the BM leaders –

which rationalizes and drives the collective understanding of value-creating and innovation activities within a specific BM. Hence, it is justifiable to depart from exploring the differences in the ontology of BMs (i.e. the compositional elements) to reasoning the discrepancies of value creation and innovation in BMs between Confucian Asia and the West. Related to this point, it is also appropriate to adopt the *Yin-Yang* harmony cognitive framework that crystallizes the relatively abstract core spirit of Confucian culture to elucidate the differences in the ontology of BMs between Western Christian and Catholic cultures (e.g. the US and UK) and Eastern Confucian cultures in the Asia Pacific (e.g. China, South Korea, Japan and Vietnam).

With an inherent cross-disciplinary nature, the *Yin-Yang* harmony cognition, as illustrated in the three laws above, embraces harmony, hierarchy and moralism; it comprehensively decodes the perceived patrimonial interaction of ruler and ruled in Confucianism (Redding 2017; Chin et al. 2018). More specifically, BMs in Western cultures generally achieve revenue and create economic value mainly through responding to or driving customer demands, while those in Confucian societies may not necessarily conform to market forces, but gain profits via undertaking social networking behaviors to benefit from elaborate institutional structures.

In light of this logic, as far as the ontology of a BM is concerned, it is indispensable to include the compositional elements that reflects the Confucian ideology based on the three laws of the *Yin-Yang* harmony cognition. In other words, the content and structure of such BMs should embody the degree to which they reconcile their work values and management practices with the social norms, beliefs and values of Confucianism, which can be seen as a distinctive manifestation of 'Confucian social legitimacy' (CSL). Extending this line of thought, the compositional elements of BMs in the Confucian Asia Pacific must be able to manifest and legitimate the complex interactions of critical institutional rationalities that *enable* or *disable* their value creation and innovation behaviours, so as to achieve CSL.

Osterwalder and Pigneur (2010) BM canvas that focuses on design and innovation is widely viewed as one of the most well-known and acceptable tools for describing, visualizing and accessing the key constituent elements and their interaction relationships of BMs (Lewandowski 2016; Joyce and Paquin 2016). The basic 12 building blocks of their canvas are classified into four pillars: 1) customer interface (i.e. customer segments, relationships and channels), 2) product and service offerings (i.e. the bundles of products and services catering to the needs of target customers), 3) infrastructure management (key activities, partners and resources), and 4) financial outcomes (revenue and costs). The nine blocks of the four pillars cover the core content of BMs and are thereby able to more explicitly and holistically address the *value logic* of a BM (Massa, Tucci, and Afuah 2017; Abdelkafi and Tauscher 2015). More specifically, as shown in Figure 1, the central block of product and service offerings actually represents the value propositions, the rightmost block and the second on the right articulate the value delivery function, the leftmost block and the next two on the left describe the value creation mechanism, and the two blocks at the bottom address the value capture condition of a BM.

Taking the architecture of this canvas as our basis to incorporate the above-mentioned CSL, we further propose a novel prototype of *Confucian BM Canvas* by adding a new pillar of *social legitimacy* as the underlying rationale for the value logic system that encompasses three new building blocks (i.e. institutional enabler, institutional disabler and Confucian social legitimacy) at the upper end of Osterwalder and Pigneur (2010) framework as above.

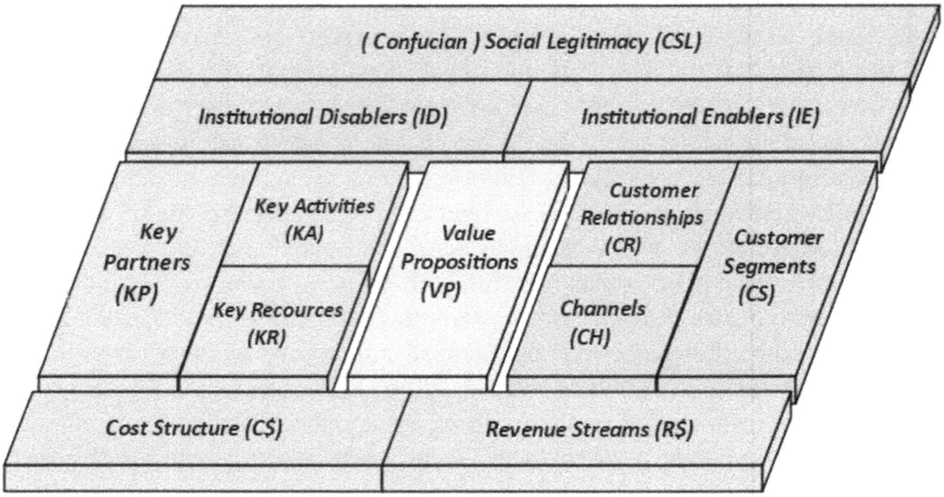

Figure 1. Confucian business model canvas.

For a better understanding, we referred to Osterwalder and Pigneur (2010) definitions of the original nine building blocks and conceptualized the three new building blocks of the new pillar of social legitimacy as per Dowling and Pfeffer (1975)'s seminal work that defines this notion as the degree to which an organization conforms to the prevailing social norms and values; the detailed definitions of the four pillars as well as their associated 12 building blocks are illustrated below.

Social legitimacy pillar- the rationale for the value logic system

Confucian social legitimacy (CSL)

This depicts the degree to which the design, content and governance of the whole BM conform to the social norms, beliefs and values of Confucianism whose mental programming system adheres to the laws of *Yin-Yang* harmony cognition.

Institutional disablers (ID)

This describes the degree to which the humanly devised constraints as social forms of order disable the access to valuable resources and the cooperation of organizations in BMs.

Institutional enablers (IE)

This characterizes the degree to which new knowledge are created in diversified markets across borders whereby the legitimacy pressures impeding innovation and value creation of a BM model can be reduced.

Customer interface pillar- value delivery

Customer segments (CS)

This reflects the various groups of individual and organizational customers, namely the diversified markets a focal organization aims to reach and serve.

Customer relationships (CR)

This addresses the types of relationships and networks a focal organization develop with its customer segments.

Channels (CH)

This characterizes how a focal organization communicates and reaches its customer segments and thereby delivers its value propositions.

Value proposition (VP) pillar

This is pivotal to a BM and illustrates the bundle of products and services offered to create value for a specific customer segment.

Infrastructure management pillar- value creation

Key partnerships (KP)

This describes the networks and alliances a focal organization builds with its suppliers, strategic partners and other critical stakeholders (except customers) that helps optimize the BM.

Key activities (KA)

This characterizes the most important things a focal organization must do to make the BM model work.

Key resources (KR)

This addresses the most vital assets required to make a BM work.

Financial outcome pillar- value capture

Cost structure (C$)

This reflects all the costs incurred by a focal organization operating its BM, which are mainly resulted from value creation.

Revenue streams (R$)

This characterizes a focal organization's overall income deriving from its customer segments during value delivery.

A networked synergistic mode of innovation for value creation

The dialectical analysis above demonstrates the critical role of the *structural discrepancies* in shaping the value creation and innovation practices of BMs, whereby we have based on the *Yin-Yang* harmony cognition proposed a new, context-specific *Confucian BM canvas* whose new pillar of CSL delineates the distinctive reciprocal interactions between the societal forms of order and shared beliefs under the environment of Confucian culture.

At the outset, we have used a real case of the flourish of Asian Pacific BMs in the electric motor industry as an exemplar, whereby an idiosyncratic form of *networked synergistic innovation for value creation* is identified. From the *Yin-Yang* harmony cognition, we think it can fit well into the *Confucian BM canvas* because this indigenous paradigm shows at least three prominent characteristics regarding value creation and innovation different from those in typical western BMs. First, it is *the government* instead of the focal firm that recognizes the valuable opportunity and thereby *network* that involved organizations along the value chain of the electronic motor industry to engage in product and service innovation for creating value together. Second, to a certain extent, the realization and amplification of value creation is made and led by the state rather than the focal firm of BMs. It is because the government support as the key resource enables participating organizations to bypass institutional constraints and create more interrelated or complementary BMs, whereby the huge *synergistic* effects can be achieved. Third, such a government-led BM in general lays almost equal emphasis on both public/social value and customer value and is partly driven reinforced state intervention. This differs from the typical linear value creation practice of BMs in Western market economies, which depending on the interactions of market demands ('market pull') and technological innovation ('technology push') often places major focus on generating 'customer value' and is amplified by the synergy of enhanced market power and limited government interference (Hall and Soskice 2001; Teece 2010).

The internationalization of China's high-speed railway (HSR) industry also provides quite a few emblematic evidences characterizing the networked synergistic mode of innovation for value creation in Confucian BM canvas. For example, the Jakarta-Bandung high-speed railway project, promoted by China's Belt and Road Initiative, seems to be a typical case, as it was the first foreign project using China's HSR standard, conducted by a joint venture formed by Chinese and Indonesian state-owned enterprises. By doing so, the institutional disablers could be bypassed smoothly. To a certain extent, this case describes how China's HSR company changed its business model for the obtain of social legitimacy in this context, and thereby achieve symbiosis with its counterpart in Indonesia. Since the memorandum of HSR cooperative project between Chinese and Indonesian governments was signed in 2015, the high-speed link has become a flagship project for China's Belt and Road Initiative and Indonesia's Global Maritime Fulcrum vision. With strong governmental support from both countries, this HSR project has not only largely promoted Indonesia's technological innovation and economic development, created numerous job opportunities for Chinese and local people, but also help China achieve a vital milestone in terms of its go-global strategy. The networked synergistic effects can be clearly identified.

For a better understanding, Figure 2 more clearly illustrates this idiosyncratic modality of innovation for value creation with the case of the electric scooter industry.

Discussion, implications, and future research

Discussion

Recognizing the existence of cross-cultural heterogeneity in the BM design in the West and Confucian Asia, we first elucidated the prominent cultural differences in the logic of value creation innovation in BMs, followed by a systematic review underpinning and justifying the aforementioned research gap on relevant issues. Second, we adopted a Yin-

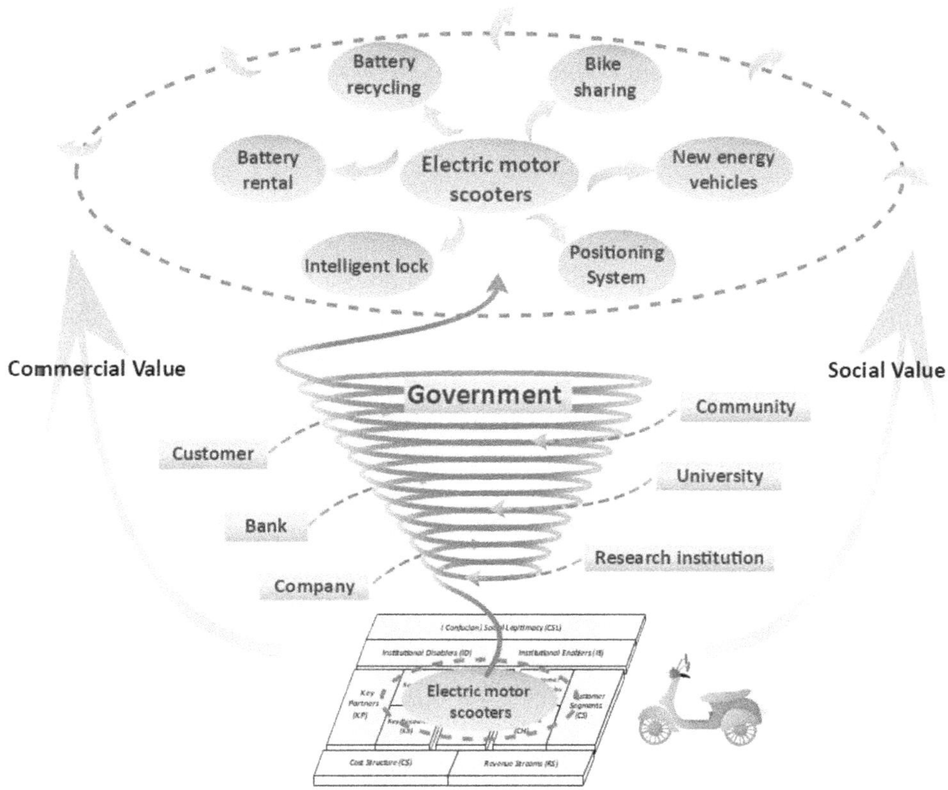

Figure 2. Networked synergistic mode of innovation for value creation.

Yang harmony cognition, a counterpart to the Western theory of paradox, proposing three new components of the BM construct as per the Confucian doctrine about gaining social legitimacy, and thereby put forward a novel- yet probably context-specific- mode of innovation for value creation. Third, we used two brief, descriptive cases illustrating the practicality and applicability of the proposed Confucian BM canvas as well as the networked synergistic mode of innovation in the Asia Pacific.

Theoretical contributions

Overall, this study makes several contributions to the existing body of knowledge about BMs in the Asia Pacific. First and foremost, we respond to appeals to fill the relevant literature gap. Teece (2010) indicated that BMs seem to be redundant in non-Western market economies, such as a planned economy where the state decides what customers can get, or a perfectly competitive economy where firms may simply capture value by selling their products at competitive market prices. Echoing this, scholars have highlighted the vital need to delve into the idiosyncratic value logic of BMs in non-Western contexts or under different kinds of economic structures (Bidmon and Knab 2018; Spieth et al. 2018). Our research, thus, can be deemed as a response to this appeal from an unconventional, interdisciplinary angle and thereby contributes to the BM literature. It refined and extended Osterwalder and Pigneur (2010) BM canvas model, putting forward a new framework of

Confucianism BM canvas based on a novel integrative lens of paradox and culture to explore the distinctive compositional elements of BMs in non-Western market economies.

Second, related to the point above, given this study allows us to more clearly situate *Yin-Yang* theory in the wider arena of social science, we also answer recent calls for developing new management theories from the less-popular Eastern philosophies rather than the widely-used Western perspectives (Barkema et al. 2015; Rowley and Oh 2020). More specifically, by building on Osterwalder and Pigneur (2010) BM canvas theory, we fill the theoretical lacuna by adopting an emic, indigenous *Yin-Yang* harmony cognition identifying a new pillar of CSL as the underlying rationale for the unique value-creating and innovation patterns of BMs in Confucian Asia and which encompasses three new building blocks (i.e. IE, ID, CSL) as shown in Figure 1.

Third, on the premise that values are understood as subjective notions of the desirable, we proposed a nuanced *networked synergistic mode of innovation* for value creation of BMs in the Asia Pacific that goes beyond the focal firm's goal of value generation as well as the limited emphasis on economic value. Explicitly, it addresses the significance of combing social and economic concerns to establish a value network for achieving synergistic innovation performance in the context of Asian Pacific BMs. Implicitly, such an intricate innovation mode led by the government often necessitates the forming of shared cultural values among multiple stakeholders, whereby the continuing development and expanding scope of the value network can be justified and legitimized. Viewed from this angle, our research also partly contributes to the current trend of taking into account the strong interdependence and complementarity of social and economic benefits in the studies of BM innovation (Breuer and Ludeke-Freund 2017; Spieth et al. 2018).

In addition, while a more context-specific manifestation of BM archetype and construct is of extraordinary importance to clarifying the currently- debatable definition of BMs (Kajanus et al. 2018; Massa, Tucci, and Afuah 2017; Fielt 2013), we also bring new insights into the BM theory through suggesting and concretizing new cognitively- based constituents of the architecture of Asian Pacific BMs. This enriches the conceptual base of BMs.

Practical implications

Our proposed *Confucian BM canvas* has high practical relevance. Evidence has shown that local institutional logic may constrain or enable the operation of BMs across borders by giving legitimacy to certain types of BMs rather than other types (Foss and Saebi 2016). For instance, the Western BM of Uber (car-hailing platform) cannot gain legitimacy in several Asia Pacific countries (e.g. China and Vietnam), while the BM of Airbnb (house and apartment rental) stagnated at an early stage of development in the Asia Pacific region due to the need of overcoming some institutional barriers to entry. These crucial facts accentuate that in practice firms must formulate suitable BMs in adaptation to the socio-economic environment where they do business.

Given this, our research that demonstrates the novel concept of a *Confucian BM canvas* may provide a more holistic picture of what a 'good' BM in the Asia Pacific should look like, whereby managers can make a retrospection about how to better pursue business opportunities in a Confucian cultural setting. Further, managers from other cultures may glean fresh insights from the networked synergistic mode of innovation and thereby to enhance their value-creating practices in this Confucian context. In addition to benefiting practitioners, considering BM-related policies must contain a better integration and acknowledgement of heterogenous stakeholders across cultural borders, our research also offers fruitful implications for policy makers to be more prudent to set measures that enables the operation of BMs.

Future research

This current study is conceptual in nature, future research is encouraged to empirically examine the applicability of the novel framework of *Confucian BM canvas* proposed here. Although we have addressed the impact of culture on the compositional structure of BMs in the Asia Pacific, future research could incorporate more variety of contingency factors, such as environmental and social conditions, with culture to gain a deeper, more comprehensive understanding of relevant issues in this context. The rapid progress of ICT has not only facilitated and accelerated, but sometimes may also jeopardize, the traditional transaction and cooperation modes between organizations and their stakeholders across borders. Future researchers may also wish to further explore the interacting effects of ICT and culture on Asia Pacific BMs. Rowley and Oh (2020) have highlighted the pivotal role of institutional repertoires as storytelling in explaining and justifying BM innovation in Western mainstream studies, future research could also take into account the use of narrative schemas to explore relevant issues in depth.

Conclusion

Without doubt, the BMs emerging from Confucian Asia have gained considerable momentum in recent years. The Confucian cultural cluster in the Asia Pacific region encompasses ten nations, namely China, Japan, South Korea, North Korea, Vietnam, Singapore, Malaysia, Indonesia, Philippines and Thailand. Despite this accounting for only 5% of the total number of countries in the world, the gross domestic product (GDP) of the 10 Confucian countries that kept rising moderately for decades has made a tremendous contribution to the global GDP of more than 27% in 2018, of which nearly 60% was generated in China. However, traditional BM theory actually stems from the US liberal market system where the institutional structure rooted in Western Christian or Catholic cultures is typically designed to support market functions, i.e. the dominant market-oriented orthodoxy (Witt and Redding 2009: 866), but in fact, there exist quite a few non-western market systems underpinned by diverse institutional logics in Confucian Asia. For instance, in a coordinated market economy like Japan (Hall and Soskice 2001) or a socialist market economy like China, the institutional structure is designed in favour of solving societal challenges, which may not be necessarily market-conforming. It is thus of vital importance to delving into the culturally-specific characters and modalities of BMs in this context. In this sense, we believe our research that suggests a novel *Confucian BM canvas* provides valuable new ways of thinking to understand the intricate and dynamic reality about value creation and innovation of BMs in the Asia Pacific.

Disclosure statement

No potential conflict of interest was reported by the authors.

References

Abdelkafi, N., and K. Tauscher. 2015. "Business Models for Sustainability from A System Dynamics Perspective." *Organization & Environment* 29 (1): 74–96. doi:10.1177/1086026615592930.

Amit, R., and C. Zott. 2001. "Value Creation in E-business." *Strategic Management Journal* 22 (67): 493–520. doi:10.1002/smj.187.

Amit, R., and C. Zott. 2012. "Creating Value Through Business Model Innovation." *MIT Sloan Management Review* 53 (3): 41–49.

Baden-Fuller, C., and S. Haefliger. 2013. "Business Models and Technological Innovation." *Long Range Planning* 46 (6): 419–426. doi:10.1016/j.lrp.2013.08.023.

Barkema, H. G., X.-P. Chen., G. George., Y. Luo., and A. S. Tsui. 2015. "West Meets East: New Concepts and Theories." *Academy of Management Journal* 58 (2): 460–479. doi:10.5465/amj.2015.4021.

Bashir, M., and R. Verma. 2018. "Internal Factors & Consequences of Business Model Innovation." *Management Decision* 57 (1): 262–290. doi:10.1108/MD-11-2016-0784.

Bidmon, C. M., and S. F. Knab. 2018. "The Three Roles of Business Models in Societal Transitions: New Linkages between Business Model and Transition Research." *Journal of Cleaner Production* 178: 903–916. doi:10.1016/j.jclepro.2017.12.198.

Bohnsack, R., J. Pinkse, and A. Kolk. 2014. "Business Models for Sustainable Technologies: Exploring Business Model Evolution in the Case of Electric Vehicles." *Research Policy* 43 (2): 284–300. doi:10.1016/j.respol.2013.10.014.

Breuer, H., and F. Ludeke-Freund. 2017. "Value-Based Network and Business Model Innovation." *International Journal of Innovation Management* 21 (3): 1–35. doi:10.1142/S1363919617500281.

Burrell, G., and G. Morgan. 1979. *Sociological Paradigms and Organizational Analysis*. London: Routledge.

Cappelli, P. 2009. "The Future of the U.S. Business Model and the Rise of Competitors." *Academy of Management Perspective* 23 (2): 5–10. doi:10.2307/27747506.

Chesbrough, H. W. 2007. "Why Companies Should Have Open Business Models." *MIT Sloan Management Review* 48 (2): 22–28. doi:10.0000/PMID48208.

Chesbrough, H. W. 2010. "Business Model Innovation: Opportunities and Barriers." *Long Range Planning* 43 (2–3): 354–363. doi:10.1016/j.lrp.2009.07.010.

Chin, T. 2015. "Harmony and Organizational Citizenship Behaviour in Chinese Organizations." *International Journal of Human Resource Management* 26 (8): 1110–1129. doi:10.10.80/09585192.2014.934882.

Chin, T., G. Li, H. Jiao, F. Addo, and I. M. Jawaha. 2019a. "Career Sustainability during Manufacturing Innovation: A Review, A Conceptual Framework and Future Research Agenda." *Career Development International* 24 (6): 509–528. doi:10.1108/CDI-02-2019-0034.

Chin, T., H. Jiao, and I. M. Jawahar. 2019b. "Sustainable Career and Innovation during Manufacturing Transformation." *Career Development International* 24 (5): 397–403. doi:10.1108/CDI-09-2019-331.

Chin, T., C. Rowley, G. Redding, and S. Wang. 2018. "Chinese Strategic Thinking on Competitive Conflict: Insights from Yin-Yang Harmony Cognition." *International Journal of Conflict Management* 29 (5): 683–704. doi:10.1108/IJCMA-09-2017-0101.

Dowling, J., and J. Pfeffer. 1975. "Organizational Legitimacy: Social Values and Organizational Behaviour." *Pacific Sociological Review* 18 (1): 122–136. doi:10.2307/1388226.

Drucker, P. F. 1954. *The Practice of Management*. New York: Harper Brothers.

Fielt, E. 2013. "Conceptualizing Business Models: Definitions, Frameworks, and Classifications." *Journal of Business Modes* 1 (1): 85–105. doi:10.5278/ojs.jbm.v1i1.706.

Fjeldstad, Q. D., and C. C. Snow. 2018. "Business Models and Organization Design." *Long Range Planning* 51 (1): 32–39. doi:10.1016/j.lrp.2017.07.008.

Foss, N. J., and T. Saebi. 2016. "Fifteen Years of Research on Business Model Innovation: How Far Have We Come and Where Should We Go?" *Journal of Management* 43 (1): 1–28. doi:10.1177/0149206316675927.

Hall, P., and D. Soskice. 2001. *The Institutional Foundations of Comparative Advantage*. Oxford: Oxford University Press.

Hofstede, G. J., and M. Minkov. 2010. *Cultures and Organizations: Software of the Mind*. Vol. 2. New York: Mcgraw-hill.

Joyce, A., and R. L. Paquin. 2016. "The Triple Layered Business Model Canvas: A Tool to Design More Sustainable Business Models." *Journal of Cleaner Production* 135: 1474–1486. doi:10.1016/j.jclepro.2016.06.067.

Kajanus, M., V. Leban., P. Glavonjic., J. Krc., J. Nedeljkovic., D. Nonic, E. Nybakk, et al. 2018. "What Can We Learn from Business Models in the European Forest Sector: Exploring the Key Elements of New Business Model Designs." *Forest Policy and Economics* 99: 145–156. doi:10.1016/j.forpol.2018/04/005.

Lai, K. 2008. *An Introduction to Chinese Philosophy*. Cambridge: Cambridge University Press.

Larissa, V. A., K. Al-Htaybat., and K. Hutaibat. 2017. "A Knowledge Management and Sharing Business Model for Dealing with Disruption: The Case of Aramex." *Journal of Business Research* 94: 400–407. doi:10.1016/j.jbusres.2017.11.037.

Lewandowski, M. 2016. "Designing the Business Models for Circular Economy-Towards the Conceptual Framework." *Sustainability* 18 (1): 1–28. doi:10.3390/su8010043.

Lloyd, G. E. R. 1996. *Adversaries and Authorities: Investigations into Ancient Greek and Chinese Science*. Vol. 42. Cambridge: Cambridge University Press.

Magretta, J. 2002. "Why Business Models Matter." *Harvard Business Review* 80 (5): 86–92.

Martins, L. L., V. P. Rindova., and B. E. Greenbaum. 2015. "Unlocking the Hidden Value of Concepts: A Cognitive Approach to Business Model Innovation." *Strategic Entrepreneurship Journal* 9 (1): 99–117. doi:10.1002/sej.1191.

Massa, L., C. Tucci, and A. Afuah. 2017. "A Critical Assessment of Business Model Research." *Academy of Management Annals* 11 (1): 73–104. doi:10.5465/annals.2014.0072.

Meng, J. W. 2012. "Chinese Approaches to the Philosophy of Scientific Culture." *Journal of Dialectics of Nature* 34 (6): 15–19. doi:10.15994/j.1000-0763.2012.06.003.

Meng, J. W. 2017. *Science and Humanities: A New Outlook*. Beijing: Science Press.

Nambisan, S., S. A. Zahra., and Y. Luo. 2019. "Global Platforms and Ecosystems: Implications for International Business Theories." *Journal of International Business Studies* 50 (9): 1464–1486. doi:10.1057/s41267-019-00262-4.

Neissuer, U. 1976. *Cognition and Reality*. New York: W. H. Freeman.
Osiyevskyy, O., and J. Dewald. 2015. "Explorative versus Exploitative Business Model Change: The Cognitive Antecedents of Firm-Level Responses to Disruptive Innovation." *Strategic Entrepreneurship Journal* 9 (1): 58–78. doi:10.1002/sej.1192.
Osterwalder, A., and Y. Pigneur. 2010. *Business Model Generation: A Handbook for Visionaries, Game Changers and Challenges*. Hoboken: NJ: John Wiley and Sons.
Paulet, E., and C. Rowley. 2017. *The China Business Model: Originality and Limits*. Oxford: Chandos Publishing.
Putnam, L. L., G. T. Fairhurst, and S. Banghar. 2016. "Contradictions, Dialectics, and Paradoxes in Organizations: A Constitutive Approach." *The Academy of Management Annals* 10 (1): 65–171. doi:10.1080/19416520.2016.1162421.
Redding, G. 2005. "The Thick Description and Comparison of Societal Systems of Capitalism." *Journal of International Business Studies* 36 (2): 123–155. doi:10.1057/palgrave.jibs.8400129.
Redding, G. 2017. "Components and Process in Social Science Explanation: Is There A Role for Yin-Yang Balancing." *Cross Cultural & Strategic Management* 24 (1): 152–166. doi:10.1108/CCSM-11-2016-0195.
Rosado-Serrano, A., J. Paul, and D. Dikova. 2018. "International Franchising: A Literature Review and Research Agenda." *Journal of Business Research* 85: 238–257. doi:10.1016/j.jbusres.2017.12.049.
Rowley, C. 2019. "'There are Nine Million Bicycles in Beijing': Booma and Bust for the Sharing Economy." *China's World* 4 (1): 86–89.
Rowley, C., and I. Oh. 2016. "Business Ethics and the Role of Context: Institutionalism, History and Comparisons in the Asia Pacific Region." *Asia Pacific Business Review* 22 (3): 1–13. doi:10.1080/13602381.2015.1129814.
Rowley, C., and I. Oh. 2020. "Trends in Chinese Management and Business: Change, Confucianism, Leadership, Knowledge & Innovation." *Asia Pacific Business Review* 26 (1): 1–8. doi:10.1080/13602381.2019.1698707.
Schaltegger, S., F. Ludeke-Freund., and E. G. Hansen. 2016. "Business Models for Sustainability: A Co-Evolutionary Analysis of Sustainable Entrepreneurship, Innovation and Transformation." *Organization and Environment* 29 (3): 264–289. doi:10.1177/1086026616633272.
Shi, X. H., A. Z. Bigdeli, and F. Li. 2015. "An Examination of NPD Models in the Context of Business Models." *Journal of Business Research* 69 (7): 2541–2550. doi:10.1016/j.jbusres.2015.10.087.
Spieth, P., S. Schneider., T. Claub., and D. Fichenberg. 2018. "Value Drivers of Social Businesses: A Business Model Perspective." *Long Range Planning* 52 (3): 427–444. doi:10.1016/j.lrp.2018.04.004.
Teece, D. J. 2010. "Business Models, Business Strategy and Innovation." *Long Range Planning* 43: 172–194. doi:10.1016/j.lrp.2009.07.003.
Tongur, S., and M. Engwall. 2014. "The Business Model Dilemma of Technology Shifts." *Technovation* 34 (9): 525–535. doi:10.1016/j.technovation.2014.02.006.
Weber, M. 1964. *The Theory of Social Economic Organization*. New York: Free Press.
Wirtz, B. W., A. Prstoia., S. Ullrich., and V. Gottel. 2016. "Business Models: Origin, Development and Future Research Perspectives." *Long Range Planning* 49 (1): 36–54. doi:10.1016/j.lrp.2015.04.001.
Witt, M. A., and G. Redding. 2009. "Asian Business Systems: Institutional Comparison, Clusters, and Implications for Varieties of Capitalism and Business Systems Theory." *Socio-Economic Review* 11 (2): 265–300. doi:10.1093/ser/mwt002.
Zott, C., R. Amit, and L. Massa. 2011. "The Business Model: Recent Developments and Future Research." *Journal of Management* 37 (4): 1019–1042. doi:10.2139/ssrn.1674384.

OPEN ACCESS

User-driven business model innovation: an ethnographic inquiry into Toutiao

Li-Chung Chang, Xin Wang, Su-Qun Zhang, Chang-Bin Chen, Zhi-Hong Yuan, Xian-Ju Zeng, Jian-Qi Chu and San-Bing Tsai

ABSTRACT

The current firm-driven business model innovation (FDBMI) has found its limits. The aim of this research is to explore the user-driven business model innovation (UDBMI) adopting the ethnographic inquiry approach in the Chinese context. The findings show that UDBMI includes five stages: co-creation of content via interaction, creation release by platform, content spread, effect and flow into cash. It is an inside-out cycle which starts from personal (both fans and creators), then platform, community, and to the whole society lifestyle (culture). In contrast to Chinese culture, western culture is an outside-in cycle which starts from the community, then creators, platform, personal (fans) and finally personal life. This study contributes to advancing the understanding of the UDBMI in the Chinese context, and explains why Toutiao has been able to grow rapidly via value co-creation.

1. Introduction

Conventional BMI (business model innovation) puts more emphasis on the role of firm-driven value creation. This is firm-driven business model innovation (FDBMI) (Debruyne 2014). FDBMI places greater emphasis on value capture (Haque 2011), profit and on maximizing shareholders' interests from the value chain. It is competitive and closed-oriented in nature and it needs to sacrifice the interests of the environment, community, society, public, and the next generation. Resources are overconsumed with the increasingly lower economic return, thus gradually reducing the value (Arjoon, Turriago-Hoyos, and Thoene 2018).

In contrast, an increasing number of scholars and practical workers have been calling for user-driven BMI (UDBMI). It features collaboration and value co-creation, and is open-oriented in nature (Arjoon, Turriago-Hoyos, and Thoene 2018). It results in positive increasing returns from a network cycle which recovers the damage in the environment to make all elements continually cycle and grow together. Such damage can be found at the gaps among durability, centrality, targets, delegation, equality, generosity, sharing, independence, reality, inspiration and cognition.

UDBMI is emerging and disrupting conventional industries. Many firms adopting UDBMI are becoming leading companies or unicorns in industries. UDBMI cooperates with users (customers) to co-create unique and personalized value and digitalization technologies which facilitate this trend. UDBMI can allow companies to better grasp opportunities and enhance legitimacy to reduce competition (Wu, Zhao, and Zhou 2019). The aim is not to search for a blue ocean market, but to better satisfy unsatisfied customers (Visnjic, Neely, and Jovanovic 2017).

Therefore, this research adopted the value co-creation theory to explore how UDBMI is running, and the pattern in the Chinese context. UDBMI in the Chinese context needs to be specified for its cultural uniqueness. China is deeply influenced by the cultural roots of 'The Book of Changes' and the later philosophies of Taoism (Chang et al. 2014, 2017), Confucianism and Buddhism (Nan 2013; Sundararajan and Sundararajan 2020). In contrast to European-centric (western) culture in management (Asante 2006), management in China places more emphasis on holistic ontology (rather than polarization), harmony (rather than fair contracts) in axiology (Chin et al. 2018), and intuitive or nonlinear (rather than linear) thinking (Chen 2013).

Therefore, we selected the representative case of Toutiao (meaning 'today's headlines') which is owned by Beijing Bytedance Technology Co. Ltd. It is valued at US$75 billion and is in second position among emerging unicorn companies. It is valued higher than many well-known global unicorns such as Uber, Airbnb, WeWork, Space X, and so on. Its success is mainly attributed to its UDBMI in China.

Toutiao announced its 'V project' which established a (mobile news media) platform to facilitate reader engagement to finally become a creator to encourage user (reader) innovation in 2018. UDBMI via VCC has experienced phenomenal growth in the media industry in China. The following provides a review of the literature on VCC to elaborate on the UDBMI pattern in order to answer the research questions for this special issue.

2. Literature review

2.1. Business model innovation (BMI)

Business model innovation (BMI) can be defined as a new combination of a set of value creation components. It can be viewed as the integration of IO (industrial organization theory) and RBT (resources-based theory) (Mitani 2015). This combination can be created from the four elements of customer value proposition, profit formula, key resources, and key process (Gellweiler and Krishnamurthi 2020) or the three elements of adding novel activities, linking activities and new activity system governance (Jost 2020), or the nine elements of customer segments, value proposition, channels, customer relationship, revenue streams, key resources, key activities, partnerships and cost structure (Baldina and Masyuk 2020).

In general, there are two main approaches to creating BMI: the itself or the mount stream (Matemba et al. 2020). An 'itself' stream asserts that the business model itself with new element combinations can make a huge change that is an innovation (Buntić, Damić, and Sesar 2020). In contrast, the 'mount' stream asserts that emerging technology can be combined into a business model to create innovative value.

In the 'itself' stream, Bower and Christensen (1995) were the first to introduce the concept of BMI. They proposed that a new concept constituted a new business which can be revolutionary or disruptive to conventional industry (Bower and Christensen 1995). A new concept to start a brand new business is creating a new blue ocean (Kim and Mauborgne 2004). For example, Prahalad (2005) suggested a new concept that firms should design a new business model for the population of 4 billion who live in poverty (rather than for those who are wealthy at the top of the pyramid). In his book, 'The Fortune at the Bottom of the Pyramid', Prahalad provides many successful cases of how BMI benefits both firms and the population living in poverty. Like the 'itself' stream, the 'mount' stream also creates BMI, especially combined with those emerging technologies such as e-business based on IT (information technology) (Zott, Amit, and Massa 2011).

Yet, current literature is rarely mentioned about UDBMI. Therefore, the following section will review and comment on the VCC theories, especially in relation to UDBMI, and will point out the progress, advantages, usability and limitations of the current theories, that is, the gap between the phenomenon and the theory.

2.2. Value co-creation

Eric von Hippwl (1988) found that customers rather than firms are the main initiators of innovation. His study showed that 77% of instruments in science and technology, and 67% in the semiconductor industry are customer-initiated innovations. In 2003, Prahalad and Ramaswamy provided a customer-engaged viewpoint of value co-creation via their book titled 'The Future of Competition: Co-creating Unique Value with Customers' which emphasizes that future business will rely on the VCC approach to create unique value to customers. Ramaswamy (2009a) further provided a holistic paradigm of VCC (VCCP) consisting of two external poles between the individual network (communities) and interaction, and two internal contact poles between the human experience environment and engagement platforms. The core of VCCP is a uniquely personal experience. These elements have been widely discussed in a large number of related studies (Chiu, Won, and Bae 2019).

2.2.1. (Social) network and community

Networks or communities based on VCC have been widely discussed, especially virtual communities. A growing number of users are relying on the Internet to obtain useful information instead of offline sources (Fieseler, Bucher, and Hoffmann 2019). They connect with one another through online channels or virtual communities to share their interests (Pang and Capek 2020), for peer-to-peer information sharing, problem-solving (Chang et al. 2020), intentional information seeking, social interactions (Chuah et al. 2020), and chatting (Dholakia, Bagozzi and Pearo 2004). The success of virtual communities, however, greatly depends on the contributions of their members (Bagozzi and Dholakia 2002).

The reasons why members contribute to the community are mainly the sense of a virtual community. People with a sense of belonging (Lin 2008), benevolence and trust (Chen et al. 2017) and who are motivated and emotionally attached (Chou, Lin, and Huang 2016) are more willing to participate by exchanging information, inviting friends to join the community, and contributing knowledge to the community. Such a sense of community will affect their loyalty, and further, their purchase intention (Kim, Yang, and Kim 2009). People's justice perceptions and subsequent sense of virtual community also positively affect their willingness to conduct knowledge contribution and online community citizenship behaviours in virtual communities (Chou, Lin, and Huang 2016).

Besides sense, the expectation of value outcome also positively affects participation, especially in the alignment of meaning-making processes among decision-makers which resonate in an ambiguous community identity (Gambetti and Graffigna 2015). Such engagement behaviours including augmenting, co-developing, influencing, and mobilizing are motivated by the focal customers' need to extend and improve the offering, either for personal or collective purposes (Gambetti and Graffigna 2015).

Despite these antecedents to drive participation behaviour (Yen, Hsu, and Huang 2011), the processes of participation during consumption and value-in-use are also important (Ramaswamy and Ozcan 2018b). Lehrer et al. (2012) found that consumer engagement in the processes of co-production will be inseparably important in the first stage of project definition and in the last stage of application of the solution. Firms need to do more alone at the middle stage of the generation of the creative solution.

Mechanisms to generate new ideas via the virtual community of VCC have also been developed. Chen, Marsden, and Zhang (2012) structured and validated a taxonomic framework of COCBs (Company-Sponsored Online Co-Creation Brainstorming) which demonstrates that the level of peer feedback and the responsiveness (speed) of sponsor company feedback have significant influences on both members' contribution levels and the duration of their active participation. The sponsoring company's feedback, however, seems to influence only the quality of the members' contribution level. On the practical side, the outcomes suggest that sponsoring companies should develop efficient processes for reviewing and responding to submitted ideas.

In brief, a VCCP-based network with elements such as a sense of belonging, benevolence and trust can attract people to participate in and contribute to the network via the in- or extra-roles.

2.2.2. Engagement platform

The use of the term *platform* has proliferated as both a metaphor and a construct in management research. It is used to describe management phenomena at the level of individual products, product systems, industry supply chains, markets, industries, and even constellations of industries (Ramaswamy and Ozcan 2016).

Thomas, Autio, and Gann (2014) presented a systematic review of the platform literature, identifying four distinct streams: organizational platforms, product family platforms, market intermediary platforms, and platform ecosystems (PE). In recent years, the PE stream has received increasing attention. PE has evolved into the 'artificial intelligence era', which has infrastructure consisting of terminals, networks and cloud levels via IT technology. A terminal is the interactive point of contact with the business scene. A network is a business network which combines different technological modules as an ecosystem to provide value. The cloud provides a virtual solution via processing storage, computing, and optimization between the terminal and the network (Liao and Cui 2017).

The PE-based VCC provides the infrastructure and rules for a marketplace that brings together producers and consumers. The players fill four main roles (producers, consumers, providers and owner) but may shift rapidly from one role to another in the ecosystem. The relationships both within (rear-end) and outside (front-end) the ecosystem are central to the platform. Such relationships mainly build on the interactive experience to create customer loyalty, shared purpose with the participants, and mutual trust (Brown 2016), and even further create engagement behaviour which is a voluntary resource making contributions rather than acting out of self-interest. Types of customer engagement include augmenting behaviour, co-developing behaviour, influencing behaviour, and mobilizing behaviour (Jaakkola and Alexander 2014).

Processes to help a producer to transit product to PE mainly include the demand or supply sides. The demand side evolution includes: structuring an external product 'love group', transforming the love group into early platform adopters, and leveraging early adopters to accelerate platform adoption. The supply-side evolution includes internal product R&D plus external complements, internal platform R&D plus blended complementary plus community management, and hybrid business model management (Furr 2016). In order to avoid the risk of transit, Zhu and Furr (2016) provided four practices to help ensure success: starting with a defensible product and a critical mass of users, applying a hybrid business model focused on creating and sharing new value, driving rapid conversion to the new platform, and identifying and acting on opportunities to deter competitive imitation. Further, Ihrig and MacMillan (2017) provided a tool kit for assessing the way in which an innovation affects each stakeholder.

A VCCP-based engagement platform enables and supports 'two-sided' interactions on a large scale (Ramaswamy and Ozcan 2018a). In the past, the product was the endpoint of the consumer experience; now it is the starting point (Greene 2008).

2.2.3. Interactions

Echeverri and Skalen (2011) identified five interaction value practices–informing, greeting, delivering, charging, and helping–and theorized how interactive value formation takes place as well as how value is inter-subjectively assessed by actors at the provider-customer interface.

VCCP-based interaction goes beyond activities to interactions anywhere in the system – the underpinning of the new source of value (Ramaswamy 2009a; Ramaswamy and Ozcan 2018a). For example, Nike offers the Nike+ *experience* kit consisting of a wireless device that transmits speed and distance information from a sensor-equipped Nike running shoe to an iPod Touch or special wristband. Then, through a website (nikeplus.com) runners can track their progress, set personal goals and challenge friends to races. With over 1 million runners and over 130 million miles uploaded, Nike+ has been a runaway success. For Nike, its market share has increased by as much as ten share points, not to mention increased revenues through the Nike+ ecosystem, in partnership with Apple and others.

2.2.4. Experience environment

Many papers focus on the study of influence factors in an experiential environment. For example, Horbel et al. (2016) empirically studied context-specific contributions of the co-creating actors and spectators' experience evaluations, and found the performance of the ball game team only makes a minor contribution to the spectators' overall event experience. This corresponds with the finding that 'fun and entertainment', 'atmosphere', and 'social contacts and interaction' are the three motives that are best satisfied by the public screening of spectators' experience, and hence represent their three most important value dimensions. Besides, Prebensen, Vittersø, and Dahl (2013) surveyed 505 tourists and revealed that tourist resources, in addition to personal service, environment and other visitors, significantly enhance the experienced value of a trip.

Besides the physical environment, IT-aided technology also enhances the experience. For example, Chen and Wang (2016) investigated the relationships among customer participation, co-created values and customer loyalty in an air transport context. In particular, three perceived values are specified to represent the passengers' co-created values. The empirical results pointed out that customer participation in using an online check-in system is positively related to all three values, which further leads to satisfaction with respect to the system.

The environments of human experiences of VCCP embody interactions of individuals with each other and with the company and its network partners' products and artefacts, places and spaces where interactions take place (whether online or offline), and interactions with the company and network partners' business processes (Ramaswamy 2009a). Designing for human experience environments goes well beyond classic product and service design, not only in terms of the complexity of the different types of interactions among individuals, communities, and the firm's enhanced network but also in terms of a deep understanding of the interaction experiences that actually generate value for those involved (Ramaswamy 2009b).

2.2.5. *Value expansion*

Through network participation, engagement on the platform, interaction and environmental experience, the level of value created will be raised by such staged experience (Ramaswamy and Ozcan 2018b). VCCP is not just about 'thinking outside the box'; it is about changing the box to the whole diamond of value creation. It is about starting with the perspective of the whole diamond of value creation, as shown in Figure 1, to drive the implications for the 'value chain'. What this fundamentally means is for us to stop thinking of individuals as mere 'passive recipients of value' that firms traditionally deliver to, and instead engage them as active co-creators of value; in this way, a whole new world of *value expansion* will open up (Ramaswamy and Ozcan 2018a).

2.3. *Value co-creation for business model design*

VCC has become a very popular theory, and many studies have extended VCC to the business model design (Hsu 2016).

2.4. *Theoretical gap: UDBMI via VCC*

To sum up, based on the abovementioned literature, Ramaswamy's five elements of VCCP create a more holistic framework (Figure 1) which is closer to the Chinese context. Besides, the framework includes all roles for a new combination of a set of value creation components.

Therefore, we adapted the framework as an initial conceptual framework for the study to explore how UDBMI is running via VCC, and to explain why Toutiao can be successful in

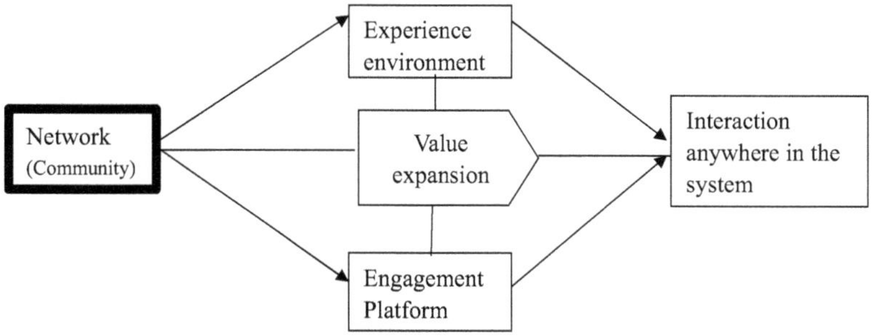

Figure 1. System framework of value co-creation.
Source: Ramaswamy (2009a) Co-Creation of Value: Towards an Expanded Paradigm of Value Creation. Marketing Review St. Gallen. # 26 (6):11–17.

the Chinese context. In this research, we also adopted this framework to collect and analyse cases to answer the research questions.

3. Methodology

3.1. Research design

A qualitative 'ethnography' approach is more suitable to explore cultural life as it places greater emphasis on depth and persistence via immersion in the representative case's life rather than quantitative research which collects wide and large-scale samples to generalize principles (Sinanan 2018).

As the world becomes increasingly digital, people are interacting more frequently with each other through online communities, and are forming unique online communities and corresponding cultures (Androutsopoulos 2008). In order to keep pace with this new cultural phenomenon, research methods must also be updated (Kozinels 2010) to make an in-depth, long-term study of a specific virtual community (as in Baym 2000). Toutiao is currently one of the hottest creative (news media) platforms (https://www.Toutiao.com/) for short videos. Its short (social) video platforms called Huoshan (https://www.huoshan.com/) and Douyin (https://www.douyin.com/) are available in more than 150 countries. In 2018 Toutiao announced the '100,000 creators V project' which can help individual readers build personal IP to become popular creators. It is an online project. Therefore we adopted the online ethnography approach to join and immerse ourselves in the news media and fan group platforms for three years (Bauwens and Genoud 2014; Dawson 2019).

The research design of online ethnography includes five steps: (1) defining research questions, social networking sites or research topics, (2) identifying and selecting communities, (3) community participation observation (participation, immersion) and data collection, (4) data analysis and repeated interpretation of findings, and (5) writing, presenting and reporting research findings, theories or policy recommendations (Kozinels 2010). Following are the details of each of these five steps.

3.2. Data collection

The first step to collect data is to define one or two core research questions, and then to develop sub-questions (Table A1) (Kozinels 2010). The core research question is how VCC shapes UDBMI, and the sub-questions are based on the VCC framework (Table A1).

Social networking or the field then needs to be defined further. Toutiao is a representative case (Patton 1990) and we focus on the '100,000 creators V project'. We firstly collected secondary data with the aim of forming a preliminary understanding of the case through the collection of current references from official websites, public announcements, books, and news about the 'creator V project'. We coded relevant data with codes such as FSXFD-P2-P41, meaning book abbreviation_chapter2_page41.

Toutiao is a news platform which allows creators, or readers, to interact. Therefore, we joined the platform to observe cultural life. We ranked and chose good Toutiao V project workers and popular creators as online interview targets (such as Du, Tu-Feng who is a high-quality creator in agriculture in rural areas) and started to interview them. The reason why we adopted on-line interviews rather than focus group or face-to-face interviews is that Toutiao is a purely on-line service without off-line activities, so we could only interview creators, project workers and readers on-line. Primary data via interviews were collected by first building relationships with Toutiao V project workers and creators. We interacted with creators on the Toutiao message board and invited them to accept our interview via WeChat or Messenger which is embedded in the Toutiao news media platform to allow private dialogues (Figure 2). The interview questions mainly focused on the 'creator V project'. Starting with the purpose of the project, we discussed with the interviewees how the platform can help creators build innovation like personal IP, and then discussed with the creators how to realize innovation like personal IP and the embodiment of multi-party value creation. We finally coded the interview materials; for example, Code 2019.03.30_A4 means interview date_interviewee number.

We verified the data via triangulation (Dawson 2019) among co-authors. If there were different interpretations expressed by the co-authors, we collected more data and re-discussed the findings. We continued the triangulation process until saturation, and finally, 30 datasets were collected. We eliminated the irrelevant data, sorted out the relevant data and sent it to the interviewees for cross-checking and supplementation, so as to make the data more reliable.

3.3. Data analysis: narrative inquiry

Based on the VCC framework (Figure 1), we collected, verified and coded dates. Through the inductive analysis, we explored and arranged the data into a narrative as a temporal and modified story (pattern). When a pattern emerged, we cross-examined the replicated pattern as the finding (Chen 2002).

4. Findings: building UDBMI pattern through five stages

4.1. Introduction to Toutiao

According to Quest Mobile's Report on China's mobile internet in the first half of 2018, the Toutiao Group ranks second only to the Tencent Group among the five major ICT groups

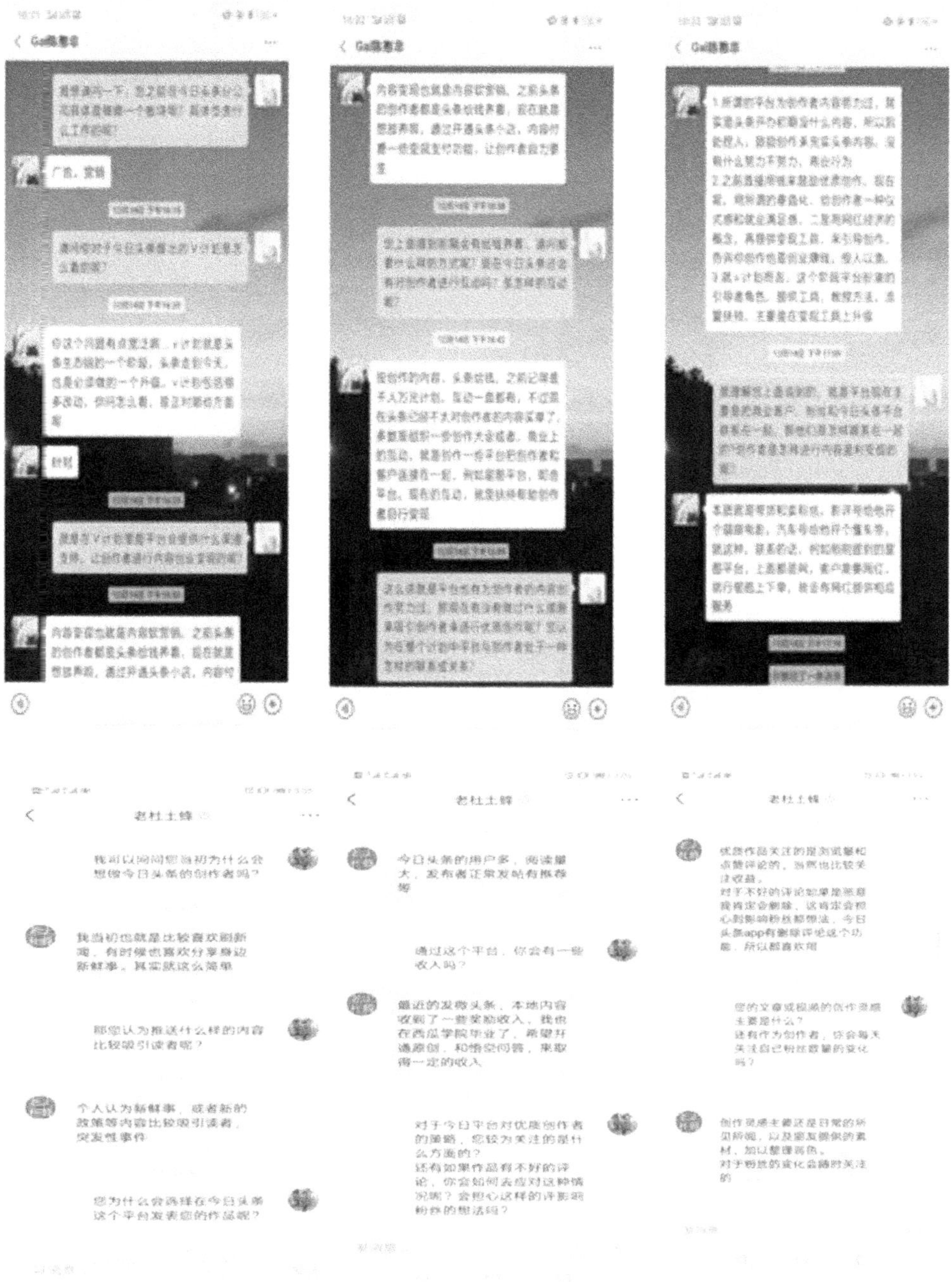

Figure 2. Examples of the on-line interview via WeChat or Toutiao messenger.
Source: this research.

in terms of total time spent on independent applications (apps). Toutiao was founded in 2012 as a flagship product of Bytedance, a data mining engine based on personalized recommendations from users.

With the rapid development of Toutiao, it has successively launched its subordinate platforms such as Douyin and Huoshan which host user self-made short videos, and acquired Flipagram, an American short video app. Now the Toutiao Group (Table A2) has became one of the leading groups in app media in the world. As Table A2 shows, Toutiao platforms include news (information), short videos, pictures, questions and answers, and language learning services, and its business has realized a vertical layout and industrial chain extension.

4.2. *Episodes and stages*

In order to encourage more self-made content creators to commit to using Toutiao's news media platform to build their personal IP and personal brand, the 'Creator V project 100,000' was launched in 2018 to revitalize original authors. With a focus on those creators with more than 1 million subscribers or more than 100,000 fans, the project planned to build and deepen an ecosystem via a large volume of watch flow and to assist 100,000 creators to build their personal IP and brand to increase their income.

This BMI can be classified into five episodes and stages described as follows.

4.2.1. *Stage 1: co-creation of content via interaction*

There are three processes to go through to become a good creator: ordinary user (reader) – creator – good creator. High-quality creators need to choose their own field before they receive certification as a creator, which also defines the orientation of the creator. Content production for creators is a content operation service based on Toutiao big data, including positioning consulting, creation consulting, specialized course training and joint customization. This series of services aims to help creators find more appropriate positioning. V project workers and creators mentioned:

> The purpose of the project is to help readers become high-quality creators and to increase the number of creators. (2019.02.15_A1)

> More than two years ago, I accidentally saw Toutiao recommend a lot of historical stories, and I felt very impressed. Toutiao is a free platform for writing and a better space for the creator. ... so, I wanted to be a creator (2019.03.30_A2)

Content innovation requires creators to have certain creative ability, but it is impossible for creators to continuously complete high-quality creations by themselves. In order to meet some basic needs of fans and to find creative highlights, creators and fans (individual users, readers) have dialogue and interaction, based on the (social media) platforms, such as the WeChat fan group or Messenger embedded in Toutiao. One creator mentioned:

> Yes, we believe that there will be no loyal fans without us; we attach great importance to the communication with fans, so we established a group, and we answer questions about food at any time. We can affect them via food. (2019.03.30_A4)

Fans will communicate with creators, and fans will give suggestions and opinions to creators from their viewpoint. Fans will also give suitable comments about the content to create collective wisdom. If the creator appreciates the fans' suggestions, such suggestions can be used as a reference to modify the later version of creation to achieve the ultimate goal of communication. One creator mentioned:

> Inspiration comes from life; when you encounter problems, you will think about how to solve them, and fans contribute by brainstorming and I will see what fans like to know. (2019.03.28_A3)

> Interaction with fans is still a lot, they will be very concerned about us when there are difficulties and they will comfort me. We also occasionally send some gifts to fans to express thanks. (2019.03.11_A4)

> I often draw some small gifts to give to my fans, read their comments and interact with them on the Toutiao platform. (2019.03.28_A4)

Besides, creators are also spreaders of creation to social media such as WeChat in one or two subject fields, and they will share their professional knowledge with readers. One creator said:

> I held an activity. I will show the Palace Museum to them and explain the Palace Museum to some fans for free so that more people can understand Chinese culture and pass on love. (2019.03.30_43)

4.2.2. *Stage 2: creation release by platform*

Toutiao, the platform of content innovation, also provides social media functions such as a message board that provides a value co-created online environment. The Toutiao news platform releases innovative content, and readers can communicate with creators interactively. In the release stage, content innovators share certain information through the social interactive function on the platform about content innovation, and share what creators have seen and heard and the professional knowledge they have mastered. Through such processes, content innovators can cultivate fans, and the platform is also a basic channel for personal IP cultivation. One creator mentioned:

> We often communicate with fans and friends; we can learn a lot to improve our creation. (2019.03.29_A4)

4.2.3. *Stage 3: content spread*

Based on the content release from the Toutiao news platform, the innovative content can be spread widely to other platforms or communities such as WeChat groups, communities or bloggers. Through the participation and interaction of the network community, the acquisition of quality information, and the experience of the personalized scene environment on the platform, the realized value will be largely increased. In this condition, the content innovation platform plays an important role in spreading innovative content and plays the role of the carrier.

Based on big data analysis and personalized preference settings, the innovator's content will be recommended and pushed to those who care about the innovative content. Readers or audience members who are interested in the content will share it with their social network. Through the large volume spreading through social networks among a wide variety of readers, the network effect will occur and will become the entire network transmission. One creator mentioned:

> Toutiao will recommend the content to users according to their personality. In normal times, I will interact with fans more often. When I publish new content, I will retweet it a few times to express my opinions. Sometimes the platform will forward it to help us spread it, and let more people know about us. (2019.03.11_A2)

4.2.4. Stage 4: effect

The effect includes the impact on communities and content innovators. To the communities, content spreading through the platform has made a difference in the life of community members. For communities, the spread of knowledge or creative content from creators not only increases community members' knowledge, but may also change their living habits, ways of doing things, and so on. For content innovators, the growth of fans and the flood of private comments are a reflection of the perceived impact of their content on community members, and such reflection could positively influence the creation of new content. One creator mentioned:

> Mainly it comes from life, it's all that happens in life. (2019.03.29_A3)

> Not long ago, a farmer uncle asked me to help him sell his unsellable products. I know nothing about e-commerce, so I communicated with a Toutiao teacher and helped him to open a store. (2019.03.11_A4)

4.2.5. Stage 5: flow into cash

The revenue of content innovators on the Toutiao platform is basically realized by the fans. As an increasing number of people change their life via the content, the readers' flow will largely be increased and the creators will further influence the fans' buying decisions. Creators will adopt 'placement marketing' to guide fans to consume recommended products from another platform, such as Taobao or Amazon. Loyal fans will follow the recommendation. When fans like the product or information from creators, they will spread the product information in the community such as via WeChat friend groups or bloggers, then creators can transfer the flow into cash from the 'placement marketing'. On the other hand, innovative content will always follow related advertising. When readers or fans click the advertising, the platform will charge firms high advertising fees.

A large volume of flow can support such UDBMI sustainability with high profit. Sustainable profit can then support creators to make more innovative content via value co-creation. V project workers and creators mentioned:

> There are several key points to support fan ecology, key areas to develop, full-link services to provide them, and realization of profit methods. (2019.02.15_A3)

> Our income is mainly from advertising, flow revenue and merchandise. (2019.03.29_A1)

5. Discussion

5.1. Discussion

After the realization of profit, the content innovator can produce the content by relying on a stable high income. In order to create and maintain the operation of fans, content innovators need to communicate with them frequently. These five steps are logical replication, which constitutes the whole process of UDBMI via VCC (Figure 3).

It is clear that Toutiao's UDBMI is based on VCC mainly between creators and fans. It is an inside-out cycle (Figure 3) which starts from an individual's personal circle (*guanxi*), (news) platform, community (such as WeChat fan groups), then the whole society lifestyle

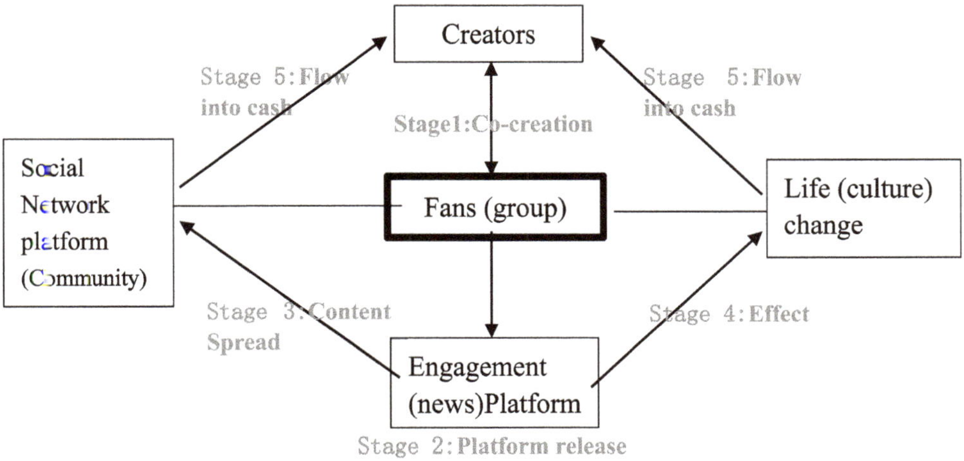

Figure 3. UDBMI via VCC in the Chinese context.
Source: this research.

(culture) in the Chinese context. This contrasts with western culture, where the pattern is outside-in, starting from a community which has a mutual interest or purpose, then creators, platform, personal interest and finally personal life.

This finding corresponds to the Chinese culture uniqueness of *'QuānZi'* (圈子) which Fei (2011) described as a 'differential mode for a different kind of association'. Social groups are built on personal networks. In contrast to Chinese culture, a community can be built for mutual interest or purpose in western culture (De Luo and Liang 2017).

5.2. Theory and theory development

This research makes theoretical developments to the understanding of UDBMI via VCC in the Chinese context. First, previous studies related to BMI were mostly FDBMI in nature. This research fills the theoretical gap regarding the process of UDMBI and the advantages gained. Second, this study advances the understanding of the holistic UDBMI pattern from creators' and fans' co-creation, platform release, spreading in the community, life change, and finally turning flow into cash.

6. Implications

This study generalizes a UDBMI pattern of VCC which includes five stages: co-creation of content via interaction, creation release by platform, content spread, effect and flow into cash.

Advantage sources of the firm have moved from industries (IO), resouces (RBV), value, then to value co-creation to satisify personalized demand. Therefore, UDBMI pattern can be applied to every field that needs to seek the advantage from satisfying personalized demand. The processes should firstly start from co-creation of value with fans by knowing fans preference, as it is the easiest way to predict the market in advance. It can then be released by the platform, and then the innovation will be spread widely in communities. When people are influenced by innovation, their life will change further. Value co-created by fans will turn flow into cash. It is an inside-out cycle (Figure 3) approach to management BMI practice, rather than the outside-in approach (Figure 1) in the Chinese context.

The success of Toutiao is the result of the collective wisdom co-created by the personal *guanxi* between creators and fans. That is, organizations that adopt the UDBMI pattern need to establish personal *guanxi*, which has been defined as personalized favour ties (Zhai 2004; Liao 2020). Such *guanxi* can be maintained and strengthened via the sustained exchange favours or *Renqing* (人情), a social norm of both emotional and material support for other in-group members (Li 2013; Ren, Chen, and Chen 2020).

7. Conclusions

7.1. Conclusions

In contrast to western culture, the UDBMI shows a different VCC cycle in the Chinese context. Western culture is community-based with mutual purpose or interest-driven VCC (Figure 1), whereas Chinese culture is personal tie driven by VCC.

This ethnographic enquiry explored the UDBMI pattern from its VCC nature to its source of advantages in the Chinese context. Through the induction of findings from the abovementioned five-stage cycle, three related conclusions are reached. First, this pattern of encouraging the co-creation of value needs to 'incubate' readers to become creators. Second, the firm needs to 'cultivate' potential readers who are interested in (Toutiao) services to become fans. Third, the firm needs to 'realize', which is the last stage of transforming flow into cash.

This generalized pattern constitutes a complete industrial chain and cycle. This five-stage cycle extends to other service fields, and constitutes the Toutiao group which occupies a leading position in many fields (Table A2). This generalized pattern cycle explains why Toutiao can grow rapidly via VCC.

7.2. Limitations

This research is limited in that it only selected one company from the ICT industry in mainland China; thus, the UDBMI pattern can only be elaborated in such settings. Different cultural contexts were not included in this study. In other words, businesses should recognize the cultural context implied in the pattern. For example, western countries like the United Kingdom or the United States are characterized by community-based UDBMI. Such a cultural context setting might not be sufficient to operate the pattern.

7.3. Future research

This research has contributed to an understanding of UDBMI in the Chinese context via VCC. Many aspects of the UDBMI are still unknown. For example, what are the success factors which influence UDBMI in the Chinese context? What will the pattern be in different industries, such as traditional industries? How does UDBMI influence managers' vision, mission, strategy, planning, organization, leadership, control and learning in the Chinese context? How does UDBMI influence the policies concerning human resources, marketing, manufacturing, finance, and research and development in the Chinese context? All of these questions warrant further investigation.

Disclosure statement

No potential conflict of interest was reported by the authors.

Funding

This study was funded by the projects of Department of Education of Guangdong Province [grant number SJY201903]; Foundation of University of Electronic Science and Technology of China, Zhongshan Institute [grant number JY201911]; Natural Science Foundation of Guangdong Province [2018A030307040] and National Natural Science Foundation of China [NO.71772130,71302107].

References

Androutsopoulos, J. 2008. "Potentials and Limitations of Discourse-Centered Online Ethnography." *Language@Internet* 5 (8): 1–20. doi:10.1017/CBO9781107415324.004.

Arjoon, S., A. Turriago-Hoyos, and U. Thoene. 2018. "Virtuousness and the Common Good as a Conceptual Framework for Harmonizing the Goals of the Individual, Organizations, and the Economy." *Journal of Business Ethics* 147 (1): 143–163. doi:10.1007/s10551-015-2969-6.

Asante, M. K. 2006. "The Rhetoric of Globalisation: The Europeanisation of Human Ideas." *Journal of Multicultural Discourses* 1 (2): 152–158. doi:10.2167/md054.0.

Bagozzi, R. P., and U. M. Dholakia. 2002. "Intentional Social Action in Virtual Communities." *Journal of Interactive Marketing* 16: 2. doi:10.1002/dir.10006.

Baldina, J., and N. Masyuk. 2020. "Organizational Business Model of State Franchising." *SHS Web of Conferences* 73: 01002. doi:10.1051/shsconf/20207301002.

Bauwens, V., and P. Genoud. 2014. "Online Ethnography." *Interactions* 21: 60–65. doi:10.1145/2642749.

Baym, N. K. 2000. *Tune In, Log On: Soaps, Fandom, and Online Community. Tune In, Log On: Soaps, Fandom, and Online Community*. Thousand Oaks, CA: Sage. doi:10.4135/9781452204710.

Bower, J., and C. Christensen. 1995. "Disruptive Technologies: Catching the Wave." *Harvard Business Review* 73 (1): 43–53 (Jan–Feb 1995).

Brown, C. 2016. "3 Questions to Ask before Adopting a Platform Business Model." *Harvard Business Review*. April.

Buntić, L., M. Damić, and D. Sesar. 2020. "Business Model Innovation as a Source of Competitive Advantage." *Quality – Yesterday, Today, Tomorrow* 21 (1): 173–183. doi:10.30657/hdmk.2020.43.

Chang, L. C., W. L. Ho, S. B. Tsai, Q. Chen, and C. C. Wu. 2017. "Dynamic Organizational Learning: A Narrative Inquiry into the Story of Huawei in China." *Asia Pacific Business Review* 23 (4): 541–558. doi:10.1080/13602381.2017.1346910.

Chang, L.-C., C.-T. Wen, Y.-M. Chang, and P.-H. Huang. 2014. "Growth Pattern of an Employee-Owned Business: A Narrative Inquiry Concerning the New Venture Creation Experience of Wowprime in Taiwan." *Asia Pacific Business Review* 20 (3): 439–460. doi:10.1080/13602381.2014.929401.

Chang, Y., R. J. Hou, K. Wang, A. P. Cui, and C. B. Zhang. 2020. "Effects of Intrinsic and Extrinsic Motivation on Social Loafing in Online Travel Communities." *Computers in Human Behavior* 109: 106360. doi:10.1016/j.chb.2020.106360.

Chen, C. F., and J. P. Wang. 2016. "Customer Participation, Value Co-Creation and Customer Loyalty - A Case of Airline Online Check-in System." *Computers in Human Behavior* 62: 346–352. doi:10.1016/j.chb.2016.04.010.

Chen, G.-M. 2013. "A Zhong Dao Model of Management in Global Context." *Intercultural Communication Studies* 1: 1–8.

Chen, J. S., D. Kerr, C. Y. Chou, and C. Ang. 2017. "Business Co-Creation for Service Innovation in the Hospitality and Tourism Industry." *International Journal of Contemporary Hospitality Management* 29 (6): 1522–1540. doi:10.1108/IJCHM-06-2015-0308.

Chen, L., J. R. Marsden, and Z. Zhang. 2012. "Theory and Analysis of Company-Sponsored Value Co-Creation." *Journal of Management Information Systems* 29 (2): 141–172. doi:10.2753/MIS0742-1222290206.

Chen, S. M. 2002. *Qualitative Research in Social Sciences*. Taipei: Wu Nan publisher.

Chin, T., C. Rowley, G. Redding, and S. Wang. 2018. "Chinese Strategic Thinking on Competitive Conflict: Insights from Yin-Yang Harmony Cognition." *International Journal of Conflict Management* 29 (5): 683–704. doi:10.1108/IJCMA-09-2017-0101.

Chiu, W., D. Won, and J. S. Bae. 2019. "Customer Value Co-Creation Behaviour in Fitness Centres: How Does It Influence Customers' Value, Satisfaction, and Repatronage Intention?" *Managing Sport and Leisure* 24 (1–3): 32–44. doi:10.1080/23750472.2019.1579666.

Chou, E.-Y., C.-Y. Lin, and H.-C. Huang. 2016. "Fairness and Devotion Go Far: Integrating Online Justice and Value Co-Creation in Virtual Communities." *International Journal of Information Management* 36 (1): 60–72. doi:10.1016/j.ijinfomgt.2015.09.009.

Chuah, S. H.-W., D. El-Manstrly, M.-L. Tseng, and T. Ramayah. 2020. "Sustaining Customer Engagement Behavior through Corporate Social Responsibility: The Roles of Environmental Concern and Green Trust." *Journal of Cleaner Production* 121348. doi:10.1016/J.JCLEPRO.2020.121348.

Dawson, C. 2019. "Online Ethnography." In *A-Z of Digital Research Methods*, edited by C. Dawson, 55–68. London: Taylor & Francis Group.

De Luo, J., and X. Y. Liang. 2017. *Community Building: Theory, Process and Cases*. Beijing: Social sciences academic press.

Debruyne, M. 2014. *Customer Innovation: Customer-CentricStrategy for Enduring Growth*. Belgium: Kogan Page Limited.

Dholakia, U. M., R. P. Bagozzi, and L. K. Pearo. 2004. "A Social Influence Model of Consumer Participation in Network- and Small-Group-Based Virtual Communities." *International Journal of Research in Marketing* 21 (3): 241–263. doi:10.1016/j.ijresmar.2003.12.004.
Echeverri, P., and P. Skalen. 2011. "Co-Creation and Co-Destruction: A Practice-Theory Based Study of Interactive Value Formation." *Marketing Theory* 11 (3): 351–373. doi:10.1177/1470593111408181.
Fei, X. 2011. *Rural China*. Beijing: Beijing press.
Fieseler, C., E. Bucher, and C. P. Hoffmann. 2019. "Unfairness by Design? the Perceived Fairness of Digital Labor on Crowdworking Platforms." *Journal of Business Ethics* 156 (4): 987–1005. doi 10.1007/s10551-017-3607-2.
Furr, N. 2016. "Transitioning Your Company from Product to Platform Transitioning Your Company from Product to Platform," 2–4.
Gambetti, R. C., and G. Graffigna. 2015. "Value Co-Creation between the 'Inside" and the "Outside" of a Company: Insights from a Brand Community Failure"'." *Marketing Theory* 15 (2): 155–178. doi 10.1177/1470593114545004.
Gellweiler, C., and L. Krishnamurthi. 2020. "Editorial: How Digital Innovators Achieve Customer Value." *Journal of Theoretical and Applied Electronic Commerce Research* 15 (1): I–VIII. doi 10.4067/S0718-18762020000100101.
Greene, J. 2008. "This Social Network Is up and Running." *BusinessWeek*.
Haque, U. 2011. *The New Capitalist Manifesto: Buildinga Disruptively Better Business*. Boston: Harvard Business Review Press.
Horbel, C., B. Popp, H. Woratschek, and B. Wilson. 2016. "How Context Shapes Value Co-Creation: Spectator Experience of Sport Events." *The Service Industries Journal* 36 (11–12): 510–531. doi:10.1080/02642069.2016.1255730.
Hsu, Y. 2016. "A Value Cocreation Strategy Model for Improving Product Development Performance." *Journal of Business and Industrial Marketing* 31 (5): 695–715. doi:10.1108/JBIM-11-2014-0221.
Ihrig, M., and L. MacMillan. 2017. "How to Get Ecosystem Buy-In." *Harvard Business Review*, March.
Jaakkola, E., and M. Alexander. 2014. "The Role of Customer Engagement Behavior in Value Co-Creation: A Service System Perspective." *Journal of Service Research* 17 (3): 247–261. doi:10.1177/1094670514529187.
Jost, J. S. 2020. "The Origins of Dislike by Amit Chaudhuri." *Eighteenth-Century Fiction* 32 (3): 508–510. doi:10.3138/ecf.32.3.508.
Kim, S. H., K. H. Yang, and J. K. Kim. 2009. "Finding Critical Success Factors for Virtual Community Marketing." *Service Business* 3 (2): 149–171. doi:10.1007/s11628-008-0059-x.
Kim, W. C., and R. Mauborgne. 2004. "Blue Ocean." *Harvard Business Review*.
Kozinels, R. V. 2010. *Nelnography: Doing Ethnographic Research Online*. SAGE Publications of London.
Lehrer, M., A. Ordanini, R. DeFillippi, and M. Miozzo. 2012. "Challenging the Orthodoxy of Value Co-Creation Theory: A Contingent View of Co-Production in Design-Intensive Business Services." *European Management Journal* 30 (6): 499–509. doi:10.1016/j.emj.2012.07.006.
Li, Y. 2013. *Traditional Chinese Thinking on HRM Practices; Heritage and Transformation in China*. Basingstoke: Palgrave Macmillan.
Liao, J. W., and Z. U. Cui. 2017. "Apocalypse of Intelligent Business Strategy." *Harvard Business Review (China Edition)*, April.
Liao, T. F. 2020. "Guanxi: How China Works." *Contemporary Sociology: A Journal of Reviews* 49 (2): 141–142. doi:10.1177/0094306120902418e.
Lin, T.-C. 2008. "Study of Knowledge Management System – Activity Theory and Critical Success Chains Perspective," 105–123.
Matemba, E. D., G. Lilves, I. C. W. Gogan, and B. Maiseli. 2020. "Technology Acceptance Model: Receent Developments, Future Directions, and Proposal for Hypothetical Extensions." *International Journal of Technology Intelligence and Planning* 12: 315. forthcoming. Doi:10.1504/IJTIP.2020.109769.
Mitani, K. 2015. *Business Model Zenshi(in Chinese)*. Beijing: Fonghong Book Co.,LTD(original japanesse edition published by Discover 21,Inc.).
Nan, H. 2013. *Nan, Hhuaijin's Collection*. Shanghai: Fudan University Press.

Pang, J., and J. Capek. 2020. "Factors Influencing Researcher Cooperation in Virtual Academic Communities Based on Principal Component Analysis." *Acta Informatica Pragensia* 9: 4–17. doi:10.18267/j.aip.128.

Patton, M. Q. 1990. *Qualitative Evaluation and Research Methods. The Modern Language Journal*. 2nd editio ed. Vol. 76. Newbury Park: Sage. Doi:10.2307/330063.

Prahalad, C. K. 2005. *Fortune at the Bottom of the Pyramid: Eradicating Poverty through Profits*. New Jersey: Dorling Kindersley Pvt.

Prebensen, N. K., J. Vittersø, and T. I. Dahl. 2013. "Value Co-Creation Significance of Tourist Resources." *Annals of Tourism Research* 42: 240–261. doi:10.1016/j.annals.2013.01.012.

Ramaswamy, V. 2009a. "Co-Creation of Value: Toward an Expanded Paradigm of Value Creation." *Marketing Review St. Gallen* 26 (6): 11–17. doi:10.1007/s11621-009-0085-7.

Ramaswamy, V. 2009b. "Leading the Transformation to Co-Creation of Value." *Strategy & Leadership* 37 (2): 32–37. doi:10.1108/10878570910941208.

Ramaswamy, V., and K. Ozcan. 2016. "Brand Value Co-Creation in a Digitalized World: An Integrative Framework and Research Implications." *International Journal of Research in Marketing* 33 (1): 93. doi:10.1016/j.ijresmar.2015.07.001.

Ramaswamy, V., and K. Ozcan. 2018a. "What Is Co-Creation? An Interactional Creation Framework and Its Implications for Value Creation." *Journal of Business Research* 84: 196–205. doi:10.1016/j.jbusres.2017.11.027.

Ramaswamy, V., and K. Ozcan. 2018b. "Offerings as Digitalized Interactive Platforms: A Conceptual Framework and Implications." *Journal of Marketing* 82 (4): 19. doi:10.1509/jm.15.0365.

Ren, H., C. W. Chen, and Y. Chen. 2020. "Between Culture and Satisfaction: Mediating Roles of Renqing Perception and Rules Perception." *Asia Pacific Journal of Human Resources*. doi:10.1111/1744-7941.12256.

Sinanan, J. 2018. "A History of the Convergence of Ethnography, Cultural Studies and Digital Media." *Cultural Studies Review* 24 (2): 181–183. doi:10.5130/csr.v24i2.6316.

Sundararajan, L., and L. Sundararajan. 2020. "A History of the Concepts of Harmony in Chinese Culture." *Oxford Research Encyclopedia of Psychology*. doi:10.1093/acrefore/9780190236557.013.679.

Thomas, L. D. W., E. Autio, and D. M. Gann. 2014. "Architectural Leverage: Putting Platforms in Context." *Academy of Management Perspectives* 28 (2): 198–219. doi:10.5465/amp.2011.0105.

Visnjic, I., A. Neely, and M. Jovanovic. 2017. "A Quest for Fit: Interplay of Service Market Strategy and Business Model Innovation." *Academy of Management Proceedings* 2017: 10358. doi:10.5465/ambpp.2017.10358abstract.

Von Hippel, E. 1988. *The sources of innovation*. New York: Oxford University Press.

Wu, X., Z. Zhao, and B. Zhou. 2019. "Legitimacy in Adaptive Business Model Innovation: An Investigation of Academic Ebook Platforms in China." *Emerging Markets Finance and Trade* 55 (4): 719–742. doi:10.1080/1540496X.2018.1429261.

Yen, H. R., S. H. Y. Hsu, and C. Y. Huang. 2011. "Good Soldiers on the Web: Under-Standing the Drivers of Participation in Online Communities of Consumption." *International Journal of Electronic Commerce* 15 (4): 89–120. doi:10.2753/JEC1086-4415150403.

Zhai, X. 2004. "Renqing, Mianzi and the Reproduction of Power." *Sociology Research* 5: 48–57.

Zhu, F., and N. Furr. 2016. "Products to Platforms: Making the Leap." *Harvard Business Review* 2016 (April): 2012–2014.

Zott, C., R. Amit, and L. Massa. 2011. "The Business Model: Recent Developments and Future Research." *Journal of Management* 37 (4): 1019–1042. doi:10.1177/0149206311406265.

Appendix A.

Table A1. Research questions.

1. How does the V project impact the growth of your innovation?
2. How has the network or community impacted your innovation?
3. How has engagement (training) impacted your innovation?
4. How has the interaction (assessment) impacted your innovation?
5. How has the environment (retention) impacted your innovation?
6. How has the value expansion (promotion) impacted your innovation?
7. Overall, what is the process or pattern of Toutiao's V project?

Table A2. Toutiao (Beijing Bytedance Technology Co. Ltd.) group.

information	short videos	pictures	Q&A	Language learning
Today's headline	Tik Tok	Insect	WuKongQ&A	Young Learners English (gogokid)
Today's headline speed edition Know Car Emperor Headline.	Watermelon video Volcano video Faceu's hot More Flash HuYa DouYu	Faceu's hot		

Sources: this research.

Business model innovation amid manufacturers' servitization transformation

Qiang Xu, Jinghui Yu, Jianxin Xu, Guangxi Zhang and Canying Liang

ABSTRACT

Servitization is important for manufacturers' strategic transition, yet applying servitization has significant barriers. Business model innovation is regarded as a systematic solution of overcoming the barriers. However, it has been insufficiently studied especially in emerging economies. Therefore, we conducted a multi-case study of two leading piano manufacturers engaging in services in China, and explore the process of business model innovation for their servitization. This study finds that, with the facilitation of dynamic capabilities, manufacturers address the barriers through business model innovation in three elements of content, structure and governance, and finally form a new business model with ambidexterity, in which efficiency-centred theme and novelty-centred theme can coexist, interact, and dynamically match with emerging economies' context. This study provides new insights on how manufacturers in emerging economies conduct business model innovation for realizing their servitization transformation.

1. Introduction

Servitization has emerged as a strategy of transformation and upgrading for global manufacturers (Kindstrom and Kowalkowski 2014; Parida et al. 2014). Servitization implies that manufacturers provide more services that are relevant to their products (Baines and Lightfoot 2014). Through servitization, manufacturers can enhance the economic efficiency and strategic advantages, and make their products more appealing to the market (Parida et al. 2014). However, servitization is not easy. Because the heterogeneity and cognitive distance between manufacturing business and service business generate transaction costs, knowledge-absorptive difficulties, and organizational culture conflicts (Xu, Wang, and Liu 2019), the process of servitization encounters great challenges. It was found that when manufacturers implemented servitization, they would face significant barriers and even failures (Benedettini, Neely, and Swink 2015; Michalik, Besenfelder, and Henke 2019). Therefore, how to overcome the servitization barriers is an interesting issue.

Our understanding of the barriers and failures for servitization remains limited (Lutjen, Tietze, and Schultz 2017). Previous researches on the solution of overcoming the servitization barriers only focused on specific aspects, respectively, such as innovation of service content, service methods, service process management, and service personnel management (Lenka et al. 2018; Reinartz and Ulaga 2008; Parida et al. 2014; Coreynen, Matthyssens, and Van Bockhaven 2017). Few of them explored the process systematically. Thus, it is necessary to explore the process and solution of overcoming the barriers during servitization transformation in a more systematic approach.

Business model innovation (BMI) is a system-oriented means that can consolidate firms' competitiveness, helps manufacturers overcome the servitization barriers and thus successfully achieves servitization (Kindstrom and Kowalkowski 2014). BMI is the reconfiguration of a company's existing business model (Wu, Ma, and Shi 2010). Facing changing contexts, companies must innovate adaptive business models (Wu and Zhao 2017), which need dynamic capabilities (Teece 2018). Yet, the mechanism of overcoming servitization barriers through BMI, and the impacts of dynamic capabilities on BMI have not been thoroughly examined. The reconfiguration of business model elements will form a new business model theme (Zott and Amit 2010). According to Amit and Zott (2001), business model is divided into efficiency-centred and novelty-centred business model themes. Servitization will bring novelty to manufacturers, but it will also lead to increased service offerings and higher costs (Cenamor, Sjodin, and Parida 2017). That is, a single-themed business model may have problems such as organizational inertia, high costs, and slow improvement (Hannan and Freeman 1984; He and Wong 2004; Hu and Chen 2016), so it is needed to implement above two business model themes at the same time to achieve greater benefits. Although implementing two business model themes during servitization is rewarding, coordinating two model themes is difficult (Zott and Amit 2007; Hu and Chen 2016). Strong dynamic capabilities are required, because firms with excellent dynamic capabilities can implement, test, and refine business model quickly in a dynamic environment (Teece 2018). Yet, how manufacturers utilize their dynamic capabilities to promote the coexistence and interaction of two business model themes is understudied.

Schneider and Spieth (2013) emphasize the necessity of exploring the process and elements of BMI in specific contexts. Chin et al. (2020) also point out the importance of studying unique value-creating and innovation patterns of BMs in the Asia Pacific. In this study, we explore the process of using BMI to overcome the barriers of manufacturing servitization in China's context. China as an emerging economy country, the specific context is different from developed countries (Makino, Isobe, and Chan 2004), and firms' strategy and behaviours are more sensitive to the institutions, such as the national strategy of 'Made in China 2025'.

This study analyzes two leading piano manufacturing companies in China, Hailun Piano and Pearl River Piano. We try to disclose the barriers manufacturers encounter during servitization, how BMI overcomes servitization barriers, the forming mechanism of business model combining two business model themes, and the role of dynamic capabilities in this process. The remaining part proceeds as follows: we first provide a brief literature review of servitization barriers and BMI, and propose an interpretive framework. Then, we carry out a case study and discuss relevant research issues. Finally, we put forward the theoretical contributions and practical implications.

2. Literature review

2.1. Servitization barriers in manufacturers

Servitization barriers refer to the difficulties of gaining positive return from manufacturers' servitization investment, and falling into the dilemma of service paradox (Michalik, Besenfelder, and Henke 2019). Servitization will bring about parallel changes within and outside organizational boundaries (Benedettini, Neely, and Swink 2015). So servitization barriers can be divided into two categories: internal barriers and external barriers. The internal barriers refer to barriers in terms of resources and capabilities. Resources barriers lie in the shortage of knowledge, technology, human resources, and other relevant resources needed for servitization. Capabilities barriers mainly lie in the inadequate ability to reconfigure resources, change organizational structure, manage the developmental process, and control cost, etc. The external barriers embrace three aspects: consumers, stakeholders (including competitors, suppliers and partners), and industry. Table 1 summarizes the servitization barriers.

Most studies on servitization barriers were conducted in developed economies (e.g. Fang, Palmatier, and Steenkamp 2008; Lutjen, Tietze, and Schultz 2017). By contrast, there are few studies on servitization barriers carried out in emerging economies. As we can see in Table 1, although literatures have analysed the internal and external barriers, insufficient attention has been paid to the servitization barriers pertaining to institutional environment. Nevertheless, Peng, Wang, and Jiang (2008) emphasize that the institution-based view is particularly suitable to be applied in research conducted in emerging

Table 1. Barriers encountered by manufacturers in the process of servitization.

Sources	Aspects	Barriers
Internal	Resources	Companies lack of technical equipment & of adopting new technologies (Caldeira and Ward 2003); Companies lack of an ideal management information system (Martinez et al. 2010); Manufacturers do not possess the resources or the experience for servitization to be implemented (Kowalkowski, Witell, and Gustafsson 2013).
	capabilities	Resource utilization faces potential changes, such as leveraging the workforce and materials across departments (Barquet et al. 2013) and acquiring new resources to reconfigure the internal structure (Neto, Pereira, and Borchardt 2015); Managers overemphasize the cognitive process of tangible characteristics, which limits the motivation to expand service (Gebauer, Fleisch, and Friedli 2005); It is a challenge to shift a cultural mindset from a product-centric to a service-centric (Kowalkowski et al. 2015; Martinez et al. 2010); It is difficult to reconfigure the organizational structure (Zhang and Banerji 2017); Lack of accurate development processes (Michalik, Besenfelder, and Henke 2019); Companies have difficulties of receiving instant feedback during the development process (Zhang and Banerji 2017); Challenges of controlling two major costs exist in servitization: competitive cost and political cost (Mathieu 2001).
External	Customers	Solution providers can not understand the importance of customer knowledge or rely too much on customers, leading solution fails to meet customer demand(Valtakoski 2017); Customers often think services are free, or unwilling to pay extra for it (Coreynen, Matthyssens, and Van Bockhaven 2017).
	Stakeholders	There is inadequate management of the service network (Martinez et al. 2010, Michalik, Besenfelder, and Henke 2019); Stakeholders may not always want to engage in a deeper collaboration (Matthyssens and Vandenbempt 2010; Coreynen, Matthyssens, and Van Bockhaven 2017).
	Industry	Market-related barriers inhibit customer acceptance and network configuration, for example, big data services require strong collaborations with network members who are versed in data management (Lutjen, Tietze, and Schultz 2017).

economies. Based on Peng's strategy tripod perspective, the strategic choice is affected by industry-based competition, firm-specific resources and capabilities as well as institutional conditions and transitions (Peng, Wang, and Jiang 2008; Peng et al. 2009). Industry-based competition as well as institutional conditions and transitions belong to the external environment analysis, while firm-specific resources and capabilities belong to internal environment analysis. Thus, it warrants paying more attention to the institutional environment when we explore servitization barriers.

Scholars have put forward countermeasures against servitization barriers, including innovating service content and service methods, strengthening service process management, and improving personnel management. In terms of innovating service content, Parida et al. (2014) suggest that advanced services and diversified product-service portfolio development, such as maintenance, R&D support, and functional services, can promote successful transformation and generate future revenue. In terms of innovating service methods, Coreynen, Matthyssens, and Van Bockhaven (2017) use four cases to illustrate the approaches for companies to increase services through digitization options: industrial, commercial and value servitization. Other researchers suggest that extending platform to the service business enables manufacturers to overcome servitization barriers (Jha, Bose, and Ngai 2016; Marion, Meyer, and Barczak 2015). In terms of strengthening service process management, Reinartz and Ulaga (2008) propose that if firms desire providing effective services, they must realize process innovation, create service sales teams, and focus on customer service processes. In terms of improving personnel management, Lenka et al. (2018) identify four tactics that staffs can apply to push forward servitization transformation and reduce organizational resistance. Eloranta and Turunen (2016) emphasize the importance of managing relationships among different partners. Because specific aspects of servitization barriers may interact with each other, focusing on a single aspect provides insufficient knowledge and partial solutions. Therefore, scholars invoke more integrated solutions and long-term strategic instruments (Gebauer et al. 2012; Michalik, Besenfelder, and Henke 2019) .

2.2. *Business model innovation*

Servitization is a new form of value creation for manufacturers (Pak et al. 2020). Servitization transformation requires manufacturers to change the way of providing value (Robinson, Chan, and Lau 2016; Barnett et al. 2013; Parida et al. 2014). However, during the process of transformation, manufacturers may encounter the servitization barriers that impede the value creation of the service business. Business model is the 'design or architecture of value creation, delivery and capture mechanisms' of companies (Teece 2010). Casadesus-Masanell and Zhu (2013) define BMI as 'the search for new logics of the firm and new ways to create and capture value for its stakeholders; it focuses primarily on finding new ways to generate revenues and define value propositions for customers, suppliers, and partners'. Therefore, BMI can provide servitization manufacturers with insights from the threat of value lost to value creation. Past studies showed that service-oriented BMI was an important way to successfully realize servitization (Frank et al. 2019; Pak et al. 2020; Chen, Zhang, and Zhang 2020). Therefore manufacturers need to change the business model fundamentally to adopt the service strategy (Storbacka et al. 2013). Companies can use BMI as a tool to visualize changes, which can reconfigure business model elements to improve service level (Kindstrom and Kowalkowski 2014). Visnjic Kastalli and Van Looy (2013) propose that forming mutual spillover effects between products and services is a way to form an integrated business model, thereby successfully realizing servitization.

Zott and Amit (2010) consider business model as the content, structure, and governance of transactions designed to take advantage of business opportunities and create value. This view decomposes the business model into three elements: content, structure and governance. The content element focuses on the value attributes created by the business model and its value-creating activity attributes. The structure element focuses on the attributes of trading partners and their interactive arrangement in the value creation network of business model. The governance element emphasizes the mechanism of benefit distribution, incentives, and constraints among trading partners in the value creation network (Johnson, Christensen, and Kagermann 2008; Voelpel et al. 2005; Zott and Amit 2010). Amit and Zott (2012) point out that changing one or more elements of a business model leads to BMI.

Based on the perspective of value creation, BMI reflects the mechanism of value creation. The innovation process of the business model is accompanied by the upgrading process of the value creation. Business model starts with the value proposition and ends with the value capture and distribution, which are linked by the value creation process (Geissdoerfer, Bocken, and Hultink 2016). Guldmann and Huulgaard (2020) summarize the value creation process of business model with three basic components, namely: the value proposition, the value creation and delivery, and the value capture.

Novelty and efficiency reflect the basic choices of companies to create value in uncertain context. Correspondingly, business model can be divided into two themes: novelty-centred business model theme and efficiency-centred business model theme (Amit and Zott 2001). Novelty-centred business model theme refers to the creative content, structure, and governance. It represents major changes to the existing business model. Efficiency-centred business model theme redesigns content, structure, and governance to reduce transaction costs and improve efficiency (Zott and Amit 2008; Zott, Amit, and Massa 2011). Although the themes of business model are not limited to these two (Zott and Amit 2010), this study mainly focuses on the theme of novelty and efficiency. Because it leads to higher development and delivery costs while innovating services to meet the special service needs of customers (Cenamor, Sjodin, and Parida 2017), the balance between novelty and efficiency is the key to successful servitization transformation. Although there are conflicting managerial demands and resource competition between the two themes, it is found that they can coexist in the same business (Zott and Amit 2007). Ambidexterity plays an important role in this process. Ambidexterity refers to ability to perform differing and competing strategic acts at the same time (Simsek et al. 2009). Markides (2013) discusses two strategies in ambidexterity literature that can manage two themes. Hu and Chen (2016) suggest that ambidexterity can realize the coexistence of two themes. Furthermore, Wilden, Devinney, and Dowling (2016) point out that it may be fruitful to link research streams of dynamic capabilities and ambidexterity. And dynamic capabilities are at the heart of the ability of a business to be ambidextrous (O'Reilly and Tushman 2008). So it is inferred that dynamic capabilities can make novelty-centred and efficiency-centred business model themes coexist. However, the mechanism has not been well studied.

Based on the rational positioning view, environmental changes require firms to make new design choices that optimize the business model to the changing environment (Amit and Zott 2001; Teece 2010; Martins, Rindova, and Greenbaum 2015). Successful application of BMI requires higher-order capabilities, namely dynamic capabilities (Teece 2018). Dynamic capabilities are ability to integrate, build and reconfigure internal and external organization skills, resources, and competences, thus to address rapid changes in the business environment (Teece and Pisano 1994; Teece, Pisano, and Shuen 1997). Strong dynamic capabilities usually mean constantly sense and seize opportunities, and periodically transform (Teece 2018). Teece (2018) points out that the construction, reorganization, implementation and transformation of business model are the output of dynamic capabilities. Zeng, Li, and Liu (2016) propose that dynamic capabilities have positive effects on BMI. Foss and Saebi (2017) point out that dynamic capabilities facilitate the exploration of internal antecedents of BMI in a changing environment. Furthermore, Teece (2018) proposes that it is urgent to understand how specific aspects of dynamic capabilities are related to different elements of BMI. Therefore, studying how dynamic capabilities affect BMI is a promising direction for future studies.

To summarize, the current literature on manufacturing servitization and BMI has three limitations. First, scholars have made significant achievements in the classification, identifying the causes, and finding the solutions of servitization barriers. However, there is a lack of systematic solution. Second, the existing studies have found that BMI can help manufacturers to overcome the servitization barriers systematically, thereby improving the level of service and creating value. Therefore, manufacturers undergoing servitization transformation are required to innovate their business models. What is more, dynamic capabilities can help companies innovate their business models in a dynamic environment. However, how BMI helps firms overcome the servitization barriers, and the role of dynamic capabilities in this process have not been thoroughly studied. Third, servitization transformation of manufacturer brings benefits as well as costs. However, dynamic capabilities can manage two conflicting themes of business model with ambidexterity. We need to have a clear understanding of how to exploit the benefits of two themes while controlling the downsides.

Based on the precedent review and discussion, this study explored how the BMI overcame the servitization barriers by proposing an interpretive framework (see Figure 1). The barriers encountered during servitization transformation require BMI. Firms with strong dynamic

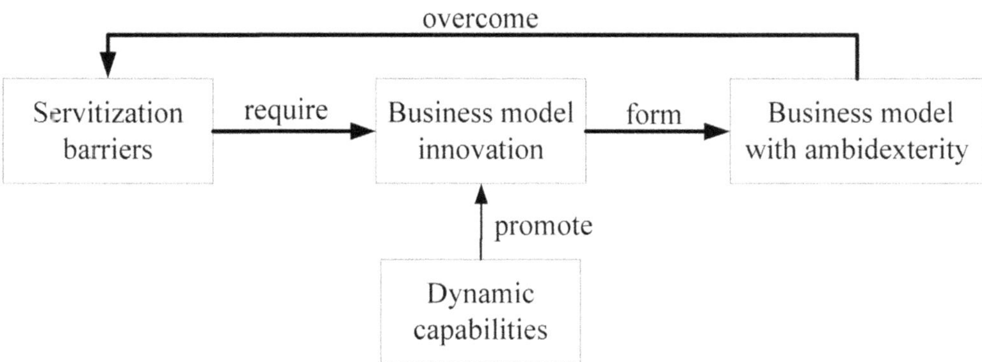

Figure 1. The interpretive framework.

capabilities are more capable to overcome the barriers through BMI. A new business model with ambidexterity ultimately formed.

3. Research methodology

3.1. Methods

This paper intends to illuminate 'how' manufacturers overcome servitization barriers in emerging economies. Case study can appropriately solve the problem of 'how' (Yin 2013). Multiple-case study can reveal horizontal comparisons through obtaining evidence from multiple analysis units (Coreynen, Matthyssens, and Van Bockhaven 2017), which has better verifiability, effectiveness, and generality than single case study. Because multiple-case study provides more information about context and process (Edmondson and McManus 2007), which is suitable for our topic and research purpose. Referring to the analysis method of multi-case in Coreynen, Matthyssens, and Van Bockhaven (2017), we carry out within-case analysis and cross-case analysis on the case data, so as to obtain evidence from them, and refine the model and theory of this study.

3.2. Data collection

Studying manufacturers in China provides valuable knowledge to understand the servitization and BMI in emerging economies. Because servitization is mainly carried out within the manufacturing industry (Baines and Lightfoot 2014), we selected two most influential and representative manufacturers in Chinese piano manufacturing industry: China Hailun Piano Co.,Ltd. (hereinafter referred to as 'Hailun Piano') and Guangzhou Pearl River Piano Group Co.,Ltd. (hereinafter referred to as 'Pearl River Piano'). The two companies originally engaged in manufacturing and selling pianos, mainly focused on improving efficiency and creating transaction value. However, the saturation of traditional piano manufacturing market prompts them to tap the potential intelligent piano training service market. The focus of our study is servitization barriers and BMI; these two companies have overcome servitization barriers through BMI realizing servitization from the piano manufacturing to related training service. The two cases are typical and similar, which increases the effectiveness and verifiability of this case study. In addition, digital technology in emerging economies is developing rapidly, and Pearl River Piano has paid more attention to the application of digital technology than Hailun Piano. This comparison enables us to better understand the impact of context on BMI.

In order to enhance the reliability and validity of data analyses, this paper utilizes the triangulation method. We analysed the case based on multiple sources of data. First, we obtained first-hand data mainly through interviews, and then we analysed the interview record. Secondly, through Hailun Piano official website, Pearl River Piano official website, Baidu.com and other search engines, we got a wide collection of information related to the servitization transformation process of Hailun Piano and Pearl River Piano. Third, we read two companies' annual reports and other documents to obtain information about their servitization. To ensure the accuracy and authenticity of data, we confirmed the important information with relevant personnel. Finally, we combined information from the interview records, web pages, and companies' documents, mutually verified information from different sources.

We analysed the verified case data in several steps. First, we identified the servitization barriers. This paper explores the servitization barriers and BMI in an emerging economy, which makes the institutional environment relevant for the analyses. We attempted to reference Peng's strategy tripod perspective to analyse servitization barriers, which considers firm-specific resources and capabilities, industry-based competition, and institutional conditions and transitions as three pillars of forming strategy. Next, as Amit and Zott (2001) decompose the business model into three elements: content, structure, and governance, we analysed the mechanisms of BMI based on those three elements. Finally, referring to the view of Guldmann and Huulgaard (2020) on value creation process and the definition of three elements of business model by Zott and Amit (2010), we discussed the value creation process based on three steps: value proposition and creation, value delivery, and value capture.

3.3. *The background of the two cases*

3.3.1. *Hailun Piano*

After being listed on the Shenzhen Stock Exchange's Growth Enterprise Market in 2012, Hailun Piano has become the second largest piano manufacturer in China. In 2014, Hailun Piano established companies related to piano training business, which engaged the R&D of intelligent piano and the developed intelligent piano training markets. From then on, Hailun Piano transformed from a traditional piano manufacturer to intelligent piano producer. Hailun Piano extended piano training services through the platform of internet. The 3-year (2017–2019) average figure on Hailun Piano's operating income of intelligent piano classroom was about 3,862,154 RMB. And in 2019, the gross margin of its intelligent piano classroom reached 29.06%, with a year-on-year increase of 7.08%.

3.3.2. *Pearl River Piano*

Pearl River Piano is the 'world's largest piano manufacturer', the leading company in Chinese musical instrument industry and the most influential Chinese brand in the global market. Since 2014, Pearl River Piano has increased its investment in cultural education and considered music training as its important future business. It successively established relative subsidiaries and training system. Pearl River Piano has incorporated new technology and changed the development model of traditional training. The 3-year (2017–2019) average figure on Pearl River Piano's operating income of culture service was about 58,315,918 RMB. In 2019, the operating income of its culture service increased by 2.92%, which accounted for 3.16% of the total operating income.

4. Findings

4.1. *Servitization barriers in piano manufacturing industry*

Hailun Piano and Pearl River Piano mainly encountered three aspects of servitization barriers when they entered into intelligent piano training services. Those barriers come from industry-based competition, firm-specific resources and capabilities, and institutional conditions and transitions. The barriers in each aspect are described in Table 2.

4.2. The process of overcoming servitization barriers

In the two cases, innovation in the content, structure, and governance of business models eventually generates new business models with ambidexterity, which are novel and efficient. The impacts of dynamic capabilities on three elements of business model are mainly manifested in their integrating, building and reconfiguring abilities, which are analysed below.

4.2.1. Hailun piano's BMI in the process of overcoming servitization barriers

4.2.1.1. Innovation in the content of the business model. Hailun Piano reasserted its value proposition as developing elementary intelligent piano, and providing novel and efficient infant piano training. To this end, Hailun Piano carried out new value-creating activities. In the early stage, Hailun Piano integrated external technical team, and in the later, set up R&D centres and technical teams, which reduced the R&D costs and solved technical difficulties. The mature technical conditions has made online and offline piano training come true, thus enabled Hailun Piano to provide the new way of intelligent piano training and expand the market. Specifically, Hailun Piano launched '6 + 1' intelligent piano classroom in which one teacher trained six students, equipped with intelligent piano–I. Piano–as the teaching instrument, the Disney Animation Smart Piano APP as a tutorial, and implemented EMP's unique teaching methods. These innovative and efficient training services met consumers' demands for fun and efficiency. In addition, Hailun Piano followed the policies in music industry to overcome institutional pressures, which was conducive to expanding the training market and making it scale operation. Outsourcing the compilation of textbooks and production of APP helped Hailun Piano to fill the knowledge gaps and standardize the teaching materials and methods for improving the teaching efficiency. Besides, through sponsoring publicity events such as children's piano competitions, Hailun Piano changed consumers' inherent cognition that traditional piano training was boring, and created an attractive atmosphere, which improved the efficiency of market expansion.

It can be seen that, in order to achieve the new value proposition, Hailun Piano reconfigured its internal resources to increase the investment in R&D and operation of intelligent piano training, reflecting its reconfiguring ability. In addition, Hailun Piano integrated external technical resources, and build its own R&D centres and technical teams to assist with other value-creating activities. At the same time, Hailun Piano integrated online and offline resources, such as novel tutorials and teaching methods, as well as music industry-related resources and policy support, to build value-creating activities such as '6 + 1' intelligent teaching mode, which reflected Hailun Piano's integrating and building abilities. The organic integration of intelligent piano and piano training formed a spillover effect of products and services. Hailun Piano's value-creating activities not only brought new experiences to consumers (created new use value), but also reduced transaction costs and created profits for stakeholders (created new transaction value), forming a business model with ambidexterity that combined novelty-centred and efficiency-centred themes.

Table 2. Servitization barriers of Hailun Piano and Pearl River Piano.

Aspects	Barriers	Specific barriers in Hailun Piano and Pearl River Piano
Industrial structure and competition	Hard-to-meet market demands	The pattern of traditional piano training is dull; The so-called intelligent piano assembled by electronic piano and tablet computer that time was expensive and lack origination.
	High industry risks	'Once there was a very good training institution with 4,000 classrooms, but it failed.' In the early stage, Hailun's intelligent piano R&D had a low return and faced the risk of failure.
	Market exploitation was challenging	The offline market expansion of the traditional piano training industry was restricted by the space. The government strictly examined and monitored the extracurricular training institutions. It was hard to develop the offline market by piano manufacturers themselves.
	Consumers needed to be educated	Consumers who were not exposed to intelligent piano training found it was hard to learn piano and the learning process was tedious. Consumers' recognition of innovative teaching methods needed time.
Institutional conditions and transactions	The industry was not well regulated	There was no unified standard for textbook. Moreover, piano teaching was not standardized. Piano teaching did not have regulation systems and regulators, making the implementation of intelligent piano training difficult.
	Unique institutions and cultures	China's institutional environment is unique. Cultural companies are more likely to be influenced by nationally and locally institutional and cultural environment. Whether the government paid attention to art training directly affected the development of intelligent piano training.
Firm-specific resources and capabilities	Positioning deviation caused by organizational routines	Hailun Piano originally produced and sold mid-to-high-end pianos. Organizational inertia initially set its position as performance-level intelligent pianos. This position involved numerous fields and large spans, also caused difficulties in R&D. It did not consider the actual needs of consumers, and it did not match the corporates' actual technical capabilities, resulting in the inability to sell products and barriers in market development.
	Lacking technical capabilities	Hailun Piano: 'The intelligent transformation of pianos meat that companies would face a new field that is completely unrelated to our previous business . . . We knew nothing about it. The idea was good, but application was difficult.' The piano manufacturer did not set foot in higher technology of intelligent development, the technical capacity was insufficient. Pearl river piano: The R&D of supporting software was the highest barrier. 'The technology of intelligent piano was not the highest barrier. An intelligent piano has many functions. If there is no corresponding software to use those functions, the functions will be useless.'
	Knowledge gaps	Piano manufacturers were unfamiliar with music theory, thus they did not know how to compile training materials. Hailun Piano outsourced the R&D of intelligent pianos to other companies, but those companies were unacquainted with pianos, therefore the final products deviated from the original ideas.
	Scarcity of key resources	In the servitization transformation of piano manufacturers, teachers are the scarce key resources. Piano manufacturers and traditional piano training teachers had conflicts of interests, making it difficult to cooperate. In addition, full-time and part-time piano teachers were mixed in the traditional piano training market, with different teaching ability and high mobility. If the piano manufacturers provided training to their own piano teachers, it would be costly and inefficient.

4.2.1.2. Innovation in the structure of the business model. First, Hailun Piano cooperated with professors in Central Conservatory of Music (CCOM), technical experts and distinguished vocal experts, solving the barriers of technology and industrial regulations. Secondly, cooperation with universities helped Hailun Piano save time and costs in training teachers, and created benefits for college students' employment, and ultimately achieved mutual benefits. Finally, the new online and offline multi-functional training systems not only expanded the market, but also changed the network structure of services.

Hailun Piano integrated technology, musical instrument training related knowledge, teachers and other external resources, built a new service network and network relationship, and achieved a win-win situation through multi-cooperation, which reflected its integrating and building abilities. The new service network showed novelty. There were participants such as upstream suppliers, outsourcers, franchisees, colleges, and kindergartens, which formed a new ecosystem in which Hailun Piano was deeply embedded. Value creators in this network shifted from companies to both companies and customers. Hailun Piano delivered the use value to customers and delivered the transaction value to other stakeholders. The service network formed by multi-cooperation and online service mode reduced operating costs and improved transaction efficiency. Hailun Piano also realized the unity of novelty and efficiency in the structure of its business model.

4.2.1.3. Innovation in the governance of the business model. Since 2014, Hailun Piano has cooperated with domestic art institutions through equity investment. By far, there are more than twenty training centres and more than two hundred music classrooms. Most of the music classrooms were franchised and operated in a profit-sharing mode, which reduced the integration degree of Hailun Piano, so that it can quickly make up for its deficiency in the knowledge and experience of service industry and facilitate the expansion of the market. The large-scale operation mode also solved the barriers of non-standard industry. Hailun Piano has built a support system and continuously updated the system to ensure that each classroom has all-round and high-quality franchise service. Hailun Piano has advanced technology, efficient teaching methods, and novel ideas, which formed the inimitable resources and capabilities. Therefore, Hailun Piano was able to reduce the risk of engaging in piano training business and prevented stakeholders' opportunism.

The building ability enabled Hailun Piano to build a new operation mode and a large-scale support system, reshaping the traditional training industry with low industrial concentration and reducing the uncertainty and complexity of transactions. The governance of Hailun Piano's business model reduced transaction costs and completed new value creation, showing novelty and efficiency.

After the above analysis, we summarized three elements of innovation of Hailun Piano's business model and the barriers which have been overcome, respectively, in Table 3, and refined the role of integrating, building, and reconfiguring abilities in the three elements of innovation in Table 4. We used similar methods to get Tables 5 and 6.

4.2.2 Pearl river piano's BMI in the process of overcoming servitization barriers

4.2.2.1. Innovation in the content of the business model. Pearl River Piano identified value proposition as providing art training combined with internet technology. Similar to

Table 3. BMI overcomes the servitization barriers in Hailun Piano.

Three elements		Specific measures	Overcome barriers
Content	Value proposition	• Offering elementary intelligent piano and playful 'online + offline' elementary intelligent piano training.	• Industry-based competition: hard-to-meet market demands, market exploitation was challenging, consumers needed to be educated.
	Value-creating activities	• Innovating technical team, developing intelligent piano. • Based on the intelligent piano classroom, it compiled unified textbooks and conducted 'online + offline' teaching mode through the '6 + 1' teaching model and novel teaching methods. • Establishing a digital platform for market expansion by integrating multiple resources. • Conducting promotional activities.	• Institutional conditions and transitions: the industry was not well regulated, with unique institutions and cultures. • Firm-specific resources and capabilities: positioning deviation caused by organizational routines, lacking technical capabilities, knowledge gaps.
Structure	Participating partners	• Upstream suppliers, outsourcers, franchisees, colleges, kindergartens, training institutions, etc.	• Industry-based competition: market exploitation was challenging.
	Network relationship	• Win-win cooperation in a new ecosystem, which has high level of embeddedness and complex relationships.	• Institutional conditions and transitions: the industry was not well regulated. • Firm-specific resources and capabilities: lacking technical capabilities, knowledge gaps, scarcity of key resources
Governance	value distribution	• Franchised music classrooms; • Profits sharing.	• Institutional conditions and transitions: market exploitation was challenging, high industry risks.
	Incentives and restricts	• Establishing a large-scale supportive system to provide high-quality service to franchisees. • Using inimitable R&D, efficient teaching methods, and novel ideas to restrict stakeholders.	• Institutional conditions and transitions: the industry was not well regulated. • Firm-specific resources and capabilities: knowledge gaps.

Table 4. Dynamic capabilities affect BMI in Hailun Piano.

Three elements	Dynamic capabilities	Business model with ambidexterity
Content	• The reconfiguring ability: Reconfigure internal resources, increase investment in R&D and operation of intelligent piano training • The integrating ability: Integrate external technical resources; integrate products and training services organically; integrate online and offline resources; integrate musical training industry-related resources and policy support; • The building ability: Build its own R&D centres and technical teams; carry out value-creating activities such as '6 + 1' intelligent teaching mode.	• Novelty-centred business model theme: New value-creating activities bring novel experiences to consumers; • Efficiency-centred business model theme: Value-creating activities improve the service efficiency of manufacturers, and reduce transaction costs between consumers and manufacturers.
Structure	• The integrating ability: Integrate external resources such as technology, musical training-related knowledge, and teachers; • The building ability: Through cooperation, build new service networks, network relationships and interaction methods.	• Novelty-centred business model theme: New network members and network structure, new value-creating subjects and delivery methods; • Efficiency-centred business model theme: Service network reduces operating costs and improves transaction efficiency.
Governance	• The building ability: Build a franchise model, a large-scale support system, and a mechanism to restrain stakeholders with inimitable resources and capabilities.	• Novelty-centred business model theme: New operation mode, support mechanisms and restraint mechanisms, capture new value; • Efficiency-centred business model theme: Reshape the traditional training industry with low industrial concentration and reduce transaction costs.

Hailun Piano, Pearl River Piano increased investment in intelligent piano training, provided diversified teaching activities with art classrooms as offline carriers, standardized teaching materials and modes, and held publicity events such as competitions. Furthermore, Pearl River Piano paid more attention to create digital service platforms for delivering mixed teaching of O2O. To this end, Pearl River Piano established internal R&D teams, and cooperated with external technical talents and companies, so as to apply artificial intelligence and cloud technology in piano training. These approaches overcame technical difficulties and met customers' demands of learning online. The innovative service model improved the convenience and flexibility of transactions, and hence facilitated the business expansion in piano education.

Pearl River Piano reconfigured and integrated internal and external technical resources and music training industry-related resources to support the intelligent piano training and the construction of digital service platforms, which essentially reflected its integrating, building and reconfiguring abilities. The innovative course system, teaching mode and service platform of Pearl River Piano have created new transaction value and use value, which was novel. At the same time, the application of digital technology improved the simplicity and flexibility of transaction, raising the teaching efficiency. It can be seen that the content of Pearl River Piano's business model was ambidexterous.

Table 5. BMI overcomes the servitization barriers in Pearl River Piano.

Three elements		Specific measures	Overcome barriers
Content	Value proposition value-creating activities	• Art Training with Modern Internet Technology. • Establishing related subsidiaries; • Based on the intelligent equipment, Pearl River Piano used an innovative course system and teaching mode to carry out the intelligent piano training. • Pearl River Piano formed a learning platform through Internet technology, built piano cloud school, and integrated cloud service platform to implement online training. • Pearl River Piano cooperated with multiple partners, integrated resources to promote the development of training business. • It held games and created a good climate of learning intelligent piano.	• Industry-based competition: hard-to-meet market demands, market exploitation was challenging, consumers needed to be educated. • Institutional conditions and transitions: the industry was not well regulated, unique institutions and cultures. • Firm-specific resources and capabilities: lacking technical capabilities.
Structure	Participating partners	• Suppliers, cooperating companies, franchisees, training institutions, parents, students, universities, experts, and governments.	• Industry-based competition: hard-to-meet market demands.
	Network relationship	• Tripartite interactions, innovative cooperation modes, win-win cooperation, a complex network, a new ecosystem, and a closed loop of the industrial chain.	• Institutional conditions and transitions: the industry was not well regulated. • Firm-specific resources and capabilities: lacking technical capabilities, knowledge gaps, scarcity of key resources.
Governance	value distribution Incentives and restricts	• Industrial operation; 'super partner' mode; Benefit sharing. • Pearl River Piano reduced partners' investment; • Pearl River Piano established teaching mode and management mode with independent intellectual property rights and spread those modes in the whole country, restricting stakeholders. • Pearl River Piano set up the reward mechanism for excess profits and formed a community of interests.	• Institutional conditions and transitions: hard-to-meet market demands, high industry risks. • Institutional conditions and transitions: the industry was not well regulated. • Firm-specific resources and capabilities: scarcity of key resources.

Table 6. Dynamic capabilities affect BMI in Pearl River Piano.

Three elements	Dynamic capabilities	Business model with ambidexterity
Content	• The reconfiguring ability: Increase the resource investment of intelligent piano training; update the internal technical resources; • The integrating ability: Integrate musical training industry-related resources; integrate digital resources; • The building ability: Build intelligent learning platforms and digital service platforms; carry out novel and efficient service activities.	• Novelty-centred business model theme: Innovative course system, teaching mode, service platform and other activities create new value; • Efficiency-centred business model theme: The application of digital technology improves the efficiency, simplicity and flexibility of transactions.
Structure	• The integrating ability: Integrate the original internal resource advantages and external stakeholders' resources; • The building ability: Build new trading platforms, industrial chain, and service ecosystem, construct a new service network.	• Novelty-centred business model theme: New trading partners and network structure, new interaction mode and value delivery mode; • Efficiency-centred business model theme: The service network reduces the complexity and uncertainty of transactions, reduces the transaction costs.
Governance	• The building ability: Build innovative operation modes such as 'super partners'; construct restraint and incentive mechanisms; form new profit distribution methods.	• Novelty-centred business model theme: Innovative governance mechanisms; • Efficiency-centred business model theme: Mature capital operation, governance mode and replicable operation mode reduce transaction cost.

4.2.2.2. Innovation in the structure of the business model. Similar to Hailun Piano, Pearl River Piano cooperated with technological companies, partners, universities, experts, and publishers. The cooperation helped Pearl River Piano absorb knowledge, overcome technical difficulties, eliminate knowledge gaps, access to key resources and standardize intelligent piano training. Pearl River Piano built digital service platforms changed the interaction with customers, it also built a 'piano service online' ecosystem and a closed-loop industrial chain of 'manufacturing-leasing-service-training', all of which promoted the expansion of the market promptly. Besides, students, parents and teachers were connected through an APP, tightening their relationships and improving service efficiency.

Pearl River Piano used the integrating ability to integrate the original internal resource advantages and external stakeholders' resources to make up for its own resource shortage and achieve a win-win situation. Pearl River Piano also used the building ability to form a new service network in which itself was deeply embedded. It delivered use value to customers, and delivered transaction value to stakeholders, forming abundant win–win relationships. The new network members, structure and interaction mode reflected the novelty, which also improved the transaction simplicity and operation efficiency, and reduced the transaction cost. Therefore, Pearl River Piano achieved the unity of novelty and efficiency in the structure of business model.

4.2.2.3. Innovation in the governance of the business model. Pearl River Piano accelerated the development of its training business through industrial operation. Pearl River Piano creatively constructed a 'super partner' mode, which not only helped it to expand the market by providing effective and standardized management, but also motivated partners by greatly reduced their investment. And, it established the teaching methods and management modes with independent intellectual property rights. These measures reduced the risk of entering the piano training industry, and increased the industrial entry barrier for latecomers. To enhance the creativity and loyalty of the core talents, Pearl River Piano set up a new incentive mechanism. The new incentive mechanism closely related the asset income of the core talents to the long-term development of Pearl River Piano, overcoming the barriers of scarcity of key resources. It also founded the national art training centres and formed a new benefit distribution system with its partners.

It was the building ability that enabled Pearl River Piano to create an innovative management and operation mode, profit distribution method, restraint and incentive mechanisms. These innovative governance methods were novel. In addition, mature capital operation and business replication methods reduced the transaction costs of Pearl River Piano. The governance of Pearl River Piano's business model had both novelty-centred and efficiency-centred themes.

5 Discussion

Past studies mainly proposed the means of overcoming the servitization barriers in specific aspects such as innovating new service contents or methods, strengthening service process management, or improving personnel management. In order to have a deeper and more systematic view of the problem, this study analyzes the servitization barriers that manufacturers in emerging economies encounter, and explores the process of the three elements of BMI (i.e. content, structure and governance) eliminates these barriers and the outcomes of BMI. We also study the role that dynamic capabilities play during the process of BMI. Figure 2 shows the process of how manufacturers overcome the servitization barriers and realize BMI.

5.1. BMI overcomes servitization barriers

5.1.1. Innovation in the content of the business model

The starting point of a successful business model is value proposition (Hwang and Christensen 2008). The two cases show that manufacturers put forward new value proposition actively based on the changing environment and customers' demand. Manufacturers reconfigure and integrate resources and capabilities to carry out value-creating activities, overcoming the barriers of lacking technical capabilities, knowledge, and forming new industry standards. These innovative and efficient activities can meet the consumers' actual needs, change their inherent cognition, and help manufacturers expand the market promptly. With policy support from the government, manufacturers carry out value-creating activities more efficiently. Thus, innovation in the content of the business model overcomes the barriers in terms of industry-based competition, institutional conditions and transitions, and firm-specific resources and capabilities.

5.1.2. Innovation in the structure of the business model

Through cooperating with members in the network, manufacturers absorb resources and capabilities that they did not have before, removing barriers of insufficient knowledge,

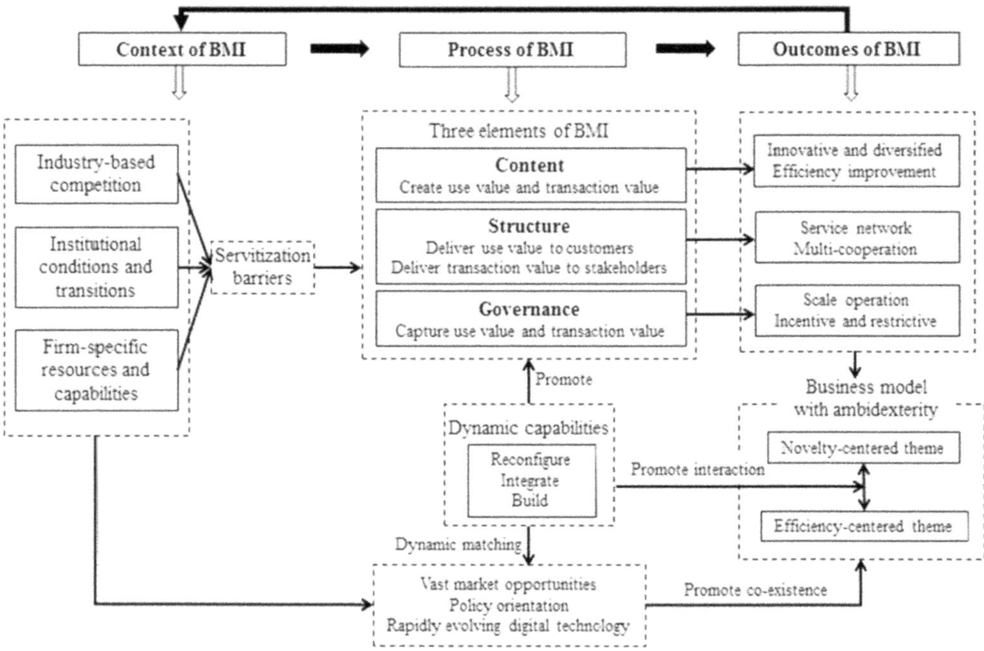

Figure 2. Process diagram for manufacturers to overcome servitization barriers and realize BMI.

technology, critical resources, and industry norms. Moreover, the adoption of digital technology to build service platform changes the transaction mode, the cooperation mode, and the network relationship, enabling manufacturers to expand the market rapidly. Thus, innovation in the structure of the business model overcomes the barriers in terms of industry-based competition, institutional conditions and transitions, and firm-specific resources and capabilities.

5.1.3. Innovation in the governance of the business model

A large-scale and efficient operation mode, and a clear profit model help manufacturers reduce transaction uncertainty, make up for knowledge shortcomings and expand the market quickly. Mechanisms of incentives and constraints enable the network members to form a community of interests, which makes it easier to obtain key resources and reduce the transaction uncertainty, thus reducing the risk of engaging in service business. Therefore, the innovation in the governance of the business model helps the manufacturers overcome the barriers in terms of industry-based competition, institutional conditions and transitions, and firm-specific resources and capabilities.

5.2. Dynamic capabilities and BMI

Cases indicate that dynamic capabilities which include integrating, building and reconfiguring abilities can affect the business model element innovation. In the process of content innovation, manufacturers with strong dynamic capabilities can capture opportunities and integrate resources to provide value-creating activities. Specifically, dynamic capabilities make manufacturers sense the trend of servitization in emerging economies, and recognize their own shortage of resources and capabilities to engage in service business. It is necessary to reconfigure and utilize internal resources, because servitization needs the support from the existing resources. However, it is not enough for a manufacturer to solely rely on its own resources. Manufacturers are motivated to obtain other complementary resources from the outside (Christensen, Johson, and Rigby 2002), such as valuable knowledge, digital technology, human resources, and government support. These resources are orchestrated astutely to carry out R&D, provide novel and efficient services, and implement other value-creating activities (Teece 2018).

In the process of structure innovation, manufacturers with strong dynamic capabilities can integrate external resources and build a new service network and new transaction means. Organizations in the Internet era need to span corporate boundaries to build cooperative relationships with various stakeholders, and need to attract participants to join the value network (Amit and Zott 2001). As found in this paper, manufacturers cooperate with stakeholders to integrate resources, innovate new service platforms and service modes, and build new service networks. These strategies create synergy of resources and capabilities among participants in the networks (Amit and Zott 2001). The structure innovation in the business model makes manufacturers pay more attention to forming win-win relationships with partners, customers, and other stakeholders (Parida et al. 2014).

In the process of governance innovation, manufacturers with strong dynamic capabilities can build new governance mode and mechanisms of incentives and constraints. Manufacturers motivate stakeholders and consolidate their loyalty (Augier and Teece 2009). By constraining stakeholders and competitors with inimitable resources and capabilities, such as teaching methods and management mode with independent intellectual property rights, manufacturers can form more competitive governance and operation modes than potential competitors, thus rapidly expanding their market shares and obtain cost advantages (Teece 2018). The clear cost and profit modes also fit manufacturers' value proposition. The benefit-sharing mechanisms among network members make the value creation process sustainable.

Based on the above analysis of three elements of BMI, we find that the dynamic capabilities enable manufacturers to respond to the changing environment quickly and capture market chances. By developing resources and capabilities related to servitization, manufacturers reconfigure elements of the business model (Kindstrom and Kowalkowski 2014), and then successfully achieve servitization transformation.

5.3. *Dynamic capabilities, emerging economies' context and business model with ambidexterity*

Cases indicate that three elements of new business model show the coexistence of two business model themes. Firstly, value-creating service activities are innovative and diversified, which can increase novelty of the business model. These activities also increase the efficiency of the business model. For example, the novel online teaching can improve the efficiency of transaction and reduce transaction costs through digital means. Secondly, the introduction of new transaction partners, the formation of new network structure, network relationship and value delivery mode increase the novelty of business model. The synergy effect of service network reduces information asymmetry, uncertainty of transaction, and complexity among stakeholders, thus increasing the efficiency of the business model. Finally, the innovative modes such as 'super partner' and the mechanisms of incentives and constraints increase the novelty of the business model. The large-scale operation mechanism reduces the defect of fragmentation of the original industry, and the incentive and restraint mechanism reduces network members' speculation and transaction uncertainty, increasing the efficiency of the business model. The coexistence of two business model themes echoes the view that companies in emerging economies are paying more attention to innovation than before while focusing on low costs (Lu and Sun 2013).

Business model is developed in a specific context (Foss and Saebi 2017), and the specific context requires companies to apply specific dynamic capabilities (Wilden, Devinney, and Dowling 2016). Therefore, dynamic capabilities can dynamically match BMI with the specific context. Based on literature review and case analysis, we find that dynamic capabilities can internalize the effects of the context in emerging economies in terms of their vast market opportunities, policy orientation, and rapidly evolving digital technology, so as to promote the coexistence of novelty-centred and efficiency-centred themes in one business. The newly formed business model with ambidexterity dynamically matches with above context characteristics. Specifically, first, the rapid development of emerging economies has brought a lot of market opportunities (Lu and Sun 2013). Dynamic capabilities help manufacturers to sense chances and threats when the environment changes. Thus, they can quickly seize market possibilities and transform, avoiding organizational inertia (Teece 2018). Manufacturers exploit and improve their original knowledge and capabilities, explore and integrate service-related sources and capabilities that can help transformation as well, thus increasing the adaptability of manufacturers in emerging economies' dynamic environment. Manufacturers with strong dynamic capabilities can make the best allocation of resources and capabilities. The two manufacturers in our case study outsourced APP R&D, textbook compilation etc., got rid of non-critical businesses, and concentrated resources and capabilities on how to better create a service-related business model. This strategy can better manage conflicting managerial demands and resource competition, and make two business model themes coexist in a business successfully. Second, the policy orientation of emerging economies, on the one hand, plays a stimulating role in new market demand, which makes the industry form a certain scale. On the other hand, the policy orientation plays a catalytic role in manufacturers' transformation, dynamic capabilities make companies integrate policy support and external resources brought by policy orientation more quickly, which enables them to reduce operation costs through mass customization, so as to realize the unity of novelty and efficiency. China's policies on music training industry enable Hailun Piano to have more support and convenience in obtaining resources and cooperating with CCOM which is the top school in music teaching. Third, the development of digital technology and internet-enabled platform can change the way organizations operate and transact (Chin, Wang, and Rowley 2020). With the rapid development of digital technology in China, the dynamic capabilities enable manufacturers to sense technological possibilities and utilize them to change transaction modes, boosting both novelty-centred theme and efficiency-centred theme. For example, Pearl River Piano built teaching online platform using digital technology, which not only innovated the transaction mode, improved the novelty, but also made the transaction more flexible, convenient and efficient. Based on the above analysis, it is found that these contextual characteristics are consistent with the view that the growth of Chinese companies are largely influenced by the Chinese unique context in terms of market regime, institutional regime and technical regime (Wei and Liu 2017).

Our case study indicates that the two themes have positive interactions between each other as well. On the one hand, efficiency-centred theme reduces the high cost and low-efficiency problems caused by service innovation, providing a solid foundation for novelty-centred theme. Dynamic capabilities ensure the existing capabilities of development and modification (He and Wong 2004), enable the original capabilities provide more basis for exploring new resources and capabilities, and thus strive for more resources and opportunities for innovation. Reducing transaction cost requires manufacturers to change and innovate the transaction mode which increases the novelty. On the other hand, novelty-centred theme makes efficiency-centred theme more flexible and innovative, avoiding manufacturers trap in suboptimal stable equilibria (March 1991). Dynamic capabilities enable the newly explored resources and capabilities supplement the original resources and capabilities (Katila and Ahuja 2002), improving the transaction mode and increasing efficiency. Novelty-centred theme boosts the efficiency in several ways. First, innovative digital methods can improve transaction efficiency. Second, the higher the novelty, the higher the conversion cost of stakeholders (Zott and Amit 2007), which can reduce the uncertainty of transactions, thereby improving efficiency. For example, the novel and inimitable training mode which was the result of Hailun Piano utilizing dynamic capabilities reduced the uncertainty and costs of transaction between it and franchisees. The operation mode with high-certainty also laid the foundation to further innovate service. Dynamic capabilities enable two contradictory business model themes, that is efficiency-centred and novelty-centred themes, to coexist and interact in a new business model through exploration and exploitation, which is the business model with ambidexterity. Business model with ambidexterity formed in the specific context of China is a balance between the two contradictory business model themes, which reflects the application of Chinese yin-yang harmony cognition in strategic management (Chin et al. 2018; Chin et al. 2020).

6. Implications

6.1. *Implications for theory and theory development*

Based on a multiple-case study involving two top piano manufacturers in China, this paper has three main theoretical contributions. First, we provide a systematic framework of BMI concerning its context, process, and outcomes. This framework studies the relationships between BMI and servitization transformation of manufacturers. Therefore, it provides a solution to the servitization barriers not only on the operational level, but on the strategical level as well, which responds to call from scholars for exploring more integrated solutions and long-term strategic instruments (Gebauer et al. 2012; Michalik, Besenfelder, and Henke 2019). At the same time, studying this framework in the context of emerging economies provides us a better understanding of how the BMI can be developed in a specific context. More specifically, in the past studies, antecedents for BMI include changes in competition, technologies, network position, stakeholder, demands, strategies, et al. (Foss and Saebi 2017). In this study, servitization barriers are regarded as antecedents of BMI. The ultimate goal of BMI is creating value, and the process of BMI enables manufacturers to overcome servitization barriers, finally forming an innovative business model with ambidexterity and realize value creation. The study systematically expands the conditions that lead to BMI (i.e. context), the measures that promote successful BMI (i.e. process), and the business model theme that manufacturing servitization companies need (i.e. outcomes). Second, this study identifies the mechanisms of dynamic capabilities to promote BMI in the context of China. That is, in view of the need for more nuanced and indigenous research in China's important topics and fields (Rowley and Oh 2019), it is of great significance to study service-oriented BMI when manufacturers transform to service becomes a trend in China. So taking the dynamic capabilities to the BMI-specific context helps us discern how dynamic capabilities can internalize the effects of the context in emerging economies in terms of their vast market opportunities, policy orientation, and rapidly evolving digital technology. Dynamic capabilities which include integrating, building and reconfiguring abilities can promote the innovation of content, structure and governance of business model, and promote the coexistence and interaction of novelty-centred and efficiency-centred themes, supporting the call of Teece (2018) for studying how specific aspects of dynamic capabilities are related to different elements of BMI. The findings not only echo the dynamic capabilities perspective on BMI, but also give us a deeper understanding of how BMI happens in emerging economies. Third, this study emphasizes the importance of implementing business model with ambidexterity. Servitization requires manufacturers to pay attention to both novelty and efficiency. In the context of emerging economies, dynamic capabilities enable novelty-centred and efficiency-centred business model themes to coexist and interact with each other in the business model of the manufacturer's servitization. From the perspective of dynamic capabilities, this study further reveals the mechanism of forming a business model with ambidexterity, and strengthens the link between dynamic capabilities and ambidexterity (Wilden, Devinney, and Dowling 2016).

6.2. *Implications for business and management practice*

This paper has managerial implications for manufacturers in emerging economies, which are undergoing servitization transformation. Firstly, our findings can guide manufacturers who planning to transform to service and facilitate them to identify and eliminate potential or existing barriers. Secondly, this paper proves that BMI is a systematic method to overcome the servitization barriers, which enlightens manufacturers in emerging economies on how to overcome barriers successfully. Therefore, encountering servitization barriers, manufacturers should carry out new value positioning proactively, conduct value-creating activities, build service network, and innovate governance methods. Thirdly, the service industry has a certain particularity, for consumers are highly sensitive to the service price and they have higher requirements for innovation and personalization of services. Therefore, it is of great practical significance to provide a solution for managers to achieve the coexistence of efficiency and novelty when manufacturers transform to service becomes a trend. Finally, in the rapidly changing era, manufacturers need to enhance their dynamic capabilities, which help them to sense chances and threats, seize chances, and adjust structure and culture to transform, and reduce transaction costs while innovating services.

6.3. Limitations and future research directions

This study has some limitations. Firstly, the two companies selected are manufacturers in the musical instrument industry, thus the findings might not be applied to other industries. Therefore, future work is required to test the findings in other industries. Secondly, there are still unanswered questions about how to develop dynamic capabilities to facilitate BMI. We suggest scholars to further analyse the relationship between dynamic capabilities and BMI based on specific situations.

7. Conclusions

This paper analyzes and explores the servitization barriers and BMI of two leading piano manufacturers in China, Hailun Piano and Pearl River Piano. We find that, in emerging economies, manufacturers who transform to service encounter barriers in three aspects, including industry-based competition, institutional conditions and transitions, as well as firm-specific resources and capabilities. Innovation in the content, structure, and governance of business model can overcome the servitization barriers. The process of three elements of innovation of business model is accompanied by the upgrading process of the value creation. Manufacturers proceed with a new value proposition, create the tangible transaction value and the intangible use value, and delivery value to the stakeholders, and finally capture the new value. Dynamic capabilities which include integrating, building and reconfiguring abilities promote three elements of innovation of business model. Strong dynamic capabilities enable novelty-centred and efficiency-centred themes coexist and interact in one business. The newly formed business model shows ambidexterity, which dynamically matches with emerging economies' context through dynamic capabilities.

Disclosure statement

No potential conflict of interest was reported by the authors.

Funding

This work was supported by Zhejiang Province Social Science Planning Project [No. 17NDJC229YB].

References

Amit, R., and C. Zott. 2001. "Value Creation in E-business." *Strategic Management Journal* 22 (6–7): 493–520. doi:10.1002/smj.187.

Amit, R., and C. Zott. 2012. "Creating Value Through Business Model Innovation." *Mit Sloan Management Review* 53 (3): 41-+.

Augier, M., and D. J. Teece. 2009. "Dynamic Capabilities and the Role of Managers in Business Strategy and Economic Performance." *Organization Science* 20 (2): 410–421. doi:10.1287/orsc.1090.0424.

Baines, T., and H. W. Lightfoot. 2014. "Servitization of the Manufacturing Firm Exploring the Operations Practices and Technologies that Deliver Advanced Services." *International Journal of Operations & Production Management* 34 (1): 2–35. doi:10.1108/ijopm-02-2012-0086.

Barnett, N. J., G. Parry, M. Saad, L. B. Newnes, and Y. Mey. 2013. "Servitization: Is a Paradigm Shift in the Business Model and Service Enterprise Required?" *Strategic Change Goh* 22 (3–4): 145–156. doi:10.1002/jsc.1929.

Barquet, B., A. Paula, M. G. De Oliveira, C. R. Amigo, V. P. Cunha, and H. Rozenfeld. 2013. "Employing the Business Model Concept to Support the Adoption of Product-service Systems (PSS)." *Industrial Marketing Management* 42 (5): 693–704. doi:10.1016/j.indmarman.2013.05.003.

Benedettini, O., A. Neely, and M. Swink. 2015. "Why Do Servitized Firms Fail? A Risk-based Explanation." *International Journal of Operations & Production Management* 35 (6): 946–979. doi:10.1108/ijopm-02-2014-0052.

Caldeira, M. M., and J. M. Ward. 2003. "Using Resource-based Theory to Interpret the Successful Adoption and Use of Information Systems and Technology in Manufacturing Small and Medium-sized Enterprises." *European Journal of Information Systems* 12 (2): 127–141. doi:10.1057/palgrave.ejis.3000454.

Casadesus-Masanell, R., and F. Zhu. 2013. "Business Model Innovation and Competitive Imitation: The Case of Sponsor-based Business Models." *Strategic Management Journal* 34 (4): 464–482. doi:10.1002/smj.2022.

Cenamor, J., D. R. Sjodin, and V. Parida. 2017. "Adopting a Platform Approach in Servitization: Leveraging the Value of Digitalization." *International Journal of Production Economics* 192: 54–65. doi:10.1016/j.ijpe.2016.12.033.

Chen, J., R. Zhang, and Y. Zhang. 2020. "The Effect of Servitization Strategy on Enterprise Performance: Based on the Mediating of Business Model Innovation." *Science Research Management* 41 (4): 131–139.

Chin, T., C. Rowley, G. Redding, and S. Wang. 2018. "Chinese Strategic Thinking on Competitive Conflict: Insights from Yin-Yang Harmony Cognition." *International Journal of Conflict Management* 29 (5): 683–704. doi:10.1108/IJCMA-09-2017-0101.

Chin, T., Y. Shi, C. Rowley, and J. W. Meng. 2020. "Confucian Business Model Canvas in the Asia Pacific: A Yin-Yang Harmony Cognition to Value Creation and Innovation." *Asia Pacific Business Review* 1–17. doi:10.1080/13602381.2020.1795481.

Chin, T., S. Wang, and C. Rowley. 2020. "Polychronic Knowledge Creation in Cross-border Business Models: A Sea-like Heuristic Metaphor." *Journal of Knowledge Management* 25 (1): 1–22. doi:10.1108/jkm-04-2020-0244.

Christensen, C. M., M. W. Johson, and D. K. Rigby. 2002. "Foundations for Growth - How to Identify and Build Disruptive New Businesses." *Mit Sloan Management Review* 43 (3): 22-+.
Coreynen, W., P. Matthyssens, and W. Van Bockhaven. 2017. "Boosting Servitization through Digitization: Pathways and Dynamic Resource Configurations for Manufacturers." *Industrial Marketing Management* 60: 42–53. doi:10.1016/j.indmarman.2016.04.012.
Edmondson, A. C., and S. E. McManus. 2007. "Methodological Fit in Management Field Research." *Academy of Management Review* 32 (4): 1155–1179. doi:10.5465/amr.2007.26586086.
Eloranta, V., and T. Turunen. 2016. "Platforms in Service-driven Manufacturing: Leveraging Complexity by Connecting, Sharing, and Integrating." *Industrial Marketing Management* 55: 178–186. doi:10.1016/j.indmarman.2015.10.003.
Fang, E., R. W. Palmatier, and J.-B. E. M. Steenkamp. 2008. "Effect of Service Transition Strategies on Firm Value." *Journal of Marketing* 72 (5): 1–14. doi:10.1509/jmkg.72.5.1.
Foss, N. J., and T. Saebi. 2017. "Fifteen Years of Research on Business Model Innovation: How Far Have We Come, and Where Should We Go?" *Journal of Management* 43 (1): 200–227. doi:10.1177/0149206316675927.
Frank, A. G., G. H. S. Mendes, N. F. Ayala, and A. Ghezzi. 2019. "Servitization and Industry 4.0 Convergence in the Digital Transformation of Product Firms: A Business Model Innovation Perspective." *Technological Forecasting and Social Change* 141: 341–351. doi:10.1016/j.techfore.2019.01.014.
Gebauer, H., E. Fleisch, and T. Friedli. 2005. "Overcoming the Service Paradox in Manufacturing Companies." *European Management Journal* 23 (1): 14–26. doi:10.1016/j.emj.2004.12.006.
Gebauer, H., G.-J. Ren, A. Valtakoski, and J. Reynoso. 2012. "Service-driven Manufacturing Provision, Evolution and Financial Impact of Services in Industrial Firms." *Journal of Service Management* 23 (1): 120–136. doi:10.1108/09564231211209005.
Geissdoerfer, M., N. M. P. Bocken, and E. J. Hultink. 2016. "Design Thinking to Enhance the Sustainable Business Modelling Process - A Workshop Based on A Value Mapping Process." *Journal of Cleaner Production* 135: 1218–1232. doi:10.1016/j.jclepro.2016.07.020.
Guldmann, E., and R. D. Huulgaard. 2020. "Barriers to Circular Business Model Innovation: A Multiple-case Study." *Journal of Cleaner Production* 243: 118160. doi:10.1016/j.jclepro.2019.118160.
Hannan, M. T., and J. H. Freeman. 1984. "Structural Inertia and Organizational Change." *American Sociological Review* 49 (2): 149–164. doi:10.2307/2095567.
He, Z. L., and P. K. Wong. 2004. "Exploration Vs. Exploitation: An Empirical Test of the Ambidexterity Hypothesis." *Organization Science* 15 (4): 481–494. doi:10.1287/orsc.1040.0078.
Hu, B., and W. Chen. 2016. "Business Model Ambidexterity and Technological Innovation Performance: Evidence from China." *Technology Analysis & Strategic Management* 28 (5): 583–600. doi:10.1080/09537325.2015.1122186.
Hwang, J., and C. M. Christensen. 2008. "Disruptive Innovation In Health Care Delivery: A Framework For Business-Model Innovation." *Health Affairs* 27 (5): 1329–1335. doi:10.1377/hlthaff.27.5.1329.
Jha, A. K., I. Bose, and E. W. T. Ngai. 2016. "Platform Based Innovation: The Case of Bosch India." *International Journal of Production Economics* 171: 250–265. doi:10.1016/j.ijpe.2015.09.037.
Johnson, M. W., C. M. Christensen, and H. Kagermann. 2008. "Reinventing Your Business Model." *Harvard Business Review* 86 (12): 50-+.
Katila, R., and G. Ahuja. 2002. "Something Old, Something New: A Longitudinal Study of Search Behavior and New Product Introduction." *Academy of Management Journal* 45 (6): 1183–1194. doi:10.2307/3069433.
Kindstrom, D., and C. Kowalkowski. 2014. "Service Innovation in Product-centric Firms: A Multidimensional Business Model Perspective." *Journal of Business & Industrial Marketing* 29 (2): 96–111. doi:10.1108/jbim-08-2013-0165.
Kowalkowski, C., C. Windahl, D. Kindstrom, and H. Gebauer. 2015. "What Service Transition? Rethinking Established Assumptions about Manufacturers' Service-led Growth Strategies." *Industrial Marketing Management* 45: 59–69. doi:10.1016/j.indmarman.2015.02.016.
Kowalkowski, C., L. Witell, and A. Gustafsson. 2013. "Any Way Goes: Identifying Value Constellations for Service Infusion in SMEs." *Industrial Marketing Management* 42 (1): 18–30. doi:10.1016/j.indmarman.2012.11.004.

Lenka, S., V. Parida, D. R. Sjodin, and J. Wincent. 2018. "Exploring the Microfoundations of Servitization: How Individual Actions Overcome Organizational Resistance." *Journal of Business Research* 88: 328–336. doi:10.1016/j.jbusres.2017.11.021.
Lu, Y., and J. Sun. 2013. "A New Perspective of the Growth Strategy of China's Firms: The Concept, the Intention,and the Method,of the Composition-based View." *Management World* 2013 (10): 106–117+141+187–188.
Lutjen, H., F. Tietze, and C. Schultz. 2017. "Service Transitions of Product-centric Firms: An Explorative Study of Service Transition Stages and Barriers in Germany's Energy Market." *International Journal of Production Economics* 192: 106–119. doi:10.1016/j.ijpe.2017.03.021.
Makino, S., T. Isobe, and C. M. Chan. 2004. "Does Country Matter?" *Strategic Management Journal* 25 (10): 1027–1043. doi:10.1002/smj.412.
March, J. G. 1991. "Exploration and Exploitation in Organizational Learning." *Organization Science* 2 (1): 71–87. doi:10.1287/orsc.2.1.71.
Marion, T. J., M. H. Meyer, and G. Barczak. 2015. "The Influence of Digital Design and IT on Modular Product Architecture." *Journal of Product Innovation Management* 32 (1): 98–110. doi:10.1111/jpim.12240.
Markides, C. C. 2013. "Business Model Innovation: What Can the Ambidexterity Literature Teach Us?" *Academy of Management Perspectives* 27 (4): 313–323. doi:10.5465/amp.2012.0172.
Martinez, V., M. Bastl, J. Kingston, and S. Evans. 2010. "Challenges in Transforming Manufacturing Organisations into Product-Service Providers." *Journal of Manufacturing Technology Management* 21 (4): 449–469. doi:10.1108/17410381011046571.
Martins, L. L., V. P. Rindova, and B. E. Greenbaum. 2015. "Unlocking the Hidden Value of Concepts: A Cognitive Approach to Business Model Innovation." *Strategic Entrepreneurship Journal* 9 (1): 99–117. doi:10.1002/sej.1191.
Mathieu, V. 2001. "Service Strategies within the Manufacturing Sector: Benefits, Costs and Partnership." *International Journal of Service Industry Management* 12 (5): 451–475. doi:10.1108/eum0000000006093.
Matthyssens, P., and K. Vandenbempt. 2010. "Service Addition as Business Market Strategy: Identification of Transition Trajectories." *Journal of Service Management* 21 (5): 693–714. doi:10.1108/09564231011079101.
Michalik, A., C. Besenfelder, and M. Henke. 2019. "Servitization of Small- and Medium-Sized Manufacturing Enterprises: Facing Barriers through the Dortmund Management Model." *Ifac Papersonline* 52 (13): 2326–2331. doi:10.1016/j.ifacol.2019.11.553.
Neto, G. Z., G. M. Pereira, and M. Borchardt. 2015. "What Problems Manufacturing Companies Can Face When Providing Services around the World?" *Journal of Business & Industrial Marketing* 30 (5): 461–471. doi:10.1108/jbim-05-2012-0090.
O'Reilly, C. A., and M. L. Tushman. 2008. "Ambidexterity as a Dynamic Capability: Resolving the Innovator's Dilemma." *Research in Organizational Behavior* 28: 185–206. doi:10.1016/j.riob.2008.06.002.
Pak, K., X. Sun, Y. Qian, and J. Kim. 2020. "A Research on the Interactive Mechanism of Technological Innovation and Business Model Innovation in Servitization Transformation of Manufacturing Enterprise——The Case Study of Shenyang Machine Tool." *Science of Science and Management of S.& T* 41 (2): 94–115.
Parida, V., D. Ronnberg-Sjodin, J. Wincent, and M. Kohtamaki. 2014. "Mastering the Transition to Product-Service Provision Insights into Business Models, Learning Activities, and Capabilities." *Research-Technology Management* 57 (3): 44–52. doi:10.5437/08956308x5703227.
Peng, M. W., D. Y. L. Wang, and Y. Jiang. 2008. "An Institution-based View of International Business Strategy: A Focus on Emerging Economies." *Journal of International Business Studies* 39 (5): 920–936. doi:10.1057/palgrave.jibs.8400377.
Peng, M. W., S. L. Sun, B. Pinkham, and H. Chen. 2009. "The Institution-Based View as a Third Leg for a Strategy Tripod." *Academy of Management Perspectives* 23 (3): 63–81. doi:10.5465/amp.2009.43479264.
Reinartz, W., and W. Ulaga. 2008. "How to Sell Services More Profitably." *Harvard Business Review* 86 (5): 90-+.

Robinson, W., P. Chan, and T. Lau. 2016. "Finding New Ways of Creating Value A Case Study of Servitization in Construction." *Research-Technology Management* 59 (3): 37–49. doi:10.1080/08956308.2016.1161405.

Rowley, C., and I. Oh. 2019. "Trends in Chinese Management and Business: Change, Confucianism, Leadership, Knowledge & Innovation." *Asia Pacific Business Review*. doi:10.1080/13602381.2019.1698707.

Schneider, S., and P. Spieth. 2013. "Business Model Innovation: Towards an Integrated Future Research Agenda." *International Journal of Innovation Management* 17 (1): 1340001(34 pp.)-1340001 (34 pp.). doi:10.1142/s136391961340001x.

Simsek, Z., C. Heavey, J. F. Veiga, and D. Souder. 2009. "A Typology for Aligning Organizational Ambidexterity's Conceptualizations, Antecedents, and Outcomes." *Journal of Management Studies* 46 (5): 864–894. doi:10.1111/j.1467-6486.2009.00841.x.

Storbacka, K., C. Windahl, S. Nenonen, and A. Salonen. 2013. "Solution Business Models: Transformation along Four Continua." *Industrial Marketing Management* 42 (5): 705–716. doi:10.1016/j.indmarman.2013.05.008.

Teece, D., and G. Pisano. 1994. "The Dynamic Capabilities of Firms: An Introduction." *Industrial and Corporate Change* 3 (3): 537–556. doi:10.1093/icc/3.3.537-a.

Teece, D. J. 2018. "Business Models and Dynamic Capabilities." *Long Range Planning* 51 (1): 40–49. doi 10.1016/j.lrp.2017.06.007.

Teece, D. J., G. Pisano, and A. Shuen. 1997. "Dynamic Capabilities and Strategic Management." *Strategic Management Journal* 18 (7): 509–533. doi:10.1002/(SICI)1097-0266(199708)18:7<509::AID-SMJ882>3.0.CO;2-Z.

Teece D. J. 2010. "Business Models, Business Strategy and Innovation." *Long Range Planning* 43 (2–3): 172–194. doi:10.1016/j.lrp.2009.07.003.

Valtakoski, A. 2017. "Explaining Servitization Failure and Deservitization: A Knowledge-based Perspective." *Industrial Marketing Management* 60: 138–150. doi:10.1016/j.indmarman.2016.04.009.

Visnjic Kastalli, I., and B. Van Looy. 2013. "Servitization: Disentangling the Impact of Service Business Model Innovation on Manufacturing Firm Performance." *Journal of Operations Management* 31 (4): 169–180. doi:10.1016/j.jom.2013.02.001.

Voelpel, S., M. Leibold, E. Tekie, and G. Von Krogh. 2005. "Escaping the Red Queen Effect in Competitive Strategy." *European Management Journal* 23 (1): 37–49. doi:10.1016/j.emj.2004.12.008.

Wei, J., and Y. Liu. 2017. "Asymmetric Innovation Strategy of Chinese Enterprises." *Tsinghua Business Review* 10: 20–26.

Wilden, R., T. M. Devinney, and G. R. Dowling. 2016. "The Architecture of Dynamic Capability Research Identifying the Building Blocks of a Configurational Approach." *Academy of Management Annals* 10 (1): 997–1076. doi:10.1080/19416520.2016.1161966.

Wu, X. B., R. F. Ma, and Y. J. Shi. 2010. "How Do Latecomer Firms Capture Value from Disruptive Technologies? A Secondary Business-Model Innovation Perspective." *Ieee Transactions on Engineering Management* 57 (1): 51–62. doi:10.1109/tem.2009.2033045.

Wu, X., and Z. Zhao. 2017. "The Antecedents of Business Model Innovation: A Literature Review and Research Agenda." *Foreign Economics & Management* 39 (1): 114–127.

Xu, S. Q. Wang, and D. Liu. 2019. "Research on the Pattern of Enterprises' Cross-Industry Innovation for Obtaining Competence." *China Industrial Economics* 2019 (3): 175–192. doi:10.19581/j.cnki.ciejournal.2019.03.020.

Yin, R. K. 2013. *Case Study Research: Design and Methods*. Thousand Oaks, CA: SAGE Publications.

Zeng, P., M. Li, and Y. Liu. 2016. "Government Support, Dynamic Capabilities, and Business Model Innovation: Mediation and Moderation Effects." *R&D Management* 28 (4): 31–38+137.

Zhang, W., and S. Banerji. 2017. "Challenges of Servitization: A Systematic Literature Review." *Industrial Marketing Management* 65: 217–227. doi:10.1016/j.indmarman.2017.06.003.

Zott, C., and R. Amit. 2007. "Business Model Design and the Performance of Entrepreneurial Firms." *Organization Science* 18 (2): 181–199. doi:10.1287/orsc.1060.0232.

Zott, C., and R. Amit. 2008. "The Fit between Product Market Strategy and Business Model: Implications for Firm Performance." *Strategic Management Journal* 29 (1): 1–26. doi:10.1002/smj.642.

Zott, C., and R. Amit. 2010. "Business Model Design: An Activity System Perspective." *Long Range Planning* 43 (2–3): 216–226. doi:10.1016/j.lrp.2009.07.004.

Zott, C., R. Amit, and L. Massa. 2011. "The Business Model: Recent Developments and Future Research." *Journal of Management* 37 (4): 1019–1042. doi:10.1177/0149206311406265.

OPEN ACCESS

Unconventional revenue models to capture value from smart services

Moritz Classen and Thomas Friedli

ABSTRACT
Western European manufacturers' difficulties in earning revenue from industrial services in Pacific Asia have been linked to cultural values. Yet, ways of creating and capturing value from smart services in the region remain unexplored. Against this backdrop, this research seeks to (1) uncover how cultural values influence smart service revenue models, and (2) derive revenue model configurations enabling value capture. To do so, the authors study six Western European manufacturers commercializing smart services in Pacific Asia. The results indicate that indirect and freemium revenue models may achieve fit with the cultural values identified.

Introduction

Service growth remains a strategic priority for manufacturing companies in the digital age. Since the 1980s, manufacturers have pursued strategic moves to offer more services to secure stable, profitable revenue growth and, potentially, competitive advantage (Cusumano, Kahl, and Suarez 2015; Oliva and Kallenberg 2003; Vandermerwe and Rada 1988). Today, the 'digital wave' based on technologies to collect, transmit and process data supports 'digital servitization', which is the 'deployment of digital technologies to support the transformation from a product-centric to a service-centric business model' (BM) (Tronvoll et al. 2020, 1; Ardolino et al. 2018; Coreynen, Matthyssens, and Van Bockhaven 2017). To recoup investments in digitalization, manufacturers need to offer new services (Kohtamäki et al. 2020; Visnjic, Neely, and Jovanovic 2018). Notably, 'smart services' for business-to-business (B2B) markets enable pre-emptive action based on field information using connected devices, software and data analysis (Allmendinger and Lombreglia 2005).

Smart services build the foundation for BM innovation. BMs describe mechanisms to create and capture value (Amit and Zott 2001; Johnson, Christensen, and Kagermann 2008; Teece 2010). Smart services have fuelled BM innovation (Klein, Biehl, and Friedli 2018; Kohtamäki et al. 2019; Porter and Heppelmann 2014, 2015; Wünderlich, Wangenheim, and Bitner 2013), creating new revenue opportunities, notably by leveraging innovative profit formulae such as subscription models (Gebauer et al. 2020; Paschou et al. 2020).

Still, mechanisms to capture value from smart services merit further study. Revenue models (RM) define the mode of capturing value from BMs (Amit and Zott 2001). Extant RM research focused on information goods and consumer markets, offering little guidance to manufacturers struggling to design profitable smart service RMs (Hasselblatt et al. 2018; Klein, Biehl, and Friedli 2018). This study addresses this knowledge gap.

Pacific Asia, encompassing East and Southeast Asia (Thompson 2004), is relevant to study smart services. In 2020, Pacific Asia accounted for over 40% of global manufacturing value added (UNIDO 2020). Facing global competition, its manufacturing industry undergoes a transformation towards stronger service orientation (Wu, Liu, and Chin 2018) and digitalization (Xu, Chin, and Cao 2020). Yet, extant research has focused on smart services in Europe (Paschou et al. 2020) and the United States (Suppatvech, Godsell, and Day 2019), leaving Pacific Asia largely unexplored (Raja and Frandsen 2017).

Cultural values are likely to influence value capture in Pacific Asia. In China, Western manufacturers tend to offer industrial services free of charge to comply with cultural values favouring long-term relationships and keeping face over short-term returns (Bao and Toivonen 2015; Gebauer et al. 2007). How this unfolds across Pacific Asia in the age of smart services remains unclear.

This research addresses three knowledge gaps. First, how prior findings apply to broader Pacific Asia. Second, how cultural values intervene in the age of smart services. Third, how Western European manufacturers can configure their smart service RMs accordingly. Thus, we seek to answer two research questions (RQ):

RQ1: How do cultural values affect Western European manufacturers' smart service RMs in Pacific Asia?

RQ2: How can smart service RMs be configured accordingly to capture value?

The qualitative study of six Western European manufacturers in Pacific Asia reveals two RMs enabling value capture. Indirect RMs monetize smart services through sales of physical goods or services. Freemium RMs generate recurrent revenues from paid advanced packages. Both RM configurations achieve fit with cultural values by helping to overcome uncertainty aversion and power distance while fostering long-term orientation.

We contribute to two literature streams. We extend the RM literature by offering a holistic RM construct for B2B smart services, suggesting cultural values as antecedents. Furthermore, we advance service research by exploring smart services in Pacific Asia. Indirect and freemium RMs align cultural values, value creation and capture.

Literature review

Smart service RMs

Smart services

Facing an ever-growing pressure on margins, manufacturing companies take strategic action to grow their service business, called 'servitization' (Baines et al. 2009; Vandermerwe and Rada 1988). Servitizing manufacturers aim at creating additional customer value (Raddats et al. 2019) to deepen customer relationships and, ultimately, generate new and stable sources of income (Oliva and Kallenberg 2003; Rust and Huang 2014) As industrial goods are increasingly equipped with systems collecting and transferring data (Lerch and Gotsch 2015), smart services harnessing digital technologies such as the internet of things (IoT), cloud computing and predictive analytics emerge (Ardolino et al. 2018; Coreynen, Matthyssens, and Van Bockhaven 2017).

We propose two necessary and sufficient conditions for an industrial service to be 'smart'. First, any smart service requires a 'smart product', physical industrial good generating data (Allmendinger and Lombreglia 2005; Klein, Biehl, and Friedli 2018; Porter and Heppelmann 2014; Wünderlich, Wangenheim, and Bitner 2013). This differentiates smart services from 'pure' information goods (Jones and Mendelson 2011) such as electronic handbooks, which can create value absent any smart product.

Second, smart services need data generated by smart products (Töytäri et al. 2018). This differentiates 'smart' from physical industrial services. For instance, spare parts may be shipped and installed without processing product-generated data.

Smart services substitute or complement physical services (Marinova et al. 2017). Remote interactive repair services substitute service missions by remote assistance, where frontline employees (FLE) and customers interact in real-time using communication technology (Wünderlich, Wangenheim, and Bitner 2013). Conversely, predictive maintenance services anticipate equipment breakdowns using data analytics and are typically complemented by physical service missions to replace components about to fail.

Smart services target two profit levers. First, complementarities with physical services enable cost savings in service delivery (Paiola and Gebauer 2020). Second, smart services create revenue opportunities. One way is to enhance the perceived value of physical goods to drive equipment sales; another is to tap into new revenue streams from digital service delivery (Gebauer et al. 2020).

To realize these revenue opportunities, a fit between value creation and value capture is essential. Value creation is an 'actor's attempt to increase value', while value capture is the 'process of securing financial or nonfinancial return from value creation' (Chesbrough, Lettl, and Ritter 2018, 933). High-performing BMs ensure coherence between value creation and value capture (Tidhar and Eisenhardt 2020), which coevolve throughout BM innovation and delivery (Sjödin et al. 2020).

Failing to achieve such a fit is a pitfall for smart service BMs. Smart services frequently require upfront investments in digital technologies to capture, analyse and visualize data (Kohtamäki et al. 2020). Collecting sufficient data to recognize patterns in asset behaviour is often lengthy, such that smart services unfold their full value only after an extended period of usage (Klein, Biehl, and Friedli 2018). However, if their customer-perceived value is lower than the price commanded, revenue opportunities will not materialize (Gebauer et al. 2020). Therefore, smart service value capture mechanisms typically need iterative improvements to better fit value creation (Töytäri et al. 2018).

Revenue models

RMs define how value is captured from BMs. The RM is a distinct element of a BM (DaSilva and Trkman 2014; George and Bock 2011; Giesen et al. 2007; Knyphausen-Aufseß et al. 2011; Sainio and Marjakoski 2009; Tidhar and Eisenhardt 2020). While a BM defines the total value created by a product or service, the share of value ultimately captured depends on the corresponding RM (Amit and Zott 2001; Zott and Amit 2010).

Table 1. Selected RM constructs.

Authors	RM dimensions	Market	Offering	RM configuration antecedents
Bonnemeier, Burianek, and Reichwald (2010)	Performance parameter; value proposition; price setting parameter	B2B	Industrial solutions	N/S
Casadesus-Masanell and Zhu (2010)	Charge; bundling with advertisement	B2C	N/S	RM of market entrant; product quality
Casadesus-Masanell and Zhu (2013)	Charge; price; monetization intensity	B2C	N/S	RM of market entrant; product quality
Chen, Fan, and Mingzhi (2016)	Transaction fees; bundling with advertisement	C2C	Information goods	RM of market entrant; product quality; advertisement aversion
Eckhardt (2016)	Charge; provider's commercial orientation	B2C	Information goods	Product quality
Knyphausen-Aufseß et al. (2011)	Revenue type; transaction dependence; revenue origin; pricing mechanism; revenue distribution	N/S	N/S	Portfolio, lock-in effects, network effects, price sensitivity, cost structure, customer perception, jurisdiction, financial resources
Sainio and Marjakoski (2009)	Revenue origin; licencing rights; usage; time; purpose-of-use; profit-sharing	B2B, B2C	Information goods	Product standardization; channel choice
Tidhar and Eisenhardt (2020)	Charge; revenue origin	B2C	Information goods	Quality signals; user resources; product complexity
Current study	Revenue distribution, offer bundling, pricing mechanism	B2B	Smart services	Cultural values

B2B: Business-to-business; B2C: Business-to-consumer; C2C: Consumer-to-consumer; N/S: Not specified.

Three RM-related knowledge gaps motivate this research. The RM constructs reviewed in Table 1 are insufficiently (1) holistic, (2) specified for B2B smart services, and (3) considering contextual factors.

First, holistic RM constructs are scant. While enumerations of RM configurations such as pay-per-X (e.g. Rapaccini 2015) abound (Tidhar and Eisenhardt 2020), a holistic RM construct is missing. Existing constructs omit relevant dimensions such as bundling (e.g. Tidhar and Eisenhardt 2020) or do not operationalize core dimensions such as the pricing mechanism (e.g. Knyphausen-Aufseß et al. 2011).

Second, the RM construct has to be specified for B2B smart services. Table 1 shows that prior research has focused on information goods and consumer markets. B2C markets feature simpler products and RMs (Tidhar and Eisenhardt 2020). Industrial RMs are typically more intricate, involving more actors and complex contractual agreements (Kim, Cohen, and Netessine 2007). To our knowledge, a B2B smart service RM construct is still missing.

In consequence, we conceptualize smart service RMs as a three-dimensional construct (Table 2). Consistent with previous research (Sainio and Marjakoski 2009; Tidhar and Eisenhardt 2020), we conceive an RM as a set of monetization parameters configured to capture revenue.

The third knowledge gap in RM literature is the role of contextual factors. Various antecedents to RM configuration were examined, notably RMs of market entrants and substitutes (Casadesus-Masanell and Zhu 2010, 2013). However, the contingent role of geographical (Tidhar and Eisenhardt 2020) or cultural factors is less clear. The next section argues why this matters in Pacific Asia.

Table 2. Smart service RM construct.

RM dimension	RM parameter	Configuration options	Example
Revenue Distribution (RD)	Revenue origin	• Direct customers • Third party	Third-party RM (Tidhar and Eisenhardt 2020)
	Revenue object	• Direct service fee • Indirect monetization	Razor-and blade RM (Gallaugher and Wang 2002)
Offer Bundling (OB)	Bundling approach	• Pure bundling • Mixed bundling • No bundling (Adams and Yellen 1976)	N/A
	Product bundle	• Any package of two or more separate products (Stremersch and Tellis 2002)	N/A
Pricing Mechanism (PM)	Charge	• 0 • >0	Freemium RM: one bundle free; others invoiced (Tidhar and Eisenhardt 2020)
	Invoicing mode	• Set-up fees • Recurring fees	Subscription RM: recurring fees (Chen, Fan, and Mingzhi 2016)
	Price metric	• Input • Output (Bonnemeier, Burianek, and Reichwald 2010)	Pay-per-use (Ardolino et al. 2018)
	Pricing logic	• Customer value • Competition • Costs (Ingenbleek et al. 2003)	Value-based pricing (VBP): based on customer-perceived net benefits of an offering (Ingenbleek, Frambach, and Verhallen 2010).
	Price level	• Share of value captured by the seller (Nagle and Müller 2018)	N/A

N/A: Not applicable.

Intertwining service and culture in Pacific Asia

Servitization in Pacific Asia

This article intertwines two service research streams. Research at the nexus of service and culture found individual service expectations and behaviours to differ with cultural backgrounds, notably between Asian and Western individuals (Donthu and Yoo 1998; Furrer, Liu, and Sudharshan 2000; Laroche et al. 2004; Liu, Shaw-Ching, and Sudharshan 2001; Mattila 1999). Servitization research focusses on the strategic implications of service growth in manufacturing, albeit with a focus on Western countries (Paschou et al. 2020; Raddats et al. 2019; Rabetino et al. 2018; Suppatvech, Godsell, and Day 2019). Recent servitization literature reviews call for studies outside the West (Paschou et al. 2020; Rabetino et al. 2018).

Pacific Asia is promising to study servitization. Overall, research is scant (Wang, Kosaka, and Xing 2016). Prior studies are limited to single countries, especially China (Bao and Toivonen 2015; Gebauer and Fischer 2009; Gebauer and Von Zedtwitz 2007; Raja and Frandsen 2017) and Japan (Kim and Toya 2019; Yorozu and Shi 2014). Future research has yet to examine servitization in other Pacific Asian countries (Lin and Chen 2018). Moreover, pockets of smart service revenue growth abound. Pacific Asia is considered the most competitive region worldwide, with Singapore ranking first (Schwab 2019). China, Japan and South Korea (Korea hereafter) are home to manufacturing giants such as Huawei, Mitsubishi and Samsung (Ulrich 2019), providing fertile ground for smart service BM innovation.

Cultural values

Cultural values affect RM configuration. In China, buyers of industrial services were found to be highly price sensitive (Gebauer and Fischer 2009), while local agents provided spare parts at a fraction of the price of Western European manufacturers (Bao and Toivonen 2015). However, since cultural values differ even within Pacific Asia (Alston 1989; Rowley, Ishikawa, and Oh 2019; Ulrich 2019), their similarities and differences in a service context require further investigation (Kim and Mclean 2007).

This research adopts Hofstede's concept of culture. Hofstede and Bond (1988, 6) defined culture as 'the collective programming of the mind that distinguishes the members of one category of people from those of another'. Hofstede introduced six universal dimensions of culture: uncertainty avoidance (UAV), power distance (PD), long-term orientation (LTO), individualism-collectivism, masculinity-femininity, and indulgence-restraint (Hofstede, Hofstede, and Minkov 2010). Three of them have been linked to service revenue in Pacific Asia (see Table 3) and are explored in this study: UAV, PD and LTO.

Gebauer et al. (2007) associated high levels of PD, UAV and LTO with low industrial service revenue in China. However, only physical services provided in China were considered in this study preceding the digital era and, therefore, the emergence of smart services. Thus, it remains unknown whether their findings apply to (1) other Pacific Asian countries and (2) smart services.

Overall, three knowledge gaps motivate this research. First, the paucity of research on servitization in Pacific Asia in general, and on smart services in particular. Second, little is known about how cultural values affect the smart service RM configuration. Third, RMs need to be operationalized for smart services. Six Western European manufacturers are studied to address these gaps.

Table 3. Negative link between cultural values and service revenue.

Cultural value	Definition[1]	Tendency in Pacific Asia[1,2]	Link to industrial service revenue[3]	Rationale[3]
UAV	'the extent to which the members of a culture feel threatened by ambiguous or unknown situations' (p. 191)	High: Japan, South Korea Middle: China Low: Singapore	Negative	Risk aversion of customers impedes availability-based price metrics
PD	'the extent to which the less powerful members of institutions and organizations within a country expect and accept that power is distributed unequally' (p. 61)	High: East Asia and Singapore	Negative	Service FLEs and managers not empowered to sell services proactively
LTO	Degree to which cultures foster 'virtues oriented toward future rewards – in particular, perseverance and thrift' (p. 239)	High: China, Hong Kong, Japan, South Korea, Singapore, Taiwan	Negative	Service offered for free to foster long-term personal relationships

Sources: [1]Hofstede, Hofstede, and Minkov (2010).
[2]Hofstede and Bond (1988).
[3]Gebauer et al. (2007).

Theory

This research is guided by contingency theory, which suggests that managerial systems should take into account the idiosyncratic conditions under which a company operates (Kast and Rosenzweig 1972; Lawrence and Lorsch 1967). Because the socio-cultural and market environment strongly influence organizations (Shetty and Carlisle 1972), they are important contingency factors considered in this study.

We investigate the contingency factors of RM configuration. Contingency factors pertaining to an organization's environment affect the feasibility and likelihood of success of different BM configurations (Pateli and Giaglis 2005). Thus, BMs require revision for certain geographic markets (Aspara, Hietanen, and Tikkanen 2010). However, despite its importance, cross-cultural research on the role of culture for BM adaptation is scarce (Saebi, Lien, and Foss 2017). We respond to this call by exploring the role of cultural values for smart service RM configuration.

Methodology

This exploratory research was conducted as a qualitative multiple-case study. Smart service RMs in Pacific Asia are a novel and contemporary phenomenon subject to contextual conditions. This called for an in-depth investigation using exploratory case study research (Yin 2018). We opted for a multiple case study design because the replication logic enhances confidence in the relationship between the study's main constructs (Eisenhardt 1989). Additionally, multiple cases are likely to yield more robust theory than single-case research (Eisenhardt and Graebner 2007).

Case overview

Cases were selected based on theoretical sampling (Glaser and Strauss 1967). Six Western European manufacturers were chosen based on four criteria: (1) strategic shift towards service BMs, (2) topicality of smart services, (3) strong footprint in Pacific Asia and (4) access to key informants. To avoid industry bias and increase the robustness of our findings, we selected manufacturers of diverse industrial goods (see Table 4). The smart services' maturity varied between cases: some have been in the market for several years, others were at an early innovation phase.

Data collection

Data were collected through in-depth interviews and participant observation. Interviews were used to understand how actors rooted in the focal region see and make sense of the world (MacCracken 1997). To ensure consistency of our findings, data were triangulated (Jick 1979) using participant observation. This allowed us to record human action in its natural environment (Arnould and Wallendorf 1994).

We interviewed 19 people in total, using semi-structured interview guidelines. Table 5 shows that sixteen participants worked for the case companies. Three participants worked for real estate developers PropertyAlpha and PropertyBeta (pseudonyms), Singaporean customers of E&E&Co. Interviews lasted between 60 and 90 minutes and were conducted face-to-face or by phone. All interviews, except for two, were audio recorded and transcribed.

Data were triangulated using elements of market-oriented ethnography (Arnould and Wallendorf 1994). The first author joined Min (pseudonym), a service technician of TexCo, on customer visits to nine weaving mills in Jiangsu province, Mainland China. The first author engaged in participant observation by conversing with Min, observing weaving mill operations, drinking tea with administrative staff and sharing meals with mill owners. Field work produced a rich dataset of field notes, photographs and videos (see Figure 1).

Data analysis

Data were analysed in three steps using ATLAS.ti software. The first step centred on in-depth analysis of raw data. We read the interview transcripts and notes several times, marking quotes relevant to the RQs. To let first-order codes emerge in the participants' language, we applied inductive coding (Glaser and Strauss 1967) to the data. In-vivo coding was used where participants' language was particularly vivid (Corbin and Strauss 2008), leading to codes such as 'Want to be the first with caution'. As data analysis

Table 4. Case companies.

Pseudonym	Products	Smart service	Global TO (2018)	Employees worldwide	HQ
EngineCorp	Diesel and gas engines	Remote monitoring	GBP 3.5bn	10,500	DE
HeavyCorp	Construction and agriculture machinery	Digital asset management	EUR 10.6bn	46,000	CH
E&E&Co.	Elevators, escalators	Digital asset management	CHF 10.9bn	64,500	CH
MachineInc	Machine tools, laser processing	Remote monitoring	EUR 3.6bn	13,500	DE
TexCo	Dobbies, weaving machines and preparation systems	Remote monitoring and support	CHF 1.3bn	5,500	CH
WirePro	Wire processing machines	Remote monitoring	CHF 480 m	2,000	CH

CH: Switzerland, DE: Germany, HQ: Headquarters, TO: Turnover.

Table 5. Interview participants.

					Territories in which participant does business										
#	Pseudo-nym	Role	Function	Company	CN	HK	ID	JP	KR	MY	PH	SG	TH	TW	VN
1	Yong	P	Senior Manager Textile After Sales Department	TexCo	•	•	•			•				•	•
2	Tom	P	Regional Head of Service Sales Eastern Europe & Asia	MachineInc	•			•	•						
3	John	P	Business Development Smart Services Laser	MachineInc	•			•	•						•
4	Ajai	P	Head of Customer Service	HeavyCorp			•			•	•	•	•		•
5	Peter	P	Sales Manager	HeavyCorp			•			•	•	•	•		•
6	Marc	P	Head of Customer Service Maritime Cranes	HeavyCorp			•			•	•	•	•		•
7	Cheng	C	Senior Manager, Retail Operation Engineering	PropertyAlpha								•			
8	Raja	C	Lead Retail Experience	PropertyBeta								•			
9	Mohd	C	Facility Operations Manager	PropertyBeta								•			
10	Liam	P	Head Sales & Service, Area Sales Manager SEA (Southeast Asia)	WirePro			•			•	•	•		•	•
11	Bob	P	Director Digital Business & Customer Experience	E&E&Co.		•	•			•	•	•	•	•	•
12	Linda	P	Head of Digitalization, Asia Pacific	E&E&Co.		•	•			•	•	•	•	•	•
13	Lei	P	Head of Digitalization, Group	E&E&Co.		•	•			•	•	•	•	•	•
14	Kate	P	Manager, Sales Service (Asia) Power Generation	EngineCorp	•		•	•	•	•	•	•	•	•	•
15	Zhuo	P	Manager, Sales Service (Asia) Marine	EngineCorp	•		•	•	•	•	•	•	•	•	•
16	Fang	P	Service Manager Domestic	WirePro	•										
17	Ji-ho	P	Group Manager Service Laser Technology	MachineInc					•						
18	Seo-jun	P	Head Application & Marketing	MachineInc					•						
19	Wei	P	Service Manager	WirePro	•										

C: Customer, P: Provider, CN: Mainland China, HK: Hong Kong, ID: Indonesia, JP: Japan, KR: Korea, MY: Malaysia, PH: Philippines, SG: Singapore, TH: Thailand, TW: Taiwan, VN: Vietnam.

progressed, codes were iteratively added, deleted and refined. In the second step, thematic patterns were distilled from the data. Analysis of links and patterns between first-order codes yielded second-order themes refined based on prior literature. The third step generated a set of aggregated dimensions. The formation of dimensions was based on the second-order themes and guided by constructs established in prior literature. We identified five aggregated dimensions grounded in empirical data and theory (see Figure 2).

Findings

The aggregated dimensions that emerged from the data build the foundation of a conceptual framework that structures the findings of this study. The framework in Figure 3 is a linear model guided by the contingency view (Otley 1980), linking contingent variables (cultural values), organizational levers (smart service RM) and a performance outcome (value capture).

Figure 1. Weaving mills visited.

Cultural values affecting smart service RMs

The data provide support for the relevance of UAV, PD and LTO in Pacific Asia. Specifics follow.

Uncertainty aversion

Customers in Pacific Asia seemed averse to the technological and financial downside uncertainty caused by smart services. Customers in Japan, Korea and China reacted differently to the technological immaturity of smart services:

> Both China and Japan use chopsticks. The reason to have different chopsticks is because when we are eating fish, we are different. Japanese pick the bones out of the meat, then they eat the meat. The Chinese grab everything, put it into the mouth and then start to spit the bones out. That is reflecting how we are dealing with matters. Japanese are trying to clarify all the potential issues before they get things started. So they take much longer time to verify the process, to verify the potential risks. Chinese are just trying to solve the matters during the process. In this sense, the Chinese customers have larger tolerance. Koreans have silver chopsticks. You know why? Because that's a symbol. In the older times, if you had some poison in your food, then the chopsticks changed the colours. It is very, very difficult to get customers' trust. Even if you are Korean, it's very difficult to get the customers' trust. (Wei)

Technological downside uncertainty surfaced to a lesser extent in Singapore. Novelty was embraced, given uncertainty-reducing quality signals. Smart service providers signalled quality by providing reference customers and tangibles such as technological equipment:

> We are not risk takers. (Zhuo)

> Singapore is known as early adopter. They wanna be the first, but they also wanna be the first with caution. So if they think they are going to get killed, they'd never want to be the first. Right, if they think the technology is really not proven. But if they have a lot of trust and they have good references and there is people [that] have a proven track record, then they wanna be the first. So this is why we have had customers from here go to Europe, Germany and

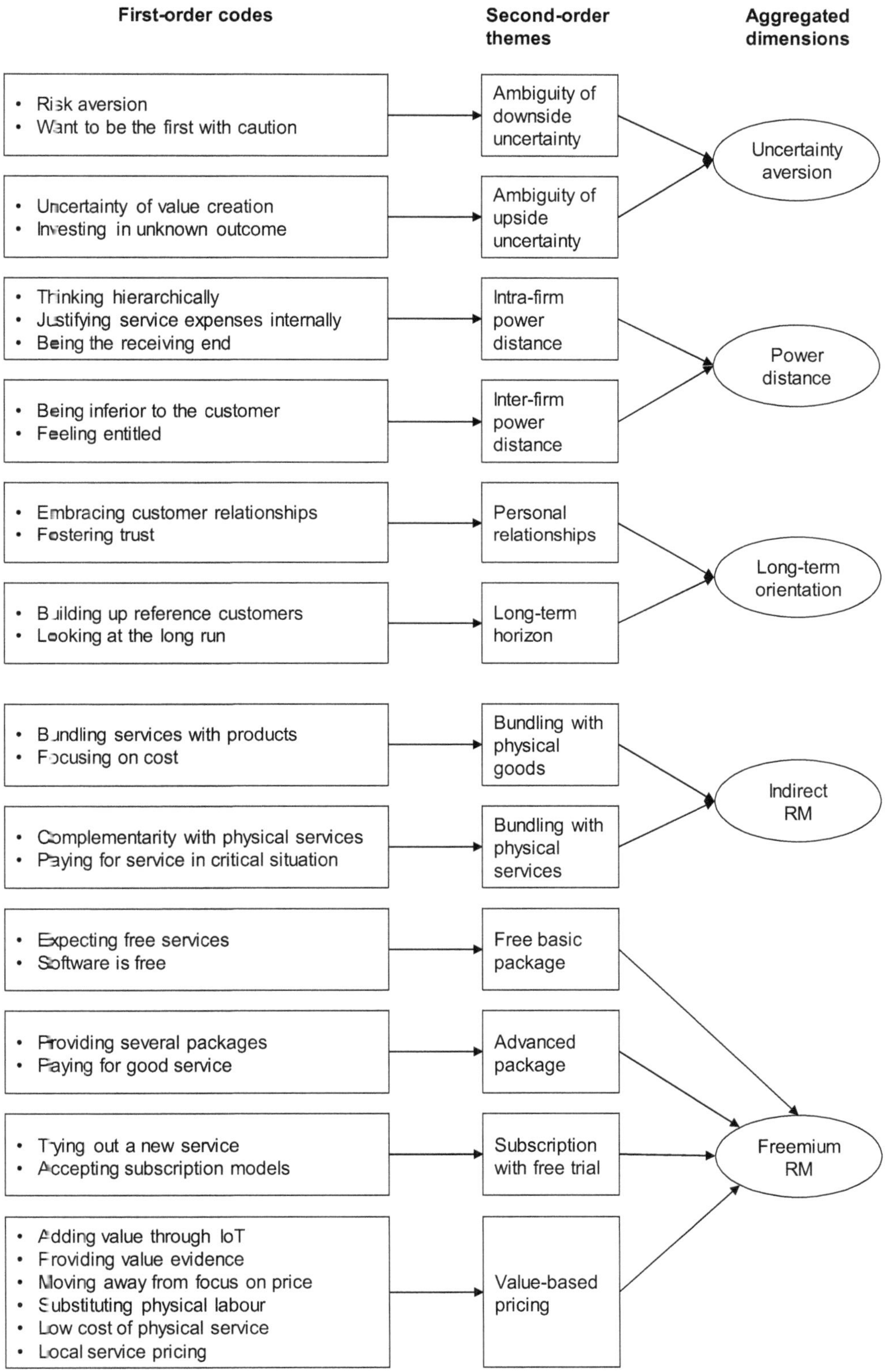

Figure 2. Data structure.

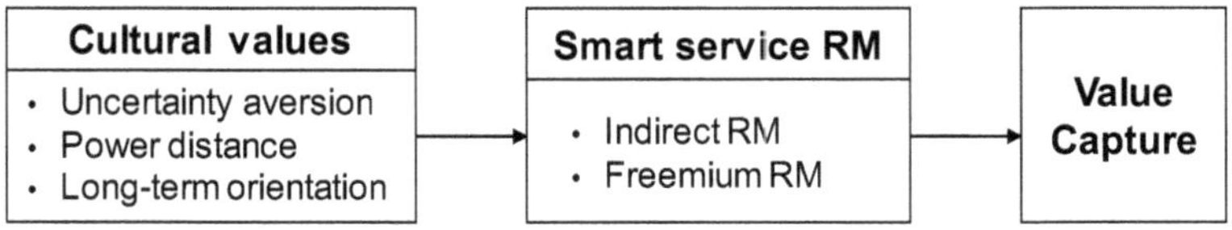

Figure 3. Conceptual framework.

> Switzerland to see our technology, get comfort ... but then they wanna be the first to do it here. (Bob)

Smart services also caused financial downside uncertainty. To cover costs for edge devices and installations, case companies charged initial setup fees to connect equipment to the internet. Additional recurring fees were billed for service delivery. Customers were cautious of the uncertain return-on-investment (ROI):

> The Asian customers are still very conservative on this topic, because they don't have this kind of experience. Also, they are conservative to put their money in. Because all you are talking about is just some figures, but not the actual things they have experienced before. (Yong)

Conversely, potential customers perceived upside uncertainty regarding the value created by new smart services. Most were recently launched, and documented evidence of value creation was scarce. Absent such evidence, customers were reluctant to become pilot users:

> 'We don't wanna be guinea pigs'. We hear that a lot. But you know, in reality, right now what we are doing – with [our smart service] – we are trying to set this expectation – is we are tweaking it all the time. This symptom happened; OK we need to manage that better. In kind of this scenario, when there was no alert, OK we have to change that ... (Bob)

Power distance

PD appeared within and beyond firm boundaries. Intra-firm, decision-making on a local and global level was highly centralized. Restrictions on the implementation of smart services applied to lower-level managers, especially when installation and operation entailed expenditure:

> Only for three [connected assets], they have to write a paper ... and the whole cost investment would be about S$15,000 to install and maintain and to have a subscription. I reckon the amount of time they have spent to write the paper would have been three times that already, in man-hours and everything. (Bob)

SEA subsidiaries were frequently the 'receiving end'. Decisions, particularly those concerning the use of smart services, were often taken in the HQ. SEA subsidiaries could hardly influence these decisions:

> Southeast Asia unfortunately is the receiving end. We have many other multinational companies here with HQ probably in Japan, in Europe or elsewhere. Sometimes the local guy may not be able to make the decision, especially for Japanese companies. (Liam)

> The Southeast Asian countries, especially the emerging countries like Vietnam, I call them a l ke a receiving country. So somehow somewhere it has been decided in the headquarter. People locally just have to follow. (Fang)

Inter-firm power distance appeared between service providers and customers. In Singapore, the socioeconomic background of FLEs was one reason. Average wages in Singapore were higher than in neighbouring countries such as Malaysia or Indonesia. This attracted a substantial number of migrant workers into occupations the local Singaporean population considered substandard. Hierarchies between FLEs and customers were pronounced:

> The paymasters in Singapore are generally Chinese Singaporeans. Very wealthy, very well-educated. The workers are foreigners that maybe have very very limited education. So in Australia you have a technician, who has probably more education and is more assertive and gets paid higher than the guy who is managing him. In Singapore, you have the customer [up here] and the technician [down] here. It's a huge gap. So the paymaster does not trust what this guy is saying. The paymaster also believes: 'You know, I'm a highly educated Chinese Singaporean. I demand a certain level of respect that you as a worker must show me'. So the way they treat them sometimes is not so nice. (Bob)

PD also materialized in the asymmetric power distribution between service providers and customers in Korea:

> The customer is the master and the supplier is the sub. (Seo-jun)

> The supplier has to serve the ordering company. (Ji-ho)

Power asymmetry was particularly visible with chaebol customers. Chaebols are large conglomerates benefitting from strategic advantages such as high market shares and capital resources (Ulrich 2019; Yoon and Suh 2019). Chaebols leveraged their bargaining power to obtain smart services for free:

> [Chaebol A] pays for the product, so they feel like they could get every information from the product. In Korea, I think the customer thinks that when they buy something, all property belongs to them when they pay for it. They think that they could buy not only the product but also the technology itself. (Seo-jun)

Long-term orientation

Personal relationships were considered fundamental for doing business in Pacific Asia. FLEs established and maintained personal rapports with customers. Min's routine customer visits were revealing. After inspecting the equipment's condition, Min spent substantial time to converse informally with factory workers, drink tea with office employees and eat with owners.

Similarly, a significant amount of time was invested to build and foster relationships before settling business issues. Establishing a certain level of trust was fundamental for subsequent sales:

> Relationship, relationship. Relationship is based on confidence. When your customer has confidence in you, or your service, or your product, this can build up a very good relationship. And then, whatever you promote to him, he will believe. This is very important in our Asian countries. (Yong)

> If you go [to Vietnam], if you are friendly, once they trust you – that means, okay, this guy doesn't cheat on me, then it's easy to do business with them. (Ajai)

Personal relationships were expected to remain paramount in the age of smart services. Face-to-face meetings with the service provider were crucial to foster the customer's trust:

> I've seen the transition from – 10 years ago – a very face-to-face, human touch kind of business to – in the last three to four years – moving to the digital world. The con is, and I really see this as a con: the lack of face-to-face discussion ... you don't need a face-to-face at all for everything based on data. I would say, in general, Asia is very much still face-to-face, especially for developing countries. Yesterday, we had a Skype meeting with Thailand, our distributors. They keep asking us to visit their Navy just to give them the assurance of proving what we can perform. Certain countries it's just that ... sometimes you just have to show face and ... you know ... present yourself, and people will have the assurance. (Zhuo)

Creating and capturing value from smart services required a long-term horizon. As many offerings were just recently introduced, user bases were embryonic. Services were expected to get 'smarter' and create superior value once extensive data were collected from the field. Yet, not all European manufacturers considered the long-term horizon required for capturing value from smart services. Our data reveal inconsistencies between short-term value capture expectations and long-term value creation:

> Whenever we come up with a digital product, we want to see results right in the third year. Even though there is no value to the customer, we just have to sell. Ideally, you are supposed to give the customer the value, because once the customer sees the value, he will stick with you a longer period. But, somehow, the company may not look at that kind of long run. Because they are looking at revenue. I may say there is a gap here. On one hand, we need to hit the target. On the other hand, we are talking about value. And the value can be a long process, it's not just a short process. (Zhuo)

Smart service RMs in Pacific Asia

Our data reveal two dominant RMs: indirect and freemium. Table 6 highlights the fundamental differences between both. In indirect RMs, no direct charge is levied for service provision. Instead, revenues come from other customers, physical goods or services sales. Freemium RMs imply direct service fees and consist of two or more product bundles. One bundle is provided for free; others are sold at a positive price.

Table 6. Differences between indirect and freemium RMs.

RM dimension	RM parameter	Indirect RM	Freemium RM
RD	Revenue origin	Customers of other services, third party	Customers of focal service
	Revenue object	Physical good, physical service	Focal service
OB	Bundling approach	Mixed bundling	Pure bundling
	Product bundle	≥1	≥2
PM	Charge	No	Yes (for advanced package)
	Invoicing mode	N/A	Recurring
	Price metric	N/A	Various
	Pricing logic	N/A	Value
	Price level	N/A	Various

N/A: Not applicable.

Indirect RM

We found two ways of monetization through indirect RM. One was bundles of physical goods. Oftentimes, customers considered services being complementary to physical goods. Services were expected to be included in equipment sales without extra charge:

> [Our customers] purchase our machine because we can provide good service. If we cannot provide good service, they will not buy our machines. So good service in their mind is a must. But they will not pay any additional cost for it. (Yong)

Service fees were not immediately visible ('the line'), but dissimulated in larger transactions:

> If we buy air-conditioning for our home, in Asia, you just buy the devices and then they will be installed. In the Western world, you buy an air condition and that device is the physical product; also you have a line for installation, a separate line to be charged. But here . . . very simply, you don't see it. Maybe it has been combined to get into this physical product, but that's the mentality. People don't really charge for this kind of service. In our quotation, you don't see this line. Even, somehow, we find a way to put it into the machine price, but you don't get this line. If you have this line showing up, except for a very, very special machine, this will be the first discussion and item that will be kicked out. (Wei)

Another way of monetizing smart services were bundles with physical services. Three types of service bundles emerged from our data: spare parts provision, maintenance agreements and outcome-based contracts. First, even if many customers were reluctant to pay for services, urgent situations left them no choice:

> [Customers in Vietnam, Taiwan and Indonesia] would keep their spare parts inventory as low as possible and only request our quick supply for the spare parts. Today, we may just receive a phone call from them: 'Ah [Yong], we need this spare part quickly, I can pay but please send me tomorrow!' [laughs] (Yong)

Second, the value was captured from smart services through maintenance agreements. EngineCorp included remote monitoring in maintenance agreements to improve the quality of physical services:

> Data collection services are an added value on our service to the customers. But the normal people-to-people contact and on-the-job is still very much higher, as compared to the [smart service] that we are giving to the customers. (Kate)

Third, smart services enabled outcome-based contracts, billed by the number of elevator rides or metres of earth cut. Smart services such as remote monitoring were included in the contract to ensure equipment availability:

> We have customers, ferry operators, [who] only pay by running hours – means if the engine runs at 800 hours, [EngineCorp] is paid 800 hours by [x] dollars. We call it 'power-by-the-hour'. We always make sure we maintain all the things and they only pay us by the running hours of the engines. (Kate)

Freemium RM

Freemium RMs consisted of bundles at zero (basic packages) and positive (advanced packages) price. Free trials and VBP were essential for advanced packages.

Basic and advanced packages were required to segment customers. Basic packages were necessary for price-sensitive customers, which appeared to predominate in the region, except for Singapore and Japan, as Figure 4 illustrates. Advanced packages targeted performance-sensitive customers. Customers were willing to pay if superior value was provided:

> If we can improve their quality, improve their yield rate, I think, for such service, they're willing to pay. (Wei)

> They're willing to pay something. So we've sold it, but then they expect much much better performance. So if today, the lift is breaking down once a month, I put this remote monitoring in, I should be able to get it to once every two months or three months. They really wanna see a visible performance. (Bob)

Subscriptions with free trial generated recurring revenues in freemium RMs. For a given duration, customers could test advanced packages without charge:

> In China, we offer a lot of apps for free for the first stage. So in this case, we can just let the customers get used to our service. For the next level, if they want more features on the service, the software, they can pay for this. (Fang)

Information goods blazed the trail for subscriptions. Instead of one-off invoices, yearly or monthly service fees were charged. Yet, to capture value for a prolonged period, value creation was to remain consistent:

> If [customers] say they can see that they are enjoying the benefit, why should they cancel? The reason why people cancel Spotify or Netflix it's because they probably no longer need it. Or they don't see that they will get benefit out of it. That's why they probably think that is good to cancel. For example, I'm personally subscribed to [Microsoft Office 365]. So every year I pay S$148 without question, because I need it. (Liam)

Prices required alignment with value creation. Three imperatives for VBP of smart services emerged from the interviews: (1) value identification, (2) value quantification, (3) price levels adjusted to substitutes. First, drivers of customer value needed to be identified, including higher equipment availability:

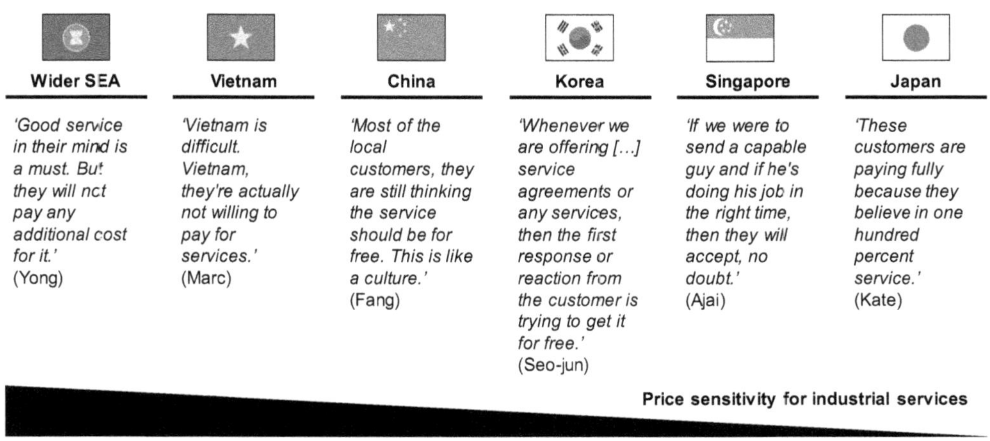

Figure 4. Heterogeneous price sensitivity.

> The outcome we seek – reliability – should improve and it's no longer based on the time we spend on the equipment and the number of times we visit, but more the availability and intervention using technology. (Bob)

Second, value needed to be quantified. Because customers in Pacific-Asia were particularly driven by numbers' (Lei), they expected financial estimates of the benefits smart services created. Calculations reflected cost savings and ROI:

> We have to find out how much money [customers] could save from their services. [A customer] asked us how much money they can save if they use our smart services. For example, maybe they don't need to buy something, they don't need to store the spare part. Then they could save the money from their working capital or storage place. (Seo-jun)

> I need to work on some of those ROI calculations. We need this kind of arguments, statements to tell them that 'Even though you're paying maybe [x] per month for the year, you will be getting double of your return'. (Liam)

Third, price levels needed to reflect substitutes. Remote monitoring services were designed to substitute physical monitoring of the status of assets, such as engines or elevators. Substituting workers was conceivable:

> If I can use this technology to substitute a physical man with it? Yeah, can. (Bob)

To fit customer value, pricing needed to consider local wages. Differences between high (e.g. Japan) and low wage countries (e.g. Indonesia) were substantial. Thus, price levels of physical services were typically country-adjusted:

> We charge, let's say 180 USD in Singapore. But maybe we charge only 60 USD in Malaysia. (Ajai)

However, this rationale was inconsistently applied to smart services. Some HQs set global prices, making the smart service unattractive compared to local substitutes:

> We are charging S$50 per month per equipment for this [smart service]. But in Indonesia, the cost of having one person sit there for eight hours monitoring this, plus he can do other things, is about US$100 a month. So the cost of very cheap labour is one reason why they might not use it. Because it's cheaper for me to sit the guy there and I can get him to clean up when he is not doing anything. Your app is not going to clean up. (Bob)

> If you want to have one year's usage, one machine, you can pay almost RMB10,000. But this is something too expensive to the customers. (Fang)

Smart service RM configurations to capture value

Table 7 and this section unfold how indirect and freemium RMs achieved fit with UAV, PD and LTO.

Fit between UAV and RM configuration

Indirect and freemium RMs reduced customer-perceived financial downside uncertainty. Fees for using a smart service were invisible (indirect RM) or deferred (freemium RM). Customers were relieved from the financial risks of experimenting with smart services:

Table 7. Fit between smart service RMs and cultural values.

Cultural value	How indirect RMs achieved fit	How freemium RMs achieved fit
UAV	Reduced perceived financial downside uncertainty	Reduced perceived financial downside uncertainty and ambiguity of upside uncertainty
PD	Circumvented intra- and inter-firm PD	Circumvented intra-firm PD
LTO	Leveraged personal relationships	Leveraged long-term horizon

> Why I mentioned about trial is: there's no loss. If you try something – at most, you stop using or you don't use [it]. It is not going to hurt you or cause you losing some money. (Fang)

Freemium RMs also reduced the ambiguity of upside uncertainty. Since uncertainty about the technological feasibility of smart services was high, providers strove to grow user bases, gather data and learn from market feedback to readjust features. Freemium RMs allowed value creation and value capture to converge over time:

> [WirePro's smart service], I will suggest that we provide the visualization for free. In this case, we can establish the infrastructure for [customers], and we can start to get data, we can start to get their feedback. Then, this feedback will help us to improve our [smart service] and also we know the customer needs for it. Then we can improve it, right? So, on top of that, we can provide value-added services. Then we can charge for that part. It's not like we can charge for everything. (Fang)

Fit between PD and RM configuration

Foregoing immediate service fees alleviated intra-firm PD. Indirect and freemium RMs allowed lower-level managers to test smart services without seeking approval:

> We can just find a deal that you just give it together, instead of we try to come back later on, so the guy needs to get the additional approval one more time. But the moment you're able to package it, maybe we can do it together. (Fang)

Indirect RMs also addressed inter-firm PD. Chaebols and others leveraged their bargaining power to obtain smart services without charge. As a countermeasure, indirect RMs were used to capture value through equipment sales.

Fit between LTO and RM configuration

Indirect RMs were designed to foster long-term personal relationships instead of maximizing short-term revenues. The TexCo case is revealing. The hours Min spent inspecting the installed base and solving ad-hoc problems were not billed. Similarly, to drive future equipment sales revenues, TexCo developed a remote support service to substitute existing mobile applications:

> They will phone us, or maybe by WhatsApp or different kind of communication apps, to send their message and then request a quick feedback or some suggestion to solve the problem immediately. (Yong)

Freemium RMs addressed customers' long-term horizon. Free basic packages or trials allowed customers to assess the value of a smart service for an extended time period. Reference customers paved the way for long-term value capture:

> Set up a reference, just as a gift to one or two customers in the market. Let them run the system for a few years and then they will say something about this system. Then the market will learn about it, the actual figures and the actual improvements. And then after that, they will think about having this system. (Yong)

Discussion

Our findings expand prior understanding of contingencies affecting RM configuration. Indirect RMs are preferred where contextual factors entail low willingness to pay for services. Our data suggest that the negative link between PD, UAV and LTO, and industrial service revenue found in China (Gebauer et al. 2007) appears in some Pacific Asian countries (e.g. Vietnam), but not in others (e.g. Singapore). We concur with prior studies that, often, Chinese customers prefer paying for tangible products and expect obtaining free services (Bao and Toivonen 2015; Gebauer et al. 2007). However, our research provides a more nuanced understanding of possible commercial responses. Services need not be offered strictly for free, as suggested by Gebauer and Von Zedtwitz (2007). Instead, indirect RMs monetize smart services through additional physical goods or service sales.

The findings allow theorizing further about three rationales for choosing freemium RMs. First, a lack of quality signals (Tidhar and Eisenhardt 2020). The smart services studied lack quality signals, which high UAV penalizes. The use of freemium RMs to let customers experience offerings at no cost is aligned with prior literature (Gu, Kannan, and Ma 2018).

Second, freemium helps to expand a service's user base (Shi, Zhang, and Srinivasan 2019). Akin to information goods, smart service quality increases with user numbers. The case companies used freemium to attract reference customers, subsequently capitalizing on word-of-mouth (Kamada and Öry 2020). The importance of personal relationships is likely to help growing the Pacific Asian user base.

Third, freemium helps to get a 'foot in the door' of new customers. Absent costs of experimentation, freemium is attractive for new users (Gu, Kannan, and Ma 2018). Our research adds another facet to this rationale. Facing high PD in Pacific Asia, smart service providers leverage freemium RMs to circumvent restrictive purchasing policies and attract users.

Implications for theory and theory development

This article contributes to the RM and service literature. The smart service RM construct we offer extends RM literature in three ways. First, it is holistic. Most of the prior research discussed specific RM configurations such as pay-per-use (Rapaccini 2015) or freemium (Gu, Kannan, and Ma 2018; Shi, Zhang, and Srinivasan 2019). Our RM construct integrates missing monetization dimensions, thus building an important bridge between the RM and pricing literature. Second, it breaks new ground in terms of markets and offerings. Existing RM constructs primarily cover information goods and consumer markets (e.g. Casadesus-Masanell and Zhu 2010, 2013). Our expansion of the RM construct domain to smart services provides B2B scholars with a theoretical framework to better describe and compare emerging RMs. Third, it considers new contingency factors. Extant research investigated several antecedents to RM configuration, but not geographical or cultural factors (Saebi, Lien, and Foss

2017; Tidhar and Eisenhardt 2020). Enriching the nomological network of RMs with cultural values enhances our understanding of boundary conditions affecting RM performance.

We contribute to service research by theorizing on RM configurations aligning value creation, capture and cultural values. Value creation and capture need alignment for service BMs to work (Sjödin et al. 2020). However, Western European manufacturers struggle to capture value from services in Pacific Asia. Particularly in China, services are offered free of charge to sustain personal relationships and reduce customer-perceived risk (Bao, Zhou, and Su 2003; Gebauer et al. 2007). The RM construct offered here allows for more nuances beyond the dichotomy of zero and nonzero prices assumed in prior studies. Between both extremes emerge indirect and freemium RMs as a middle way to capture value in line with cultural values.

Implications for business and management practice

Our findings entail four business imperatives. Importantly, managers must localize smart service RMs. Cultural values and the relevance of physical substitutes differ greatly between regions. To drive global penetration and value capture, smart service providers must move from a one-size-fits-all approach to RM configuration to one that truly considers local idiosyncrasies.

Moreover, managers should zero in on lifetime value (CLV) when evaluating smart service customers. That is because indirect and freemium RMs entail time-lagged cash in- and outflows. In indirect RMs, service delivery and revenue generation are decoupled. In freemium RMs, not all users generate revenue. Certain users remain in the 'free' tier; others switch to paid tiers. Yet in both RMs providers still incur costs to serve customers. Therefore, industry executives should follow their peers in consumer markets and start monitoring customer acquisition costs, average revenue per user and CLV (McCarthy, Fader, and Hardie 2017) to manage their smart service user base.

Additionally, RMs should leverage complementarities between smart and physical services. Face-to-face interactions remain decisive in Pacific Asia in the digital age, so the managerial focus should move away from unbundled smart services sales as the sole revenue driver. Instead, RMs should capitalize on complementarities with physical services to grow revenue in the region.

Finally, providers of smart services must develop a VBP capability. Customers in Pacific Asia accept paying for smart services that clearly provide value. Thus, providers need processes and tools to quantify value and derive according prices. To develop this capability, change initiatives affecting organizational routines, roles and metrics are effortful but necessary.

Conclusion

We seek to answer two questions. First, how do cultural values affect smart service RMs in Pacific Asia? We find RMs to be shaped by up- and downside UAV, intra- and interfirm PD, and the importance of personal relationships and long-term orientation. Second, how can RMs be configured accordingly? Our findings point to indirect and freemium RMs enabling value capture and fitting cultural values.

This study comes with limitations that offer avenues for future research. As with any qualitative inquiry, our results are not generalizable. Furthermore, the findings suffer from two cultural biases. First, the case companies are headquartered in just two countries, Germany and Switzerland. Second, since the authors are German native speakers, interviews were held in English and German. Adding the perspective of an Asian researcher or conducting the interviews in the participants' native languages may have provided additional insights. Moreover, this study stretches over Pacific Asia, which is not culturally homogeneous (Thompson 2004). The cultural differences within the region uncovered in this research call for further exploration.

Finally, VBP for smart services merits further study. Pricing is a crucial piece in the RM puzzle because it determines the share of value captured. Our findings confirm VBP as the preferred pricing logic for smart services (Classen and Friedli 2019; Töytäri et al. 2018). More research is needed to understand how VBP practices unfold in industrial firms in Pacific Asia and beyond.

Acknowledgements

Earlier versions of this paper were presented at the Exploring new business models conference at the Zhejiang University of Technology, Hangzhou in December 2019 and the Same Same, But Different: Adapting Smart Service Innovation and Sales for Pacific Asia online seminar in June 2020. The authors thank the Guest Editor, two anonymous reviewers and all participants for their valuable feedback, resulting in a much improved paper. This work was supported by the Swiss Innovation Agency Innosuisse under grant 34121.1 IP-SBM.

Disclosure statement

No potential conflict of interest was reported by the authors.

ORCID

Moritz Classen http://orcid.org/0000-0002-5183-9995

References

Adams, W. J., and J. L. Yellen. 1976. "Commodity Bundling and the Burden of Monopoly." *The Quarterly Journal of Economics* 90 (3): 475. doi:10.2307/1886045.

Allmendinger, G., and R. Lombreglia. 2005. "Four Strategies for the Age of Smart Services." *Harvard Business Review* 83 (10): 131–4, 136, 138 passim.

Alston, J. P. 1989. "Wa, Guanxi, and Inhwa: Managerial Principles in Japan, China, and Korea." *Business Horizons* 32 (2): 26–31. doi:10.1016/S0007-6813(89)80007-2.
Amit, R., and C. Zott. 2001. "Value Creation in E-Business." *Strategic Management Journal* 22 (6–7): 493–520. doi:10.1002/smj.187.
Ardolino, M., M. Rapaccini, N. Saccani, P. Gaiardelli, G. Crespi, and C. Ruggeri. 2018. "The Role of Digital Technologies for the Service Transformation of Industrial Companies." *International Journal of Production Research* 56 (6): 2116–2132. doi:10.1080/00207543.2017.1324224.
Arnould, E. J., and M. Wallendorf. 1994. "Market-Oriented Ethnography: Interpretation Building and Marketing Strategy Formulation." *Journal of Marketing Research* 31 (4): 484–504. doi:10.1177/002224379403100404.
Aspara, J., J. Hietanen, and H. Tikkanen. 2010. "Business Model Innovation Vs Replication: Financial Performance Implications of Strategic Emphases." *Journal of Strategic Marketing* 18 (1): 39–56. doi:10.1080/09652540903511290.
Baines, T., H. W. Lightfoot, O. Benedettini, and J. M. Kay. 2009. "The Servitization of Manufacturing." *Journal of Manufacturing Technology Management* 20 (5): 547–567. doi:10.1108/17410380910960984.
Bao, S., and M. Toivonen. 2015. "Cultural Differences in Servitization: Nordic Manufacturers in China." *Journal of Science and Technology Policy Management* 6 (3): 223–245. doi:10.1108/JSTPM-01-2015-0001.
Bao, Y., K. Z. Zhou, and C. Su. 2003. "Face Consciousness and Risk Aversion: Do They Affect Consumer Decision-Making?" *Psychology and Marketing* 20 (8): 733–755. doi:10.1002/mar.10094.
Bonnemeier, S., F. Burianek, and R. Reichwald. 2010. "Revenue Models for Integrated Customer Solutions: Concept and Organizational Implementation." *Journal of Revenue and Pricing Management* 9 (3): 228–238. doi:10.1057/rpm.2010.7.
Casadesus-Masanell, R., and F. Zhu. 2010. "Strategies to Fight Ad-Sponsored Rivals." *Management Science* 56 (9): 1484–1499. doi:10.1287/mnsc.1100.1199.
Casadesus-Masanell, R., and F. Zhu. 2013. "Business Model Innovation and Competitive Imitation: The Case of Sponsor-Based Business Models." *Strategic Management Journal* 34 (4): 464–482. doi:10.1002/smj.2022.
Chen, J., M. Fan, and L. Mingzhi. 2016. "Advertising versus Brokerage Model for Online Trading Platforms." *MIS Quarterly* 40 (3): 575–596. doi:10.25300/MISQ/2016/40.3.03.
Chesbrough, H., C. Lettl, and T. Ritter. 2018. "Value Creation and Value Capture in Open Innovation." *Journal of Product Innovation Management* 35 (6): 930–938. doi:10.1111/jpim.12471.
Classen, M., and T. Friedli. 2019. "Value-Based Marketing and Sales of Industrial Services: A Systematic Literature Review in the Age of Digital Technologies." *Procedia CIRP* 83: 1–7. doi:10.1016/j.procir.2019.02.141.
Corbin, J. M., and A. L. Strauss. 2008. *Basics of Qualitative Research: Techniques and Procedures for Developing Grounded Theory*. 3rd ed. Los Angeles, CA: Sage Publ.
Coreynen, W., P. Matthyssens, and W. Van Bockhaven. 2017. ""Boosting Servitization through Digitization: Pathways and Dynamic Resource Configurations for Manufacturers." *Industrial Marketing Management* 60: 42–53. doi:10.1016/j.indmarman.2016.04.012.
Cusumano, M. A., S. J. Kahl, and F. F. Suarez. 2015. "Services, Industry Evolution, and the Competitive Strategies of Product Firms." *Strategic Management Journal* 36 (4): 559–575. doi:10.1002/smj.2235.
DaSilva, C. M., and P. Trkman. 2014. "Business Model: What It Is and What It Is Not." *Long Range Planning* 47 (6): 379–389. doi:10.1016/j.lrp.2013.08.004.
Donthu, N., and B. Yoo. 1998. "Cultural Influences on Service Quality Expectations." *Journal of Service Research* 1 (2): 178–186. doi:10.1177/109467059800100207.
Eckhardt, J. T. 2016. "Welcome Contributor or No Price Competitor? The Competitive Interaction of Free and Priced Technologies." *Strategic Management Journal* 37 (4): 742–762. doi:10.1002/smj.2365.
Eisenhardt, K. M. 1989. "Building Theories from Case Study Research." *The Academy of Management Review* 14 (4): 532. doi:10.2307/258557.

Eisenhardt, K. M., and M. E. Graebner. 2007. "Theory Building from Cases: Opportunities and Challenges." *Academy of Management Journal* 50 (1): 25–32. doi:10.5465/amj.2007.24160888.
Furrer, O., B. S.-C. Liu, and D. Sudharshan. 2000. "The Relationships between Culture and Service Quality Perceptions." *Journal of Service Research* 2 (4): 355–371. doi:10.1177/109467050024004.
Gallaugher, J. M., and Y.-M. Wang. 2002. "Understanding Network Effects in Software Markets: Evidence from Web Server Pricing." *MIS Quarterly* 26 (4): 303. doi:10.2307/4132311.
Gebauer, H., and T. Fischer. 2009. "Exploring Service Needs in the Chinese Manufacturing Industry." *Chinese Management Studies* 3 (2): 143–154. doi:10.1108/17506140910963657.
Gebauer, H., E. Fleisch, C. Lamprecht, and F. Wortmann. 2020. "Growth Paths for Overcoming the Digitalization Paradox." *Business Horizons* 63 (3): 313–323. doi:10.1016/j.bushor.2020.01.005.
Gebauer, H., and M. Von Zedtwitz. 2007. "Differences in Orientations between Western European and Chinese Service Organizations." *Asia Pacific Journal of Marketing and Logistics* 19 (4): 363–379. doi:10.1108/13555850710827869.
Gebauer, H., C. Wang, B. Beckenbauer, and R. Krempl. 2007. "Business-to-business Marketing as a Key Factor for Increasing Service Revenue in China." *Journal of Business & Industrial Marketing* 22 (2): 126–137. doi:10.1108/08858620710730249.
George, G., and A. J. Bock. 2011. "The Business Model in Practice and Its Implications for Entrepreneurship Research." *Entrepreneurship Theory and Practice* 35 (1): 83–111. doi:10.1111/j.1540-6520.2010.00424.x.
Giesen, E., S. J. Berman, R. Bell, and A. Blitz. 2007. "Three Ways to Successfully Innovate Your Business Model." *Strategy & Leadership* 35 (6): 27–33. doi:10.1108/10878570710833732.
Glaser, B. G., and A. L. Strauss. 1967. *The Discovery of Grounded Theory: Strategies for Qualitative Research*. 1st ed. New Brunswick: Aldine.
Gu, X. P., K. Kannan, and L. Ma. 2018. "Selling the Premium in Freemium." *Journal of Marketing* 82 (6): 10–27. doi:10.1177/0022242918807170.
Hasselblatt, M., T. Huikkola, M. Kohtamäki, and D. Nickell. 2018. "Modeling Manufacturer's Capabilities for the Internet of Things." *Journal of Business & Industrial Marketing* 33 (6): 822–836. doi:10.1108/JBIM-11-2015-0225.
Hofstede, G., and M. H. Bond. 1988. "The Confucius Connection: From Cultural Roots to Economic Growth." *Organizational Dynamics* 16 (4): 5–21. doi:10.1016/0090-2616(88)90009-5.
Hofstede, G., G. J. Hofstede, and M. Minkov. 2010. *Cultures and Organizations: Software for the Mind*. 3rd ed. New York, NY: McGraw-Hill.
Ingenbleek, P., M. Debruyne, R. T. Frambach, and T. M. M. Verhallen. 2003. "Successful New Product Pricing Practices: A Contingency Approach." *Marketing Letters* 14 (4): 289–305. doi:10.1023/B:MARK.0000012473.92160.3d.
Ingenbleek, P., R. T. Frambach, and T. M. M. Verhallen. 2010. "The Role of Value-Informed Pricing in Market-Oriented Product Innovation Management." *Journal of Product Innovation Management* 27 (7): 1032–1046. doi:10.1111/j.1540-5885.2010.00769.x.
Jick, T. D. 1979. "Mixing Qualitative and Quantitative Methods: Triangulation in Action." *Administrative Science Quarterly* 24 (4): 602. doi:10.2307/2392366.
Johnson, M. W., C. M. Christensen, and H. Kagermann. 2008. "Reinventing Your Business Model." *Harvard Business Review* 86 (12): 50–59.
Jones, R., and H. Mendelson. 2011. "Information Goods Vs. Industrial Goods: Cost Structure and Competition." *Management Science* 57 (1): 164–176. doi:10.1287/mnsc.1100.1262.
Kamada, Y., and A. Öry. 2020. "Contracting with Word-of-Mouth Management." *Management Science* 66 (11): 5094–5107. doi:10.1287/mnsc.2019.3417.
Kast, F. E., and J. E. Rosenzweig. 1972. "General System Theory: Applications for Organization and Management." *Academy of Management Journal* 15 (4): 447–465. doi:10.2307/255141.
Kim, H., and G. N. Mclean. 2007. "Customer Service Behaviours in Korea and Implications for Training: Lessons from an Exploratory Critical Incidents Study of Customer and Employee Service Encounters." *Asia Pacific Business Review* 13 (1): 1–20. doi:10.1080/13602380600647581.
Kim, S.-H., M. A. Cohen, and S. Netessine. 2007. "Performance Contracting in After-Sales Service Supply Chains." *Management Science* 53 (12): 1843–1858. doi:10.1287/mnsc.1070.0741.

Kim, S., and K. Toya. 2019. "Leadership Style Required for the Transition to Servitization in Japan." *Journal of Manufacturing Technology Management* 30 (2): 335–352. doi:10.1108/JMTM-02-2018-0034.

Klein, M., S. Biehl, and T. Friedli. 2018. "Barriers to Smart Services for Manufacturing Companies – An Exploratory Study in the Capital Goods Industry." *Journal of Business & Industrial Marketing* 33 (6): 846–856. doi:10.1108/JBIM-10-2015-0204.

Knyphausen-Aufseß, D. Z., E. Van Hettinga, H. Harren, and T. Franke. 2011. "Das Erlösmodell Als Teilkomponente Des Geschäftsmodells." In *Innovative Geschäftsmodelle*, edited by T. Bieger, D. Z. Knyphausen-Aufseß, and C. Krys, 163–184. Berlin, Heidelberg: Springer Berlin Heidelberg.

Kohtamäki, M., V. Parida, P. Oghazi, H. Gebauer, and T. Baines. 2019. "Digital Servitization Business Models in Ecosystems: A Theory of the Firm." *Journal of Business Research* 104: 380–392. doi:10.1016/j.jbusres.2019.06.027.

Kohtamäki, M., V. Parida, P. C. Patel, and H. Gebauer. 2020. "The Relationship between Digitalization and Servitization: The Role of Servitization in Capturing the Financial Potential of Digitalization." *Technological Forecasting and Social Change* 151: 119804. doi:10.1016/j.techfore.2019.119804.

Laroche, M., L. C. Ueltschy, S. Abe, M. Cleveland, and P. P. Yannopoulos. 2004. "Service Quality Perceptions and Customer Satisfaction: Evaluating the Role of Culture." *Journal of International Marketing* 12 (3): 58–85. doi:10.1509/jimk.12.3.58.38100.

Lawrence, P. R., and J. W. Lorsch. 1967. "Differentiation and Integration in Complex Organizations." *Administrative Science Quarterly* 12 (1): 1. doi:10.2307/2391211.

Lerch, C., and M. Gotsch. 2015. "Digitalized Product-Service Systems in Manufacturing Firms: A Case Study Analysis." *Research-Technology Management* 58 (5): 45–52. doi:10.5437/08956308X5805357.

Lin, C.-A., and H. Chen. 2018. "Deconstructing B2B, Co-Creation and Service Deployment in East Asia: Evidence from Taiwan and PRC Manufacturers." *Asia Pacific Business Review* 24 (3): 351–370. doi:10.1080/13602381.2018.1429124.

Liu, B., O. F. Shaw-Ching, and D. Sudharshan. 2001. "The Relationships between Culture and Behavioral Intentions toward Services." *Journal of Service Research* 4 (2): 118–129. doi:10.1177/109467050142004.

MacCracken, G. 1997. *The Long Interview*. Qualitative research methods 13. 12th ed. Newbury Park: SAGE.

Marinova, D., K. De Ruyter, M.-H. Huang, M. L. Meuter, and G. Challagalla. 2017. "Getting Smart." *Journal of Service Research* 20 (1): 29–42. doi:10.1177/1094670516679273.

Mattila, A. S. 1999. "The Role of Culture in the Service Evaluation Process." *Journal of Service Research* 1 (3): 250–261. doi:10.1177/109467059913006.

McCarthy, D. M., P. S. Fader, and B. G. S. Hardie. 2017. "Valuing Subscription-Based Businesses Using Publicly Disclosed Customer Data." *Journal of Marketing* 81 (1): 17–35. doi:10.1509/jm.15.0519.

Nagle, T. T., and G. Müller. 2018. *The Strategy and Tactics of Pricing: A Guide to Growing More Profitably*. 6th ed. New York, NY, Abingdon, Oxon: Routledge. http://search.ebscohost.com/login.aspx?direct=true&scope=site&db=nlebk&AN=1639137.

Oliva, R., and R. Kallenberg. 2003. "Managing the Transition from Products to Services." *International Journal of Service Industry Management* 14 (2): 160–172. doi:10.1108/09564230310474138.

Otley, D. T. 1980. "The Contingency Theory of Management Accounting: Achievement and Prognosis." *Accounting, Organizations and Society* 5 (4): 413–428. doi:10.1016/0361-3682(80)90040-9.

Paiola, M., and H. Gebauer. 2020. "Internet of Things Technologies, Digital Servitization and Business Model Innovation in BtoB Manufacturing Firms." *Industrial Marketing Management* 89: 245–264. doi:10.1016/j.indmarman.2020.03.009.

Paschou, T., M. Rapaccini, F. Adrodegari, and N. Saccani. 2020. "Digital Servitization in Manufacturing: A Systematic Literature Review and Research Agenda." *Industrial Marketing Management* 89: 278–292. doi:10.1016/j.indmarman.2020.02.012.

Pateli, A. G., and G. M. Giaglis. 2005. "Technology Innovation-induced Business Model Change: A Contingency Approach." *Journal of Organizational Change Management* 18 (2): 167–183. doi:10.1108/09534810510589589.

Porter, M. E., and J. E. Heppelmann. 2014. “How Smart, Connected Products Are Transforming Competition.” *Harvard Business Review* 92 (11): 64–88.

Porter, M. E., and J. E. Heppelmann. 2015. “How Smart, Connected Products Are Transforming Companies.” *Harvard Business Review* 93 (10): 96–16.

Rabetino, R., W. Harmsen, M. Kohtamäki, and J. Sihvonen. 2018. “Structuring Servitization-Related Research.” *International Journal of Operations & Production Management* 38 (2): 350–371. doi:10.1108/IJOPM-03-2017-0175.

Raddats, C., C. Kowalkowski, O. Benedettini, J. Burton, and H. Gebauer. 2019. “Servitization: A Contemporary Thematic Review of Four Major Research Streams.” *Industrial Marketing Management* 83: 207–223. doi:10.1016/j.indmarman.2019.03.015.

Raja, J. Z., and T. Frandsen. 2017. “Exploring Servitization in China.” *International Journal of Operations & Production Management* 37 (11): 1654–1682. doi:10.1108/IJOPM-12-2015-0755.

Rapaccini, M. 2015. “Pricing Strategies of Service Offerings in Manufacturing Companies: A Literature Review and Empirical Investigation.” *Production Planning & Control* 26 (14–15): 1247–1263. doi:10.1080/09537287.2015.1033495.

Rowley, C., J. Ishikawa, and I. Oh. 2019. “Changing Facets of Leadership in East Asia: Globalization, Innovation and Performance in Japan, South Korea and China.” *Asia Pacific Business Review* 25 (2): 161–172. doi:10.1080/13602381.2018.1557425.

Rust, R. T., and M.-H. Huang. 2014. “The Service Revolution and the Transformation of Marketing Science.” *Marketing Science* 33 (2): 206–221. doi:10.1287/mksc.2013.0836.

Saebi, T., L. Lien, and N. J. Foss. 2017. “What Drives Business Model Adaptation? The Impact of Opportunities, Threats and Strategic Orientation.” *Long Range Planning* 50 (5): 567–581. doi:10.1016/j.lrp.2016.06.006.

Sainio, L.-M., and E. Marjakoski. 2009. “The Logic of Revenue Logic? Strategic and Operational Levels of Pricing in the Context of Software Business.” *Technovation* 29 (5): 368–378. doi:10.1016/j.technovation.2008.10.009.

Schwab, K., ed. 2019. *The Global Competitiveness Report 2019*. Cologny/Geneva. Accessed 26 February 2020. http://www3.weforum.org/docs/WEF_TheGlobalCompetitivenessReport2019.pdf.

Shetty, Y. K., and H. M. Carlisle. 1972. “A Contingency Model of Organization Design.” *California Management Review* 15 (1): 38–45. doi:10.2307/41164398.

Shi, Z., K. Zhang, and K. Srinivasan. 2019. “Freemium as an Optimal Strategy for Market Dominant Firms.” *Marketing Science* 38 (1): 150–169. doi:10.1287/mksc.2018.1109.

Sjödin, D., V. Parida, M. Jovanovic, and I. Visnjic. 2020. “Value Creation and Value Capture Alignment in Business Model Innovation: A Process View on Outcome-Based Business Models.” *Journal of Product Innovation Management* 37 (2): 158–183. doi:10.1111/jpim.12516.

Stremersch, S., and G. J. Tellis. 2002. “Strategic Bundling of Products and Prices: A New Synthesis for Marketing.” *Journal of Marketing* 66 (1): 55–72. doi:10.1509/jmkg.66.1.55.18455.

Suppatvech, C., J. Godsell, and S. Day. 2019. “The Roles of Internet of Things Technology in Enabling Servitized Business Models: A Systematic Literature Review.” *Industrial Marketing Management* 82: 70–86. doi:10.1016/j.indmarman.2019.02.016.

Teece, D. J. 2010. “Business Models, Business Strategy and Innovation.” *Long Range Planning* 43 (2–3): 172–194. doi:10.1016/j.lrp.2009.07.003.

Thompson, M. R. 2004. “Pacific Asia after ‘Asian Values’: Authoritarianism, Democracy, and ‘Good Governance’.” *Third World Quarterly* 25 (6): 1079–1095. doi:10.1080/0143659042000256904.

Tidhar, R., and K. M. Eisenhardt. 2020. “Get Rich or Die Trying … Finding Revenue Model Fit Using Machine Learning and Multiple Cases.” *Strategic Management Journal* 41: 1245–1273. doi:10.1002/smj.3142.

Töytäri, P., T. Turunen, M. Klein, V. Eloranta, S. Biehl, and R. Rajala. 2018. “Aligning the Mindset and Capabilities within a Business Network for Successful Adoption of Smart Services.” *Journal of Product Innovation Management* 35 (5): 763–779. doi:10.1111/jpim.12462.

Tronvoll, B., A. Sklyar, D. Sörhammar, and C. Kowalkowski. 2020. “Transformational Shifts Through Digital Servitization.” *Industrial Marketing Management* 89: 293–305. doi:10.1016/j.indmarman.2020.02.005.

Ulrich, D. 2019. "Changing Facets of Leadership in East Asia: Globalization, Innovation and Performance in Japan, South Korea and China." *Asia Pacific Business Review* 25 (2): 159–160. doi:10.1080/13602381.2019.1556524.

UNIDO. 2020. "World Manufacturing Production: Statistics for Quarter I, 2020." Accessed 18 July 2020. https://stat.unido.org/admin/publicationPdf;jsessionid=DFADC4169CA2EACAB372CA6260CEC0BA?World_manufacturing_production_2020_Q1.pdf.

Vandermerwe, S., and J. Rada. 1988. "Servitization of Business: Adding Value by Adding Services." *European Management Journal* 6 (4): 314–324. doi:10.1016/0263-2373(88)90033-3.

Visnjic, I., A. Neely, and M. Jovanovic. 2018. "The Path to Outcome Delivery: Interplay of Service Market Strategy and Open Business Models." *Technovation* 72-73: 46–59. doi:10.1016/j.technovation.2018.02.003.

Wang, J., M. Kosaka, and K. Xing, eds. 2016. *Manufacturing Servitization in the Asia-Pacific*. 1st ed. Singapore: Springer. https://link.springer.com/book/10.1007%2F978-981-287-757-4.

Wu, W., Y. Liu, and T. Chin. 2018. "The Effect of Technology Management Capability on New Product Development in China's Service-Oriented Manufacturing Firms: A Social Capital Perspective." *Asia Pacific Business Review* 24 (2): 212–232. doi:10.1080/13602381.2018.1431256.

Wünderlich, N. V., F. V. Wangenheim, and M. J. Bitner. 2013. "High Tech and High Touch." *Journal of Service Research* 16 (1): 3–20. doi:10.1177/1094670512448413.

Xu, Z., T. Chin, and L. Cao. 2020. "Crafting Jobs for Sustaining Careers during China's Manufacturing Digitalization." *Sustainability* 12 (5): 2041. doi:10.3390/su12052041.

Yin, R. K. 2018. *Case Study Research and Applications: Design and Methods*. Sixth ed. Los Angeles, London, New Dehli, Singapore, Washington DC, Melbourne: SAGE.

Yoon, J., and M.-G. Suh. 2019. "Determinants of Organizational Performance: Some Implications for Top Executive Leadership in Korean Firms." *Asia Pacific Business Review* 25 (2): 251–272. doi:10.1080/13602381.2018.1548545.

Yorozu, C., and V. Shi. 2014. "Servitization and Japan's Keiretsu Organization." In *Spring Servitization Conference*. Birmingham, UK.

Zott, C., and R. Amit. 2010. "Business Model Design: An Activity System Perspective." *Long Range Planning* 43 (2–3): 216–226. doi:10.1016/j.lrp.2009.07.004.

New business models and their government-oriented features

Haixu Bao, Xiao Hu and Lijuan Si

ABSTRACT
A number of innovative business models involve public infrastructure service, such as shared cars. Considering the regulating role of government in these industries, it is important to know what governmental features influence the development of such models. With data of 102 cities in China, we find that government service quality is positively associated with the speed with which car sharing companies are established in a city, and cities with south-born mayors have higher service quality than those with north-born mayors. The mayor's region of birth has an indirect effect on the speed with which car sharing is established.

Introduction

New business models emerge not only in the private sector, but also in the infrastructure service sector. Public-sector organizations have started to adopt new business models to deliver infrastructure services more effectively and innovatively, such as shared bikes and autos. In the past few years, the birth and development of the shared transportation industry have greatly improved the convenience of people's travelling and contributed to energy conservation, in addition to creating new jobs. According to Chinese shared travel green development report released in 2018, Didi, Chinese biggest mobile transportation platform, contributed to the emission reduction by 1.507 million tons CO_2.Given that the introduction of new business models in the infrastructure service sector is beneficial for the public, it is important to study their antecedents.

While it has been acknowledged that business models are important for generating innovative practices in the private sector (Yun et al. 2020), there has been little focus on the deployment of new business models in government or in infrastructure service (Moore and Hartley 2008). A few studies, however, have examined the business models of public-sector organizations. These include the studies undertaken by Chambers and Patrocínio (2012), who analysed the business model of New York City's economic development agency, and Ranerup, Henriksen, and Hedman (2016), who looked at public service platforms in four public sectors in Sweden: education, healthcare, elder care, and public pensions. Also, Li, Bai, and Xue (2020) focused on how did the OEM cooperate with sharing platform.

However, how new business models affect the develop of the infrastructure service sector remains unknown. As the infrastructure service sector is regulated by the government, the government plays an important role in the adoption and development of new business models in infrastructure services. Local governments, especially prefectural-level governments, are responsible for providing local infrastructure services in cooperation with the private sector. Local government often resorts to employing the private sector, i. e., enterprises, to provide infrastructure services. Enterprises also require access to public resources, which are usually regulated by government, to provide infrastructure services. Thus, the way prefectural governments provide services to the private sector may influence the introduction and adoption of new business models in the public sector. Theoretically, it is important to take into consideration the institutional backgrounds when exploring the development of business models in the Asia Pacific context (Rowley and Oh 2016; Rowley, Oh, and Jang 2019), particularly the newly opening economies such as China (Chin, Jiao, and Jawahar 2019). Furthermore, it is also meaningful to know how to develop a government with high service quality. According to upper echelon theory (Hambrick and Mason 1984), the characteristics of mayors (local government leaders) influence the performance of local government. We thus focus on which characteristics of mayors influence government performance, and in turn influence the development of new business models in city infrastructure services.

In this paper, we investigate whether government service quality contributes to the introduction of new business models in the local infrastructure service sector, and in particular the speed of establishing a shared auto service. Furthermore, we explore the characteristics of local government officials associated with government service quality. In particular, we examine whether the mayor's region of birth influences local government service quality, based on upper echelon theory (Hambrick and Mason 1984) and evolutionary modernization theory (Inglehart 1997, 2008).

Our paper makes several contributions. First, we extend research on business models from the private to the public sector. Second, we identify government factors that influence the adoption of new business models in local infrastructure services. These findings provide a new perspective on the antecedents of the introduction of new business models. Lastly, we identify a new attribute of mayors, the region of their birth, that influences government service quality. These findings contribute a new demographic attribute to upper echelon theory.

Theoretical background

Shared autos as a new business model in the infrastructure service sector

The business model concept has been used not only in the context of the digital economy, but also in the context of enterprises seeking to address social problems. Seelos and Mair (2007), for instance, described a business model as a 'set of capabilities that is configured to enable value creation consistent with either economic or social strategic objectives' (p. 53). This was echoed by Thompson and MacMillan (2010), who proposed a framework for new business models to reduce poverty and human suffering.

Business models have also been used to address environmental sustainability in business and industry (Bocken et al. 2014). Public-sector organizations have started to adopt new business models to deliver services more effectively and innovatively, such as Uber, a product of the shared economy. Another example of the sharing economy in infrastructure services is shared autos.

In recent years, online platforms providing consumers with temporary access to goods and services have proliferated (Owyang 2016). Research on these platforms has focused on the analysis and classification of their underlying business models: that is, 'the design or architecture of [their] value creation, delivery, and capture mechanisms' (Teece 2010). In the shared mobility sector, for example, 'carsharing', 'bikesharing' and 'ridesharing' have been identified as different business model categories (Cohen and Kietzmann 2014). The sharing economy is a socio-economic system enabling an intermediated set of exchanges of goods and services between individuals and organizations, which aim to increase the efficiency and optimization of under-utilized resources in society (McLaren and Agyeman 2015; Martin, Upham, and Budd 2015). Sharing-based business models are often held to have positive environmental and social effects (e.g. a more efficient use of existing resources, building social capital) and to provide profitable business opportunities (Frenken and Schor 2017; Amatuni et al. 2019).

Government's role in the adoption of new business models in the infrastructure service sector

We situated our study in China, an authoritarian country where the government has strong control over the economy and society (Lin 2011; Marquis and Bird 2018; Chin and Rowley 2018). Local government officials at the county and township/town levels are the foot soldiers and functionaries of the central government, and govern over 70% of the Chinese population. Any study of political, social, and economic changes in China that does not touch upon rural areas cannot provide an accurate picture of these issues and changes. Many studies have confirmed that the characteristics and incentives of officials often drive economic growth (Lawer, Lukas, and Jørgensen 2017; Namhoon 2020; Chen, Li, and Zhou 2005). In China, the top leaders of local governments are mayors. Municipal governments are mainly responsible for administrating urban affairs according to the law (the constitution, administrative regulations, and local regulations). In this study, we specifically examine the influence of city mayors' region of birth and government performance on the establishment of shared auto services.

Hypothesis development

Government performance and the adoption of new business models

Public-sector organizations have started to adopt new business models, especially engagements with private-sector partners, to streamline and improve their operations (Micheli et al. 2012). We hypothesize that governments with high service quality may adopt new business models earlier, because high service quality implies that the government values public welfare, and thus the government may be motivated to promote efficient infrastructure services. New business models such as the sharing economy have the potential to include low-income consumers and increase service efficiency. Fraiberger and Sundararajan (2015) emphasize that the sharing economy leads to greater inclusion because lower-income consumers traditionally excluded from participation gain access to products through peer-to-peer marketplaces.

Furthermore, high-quality government service facilitates the adoption and development of new business models in infrastructure services. Through deploying regulation, legislation, directives, and guidelines for the infrastructure service sector, local government provides easy access for the private sector to infrastructure service and information, which enables the generation of new business models in infrastructure services. Moreover, high service quality enables the private sector to cooperate with the public sector to develop new business models, making it easier to connect with the relevant departments. High service quality means less red tape, so that private-sector enterprises with new business models may obtain necessary certification and permission more quickly. Based on these two arguments, we hypothesize that the better the local government's service, the more rapidly new business models will be established in a city.

H1: The higher the local government's service quality, the faster car sharing will be established in the city.

Evolutionary modernization theory posits that the prevailing conditions during an individual's pre-adult years will have a sustained influence on their values (Inglehart 1997, 2008). According to evolutionary modernization theory, different socialization experiences in people's formative years (Inglehart 1997; Inglehart Ronald 2008; Welzel, Inglehart, and Kligemann 2003) have long-term effects on their development. In particular, earlier experiences form 'habitual mind-sets' as an enduring cognitive orientation and establish 'habitual actions' as 'learned sequences of acts that have become automatic response' (Verplanken and Aarts 1999), which highlights the role of socialization in the development of generational values.

Based on evolutionary modernization theory, we hypothesize that different prevailing conditions in north and south China influence the formation of mayors' lifelong values, including their governance values. It is well known that there are many differences in economic development, credit systems, cultural characteristics, historical background, and business culture across China, especially between north and south (Fan 2000; Tung, Worm, and Fang 2008; Tsai, Ren, and Eisingerich 2020). In general, prevailing conditions are better in southern China than in the north, because the economy in southern China is stronger. This economic imbalance has two causes. First, superior geographical and climatic conditions in the south have made the south more productive than the north for long periods of time. The climate in southern China is much more conducive to the growth of crops than that of northern China. Second, cities in the south opened up earlier and more extensively after the economic revolution than cities in the north. The high degree of openness has meant less government regulation over the regional economy, and more attractive policies for enterprises such as low land prices and low taxes, which facilitates the development of the local economy.

This better-developed economy has improved the living standards of southern Chinese. Compared to northern Chinese, southern Chinese have enjoyed greater economic security. Such economic growth parallels the more rapid development of science and technology, which has exposed southern Chinese to larger amounts of diverse information. An affluent environment leads to a shift from emphasizing self-security and self-achievement to promoting the well-being of all (Inglehart 1997). As the traditional Chinese saying puts it, 'The poor care about themselves; the wealthy care about the world'. Thus, we hypothesize that the southern Chinese have more benevolent and universalist values, i.e., caring for universal well-being and the protection of everybody's welfare. In a related finding, southerners are more collectivistic than northerners (Xinran, Xiaopeng, and Jiang 2016). Thus, we hypothesize that mayors from southern China may have more motivation to develop the local economy and provide high-quality service to the public.

Furthermore, we hypothesize that southern Chinese are more open to new business than northern Chinese because of their long business history. Northern China has always been a stronghold of feudal conservative thinking. Northerners have always attached great importance to agriculture rather than business; but business and markets are precisely what promotes industrialization and modernization. Southerners, such as the inhabitants of Wenzhou and Anhui, have very strong business consciousness. Because of this openness to business, mayors from southern China may lead their governments to be more friendly to enterprises, and to maintain good government–business relations.

H2: South-born mayor-led governments provide higher quality of government service than north-born mayor-led governments.

Indirect effect

In conjunction with the relationship between government service quality and the speed of establishing shared auto services, as described in the previous section, we expect an indirect relationship between the region of mayors' birth and the speed of establishing shared auto services via government service quality. Figure 1 depicts the theoretical model of this study. Therefore, we propose the following hypothesis:

H3: The region of mayors' birth influences the speed of establishing new business models in the city through local government service quality.

Methods

Sample

We used data on the second largest shared auto company, GoFun China. GoFun is a car sharing app that provides convenient, green, fast, and economical travel services. GoFun

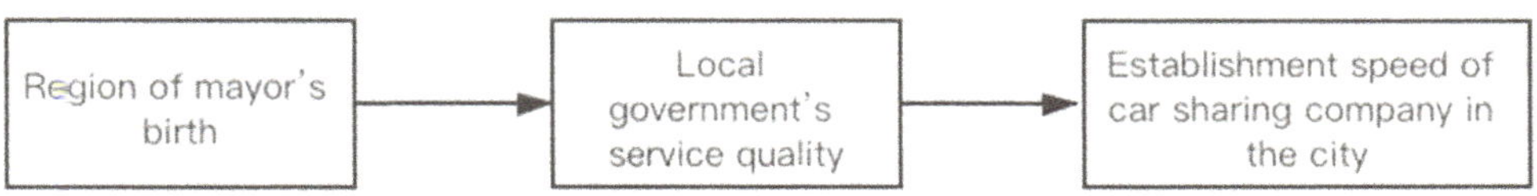

Figure 1. Theoretical framework.

is a new form of car rental business. GoFun offers a totally self-serviced car rental service. Customers can select, pick up, and return a car via the app. Service fees are charged according to usage, as measured in minutes and kilometres. GoFun now offers service in 60+ cities in China. We chose this company because it is large, and because we can access their development information via public news websites.

The theoretical population of this study would be municipal cities across China. However, there are no shared autos now in most less developed cities. We, therefore, target the most developed cities (cities on top 100 GDP list and provincial capital cities), and obtain a sample of 104 cities. After excluding cities governed by mayors whose birthplace we cannot determine, we obtain a sample of 102 cities.

Measures

Establishment speed

We collected data on the establishment of GoFun in a city through public news websites. We calculated the days from that time to 31 December 2019, as the measure of establishment speed. For the cities lacking GoFun service, we set the GoFun establishment speed as 0. Higher scores indicate greater establishment speed.

Government service quality

Government service quality is collected from the report published in 2017 by the National Academy of Development and Strategy, RUC, which provides four indices: 1) quality of infrastructure, 2) quality of financial services, 3) quality as market intermediary, and 4) efficiency of E-government. The index is developed annually based on a research and ratings process using a broad range of information sources (https://www.baidu.com/link?url=YNYL8apVjDP95v_8xUAzUZIeBRixtTrYixx3SGDUI-CouBEdzNDwMkNL0JqOdYBUEzdTyRjGkE5TE7pBIVHma_&wd=&eqid=a9e3d5d4001eb3f0000000035df9e451).

Region of mayor's birth

We collected demographic information on mayors who were incumbent in 2016. We obtained their names from hotelaah.com, which lists the officials of most Chinese cities. Then, we collected demographic information on the mayors from Baidu Encyclopaedia. We classified the region of birth as north versus south relative to the dividing line of the Huai River and Qin Mountain (Zhang Jian, Zhong-Hou, and Quan-gong 2012).

Controls

We controlled for GDP (2015) and population size (2015) as our primary control variables. Consistent with past research, we used the logs of these two variables. We also included the number of buses per 10,000 people and number of taxis in 2015 to control for transportation convenience in the city. Finally, we controlled for city classification. We coded provincial capitals, province-level municipalities, and special administrative regions as 1, and others as 0.

Results

We used hierarchical multiple regression to analyse the data. Table A1 presents the descriptive statistics and correlations between variables. GDP ($r = 0.66$, $p < 0.01$), number of buses per 10,000 people (abbreviated as number of buses, $r = 0.24$, $p < 0.01$), number of taxis ($r = 0.61$, $p < 0.01$), and city classification ($r = 0.43$, $p < 0.01$) are all highly correlated with establishment speed of GoFun, indicating that GoFun was established earlier in cities that are wealthier, have larger populations, have more buses and taxis, and are provincial capitals, province-level municipalities, or special administrative regions. Government service quality ($r = 0.59$, $p < 0.01$) is also highly correlated with the establishment speed of GoFun, indicating that GoFun established itself in cities with better government–business relations. Table A1 further reveals that the region of mayors' birth is highly correlated with government service quality ($r = 0.25$, $p < 0.05$), indicating that a mayor's birthplace may influence government–business relations.

Table A2 reports the regression results. Models 1–2 report the regression models testing the impact of government–business relations on the establishment speed of GoFun. We first examined the effects of our control variables in Model 1.Log GDP and population size are positively associated with the establishment speed of GoFun ($b = 0.62$, $p < 0.001$; $b = -0.20$, $p < 0.05$; $b = 0.20$, $p < 0.05$). Model 2 shows that government service quality is positively and significantly related to the establishment speed of GoFun ($b = 0.27$, $p < 0.01$). Thus, Hypothesis 1, which posits that government service quality is positively related to the establishment speed of GoFun, is supported.

Hypothesis 2 posits that the mayor's region of birth influences government service quality. Model 3 shows the regression results on the effect of control variables. Log GDP and number of buses are positive related to government service quality ($b = 0.52$, $p < 0.01$; $b = 0.23$, $p < 0.05$). Model 4 shows that the region of birth is significantly related to government service quality ($b = 0.21$, $p < 0.05$). This indicates that cities with mayors from the south have higher service quality than those with mayors from the north. Thus, Hypothesis 2 receives support.

Hypothesis 3 posits that mayors' region of birth influences the establishment speed of GoFun through government service quality. We use the SPSS macro (PROCESS) to examine these indirect models. Our analysis supports Hypothesis 3, which predicts an indirect path linking mayors' region of birth and the establishment speed of GoFun through government service quality, 95% CI [4.03, 90.69] (excluding 0).

Discussion

Theoretical implication

This study makes a significant contribution to the literature on business models by focusing on the adoption of new business models in the public sector. Business models have attracted increasing attention from researchers. Many notable findings have been made, such as the definition of a business model (Lorenzo, Tucci Christopher, and Allan 2017) and the antecedents of generation of new business models (Amit and Zott 2015; Martin, Upham, and Budd 2015; Normann and Ramirez 1993; Tikkanen et al. 2005). However, most research has taken place in the business administrative field, while little attention has been paid to business models in the public infrastructure sector. Focusing on the development of a car-sharing company, which constitutes one type of infrastructure service, we examine the adoption of new business models in infrastructure service, which extends research on business models from the private to the public sector.

Next, we identify the antecedents of the adoption or development of new business models from the perspective of local government. Although there have been many efforts to identify such antecedents, for example industry structure (Florian Waldner, Poetz, and Eurich 2015), and firm-level antecedents, such as organizational inertia (Sosna, Trevinyo-Rodríguez, and Velamuri 2010), inertia at upper management levels (Chesbrough and Rosenbloom 2002; Tripsas and Gavetti 2000), cognitive closure of firms (Chesbrough 2010), and conflicts with existing assets (Amit and Zott 2001). Most of these studies are from the industry, enterprise, or entrepreneurial perspectives. Little attention has been paid to the role of government in the development of new business models. By demonstrating that the government context has important consequences for whether new business models are adopted in the public sector, we examine the antecedents from a government perspective. In particular, we find that government service quality facilitates the development of car sharing companies in cities. This paper is the first to demonstrate the importance of government for research on new business models, and links the business model literature to the public administration literature.

Lastly, our results contribute to the literature on upper echelon theory. Upper echelon theory (Hambrick and Mason 1984) proposes that the characteristics of top executives can predict organizational behaviours and performance. Based on upper echelon theory, several studies have found that mayors' characteristics are associated with government performance, including mayors' demographic attributes (age, sectorial experience, education level and type) (Avellaneda 2012); motives, capacity, and networks (Avellaneda 2016); and experience such as work type, number of jobs, and years of work experience (Olvera and Avellaneda 2019). However, even in the business administration literature, few studies have examined the influence of the birthplace of top executives on organizational performance. Focusing on whether the mayors' birthplace is located in north or south China, we found that the region predicted their government performance. Through this finding, we contribute to upper echelon theory by identifying a new dimension of characteristics of top executives that may influence government performance.

Practical implications

Our findings have important implications for Asian especially Chinese governments and enterprises. Government is responsible for the management, planning and policy of the country's transport. Many of China's major cities and metropolitan areas suffer considerably from air pollution. Moves to improve the air, and reduce the health impact on inhabitants are urgently needed by governments. Much more efficient using of existing cars and large-scale using of electronic fleet, car-sharing is expected as an efficient tool. Car sharing market booming in China, but industry still in nascent stage as a new business model in the Chinese transportation industry. How to facilitate this beneficial new business model is an important issue for governments.

Our findings suggest that 1) new business models in the transportation sector can be utilized more effectively in cities with higher government service quality. Thus, governments that intend to introduce new business models in infrastructure service should increase their service quality to attract and foster new business models. 2) We found that governments with mayors from the south exhibit higher government service quality, which eventually facilitates the adoption of new business models in infrastructure service. As a result, in China, governments that intend to improve government service quality, especially in lower levels of government, can appoint officials from southern China as mayors. Countries should also pay attention to the influence of officials' birthplace. When appointing new officials, they should be conscious of the influence of their birthplace's culture and economy on their values and probably on their government's performance.

Besides to China, our research also has implications for other Asian countries who would like to facilitate the adoption and development of new business models in industries that closely related to public benefits. Through improving governmental service quality, local governments in Asian countries may speed up the development of new business models. However, the features of mayors which influence the governmental service quality need to be contextualized according to the actual conditions in these countries.

Limitations and future research directions

This study's limitations should be addressed in future research. Because we examined the impact of government performance on the development of a major car sharing company, it remains unclear whether our findings extend beyond the car sharing and sharing economy domain. As the sharing economy is a popular topic, government may facilitate the development of this new business model to improve its reputation. Future research should explore whether the effects of government performance are contingent upon the extent that the new business model is generally accepted.

Furthermore, because of China's vast territory and diverse geographic features, different native regions may shape different values and characteristics, which may present themselves as differences in mayor-led governments. We do not know whether such regional differences can apply to other countries, especially smaller and more homogenous ones. Although existing research has found region differences in several Asian countries, such as India (Thampi, Jyotishi, and Bishu 2020) and Thailand (Jory and Saengthong 2020).

Lastly, we only collected historical data from one car sharing company. As a result, the relationship between government performance and speed of establishment may be biased by the company level factor, such as company strategy. Future research should examine whether our findings can be replicated with data from other car sharing companies.

Conclusion

In public infrastructure service industries, governmental features take unneglected influence over the development of new business models. With data of 102 cities in China, we found mayor's region of birth had an indirect effect on the speed with which car sharing was established in a city through government service quality. Our findings extend research on business models from the private to the public sector, demonstrate the importance of government for research on new business models, and links the business model literature to the public administration literature and upper echelon theory.

Disclosure statement

No potential conflict of interest was reported by the author.

Funding

This research is supported by the MOE (Ministry of Education in China) Project of Humanities and Social Sciences [Project No.19YJC630002], the Fundamental Research Funds for the Central Universities [Project No.2020jbkyzy035, and No. 2019jbkyzx031]; Key Program of National Natural Science Foundation of China [Project No.71433005]; and Key project of the National Social Science Foundation of China [Project No.20AZD032].

Geolocation information

36°03′40″N 103°49′55″E, Lanzhou, China

References

Amatuni, L., J. Ottelin, B. Steubing, and J. Mogollon. 2019. *Does Car Sharing Reducegreenhouse Gas Emissions? Life Cycle Assessment of the Modal Shift and Lifetime Shift Rebound Effects*. arXiv:1910.11570 [econ.GN].

Amit, R., and C. Zott. 2001. "Value Creation in E-business." *Strategic Management Journal* 22: 6–7.

Amit, R., and C. Zott. 2015. "Crafting Business Architecture: The Antecedents of Business Model Design." *Strategic Entrepreneurship Journal* 9 (4): 331–350. doi:10.1002/sej.1200.

Avellaneda, C. N. 2012. "Do Politics or Mayors' Demographics Matter for Municipal Revenue Expansion?" *Public Management Review* 14 (8): 1–26. doi:10.1080/14719037.2012.662442.

Avellaneda, C. N. 2016. "Government Performance and Chief Executives' Intangible Assets: Motives, Networking, And/or Capacity?" *Public Management Review* 18 (5–6): 918–947. doi:10.1080/14719037.2015.1051574.

Bocken, N. M. P., S. W. Short, P. Rana, and S. Evans. 2014. "A Literature and Practice Review to Develop Sustainable Business Model Archetypes." *Journal of Cleaner Production* 65: 42–56. doi:10.1016/j.jclepro.2013.11.039.

Chambers, E., and M. Patrocínio. 2012. *Business Models and Value Creation: A Case Study of New York City Economic Development Corporation*. Retrieved from http://urn.kb.se/resolve?urn=urn:nbn:se:umu:diva-52335

Chen, Y., H. Li, and L. Zhou. 2005. "Relative Performance Evaluation and the Turnover of Provincial Leaders in China." *Economics Letters* 88: 421–425. doi:10.1016/j.econlet.2005.05.003.

Chesbrough, H. 2010. "Business Model Innovation: Opportunities and Barriers." *Long Range Planning* 43 (2–3): 0–363. doi:10.1016/j.lrp.2009.07.010.

Chesbrough, H., and R. S. Rosenbloom. 2002. "The Role of the Business Model in Capturing Value from Innovation: Evidence from Xerox Corporation's Technology Spin-Off Companies." *Industrial and Corporate Change* 11 (3): 529–555. doi:10.1093/icc/11.3.529.

Chin, T., and C. Rowley. 2018. *The Future of Chinese Manufacturing, Elsevier S & T Books*. UK: Elsevier.

Chin, T., H. Jiao, and I. M. Jawahar. 2019. "Sustainable Career and Innovation during Manufacturing Transformation." *Career Development International* 24 (5): 397–403. doi:10.1108/CDI-09-2019-331.

Cohen, B. D., and J. Kietzmann. 2014. "Ride On! Mobility Business Models for the Sharing Economy." *Organization & Environment*, 27 (3): 279–296. doi:10.1177/1086026614546199

Fan, Y. 2000. "A Classification of Chinese Culture." *Cross Cultural Management: An International Journal* 7 (2): 3–10. doi:10.1108/13527600010797057.

Fraiberger, S. P., and A. Sundararajan. 2015. "Peer-to-Peer Rental Markets in the Sharing Economy." *SSRN Electronic Journal*. doi:10.2139/ssrn.2574337.

Frenken, K., and J. Schor. 2017. "Putting the Sharing Economy Intoperspective." *Environmental Innovation and Societal Transitions* 23: 3–10.

Hambrick, D. C., and P. A. Mason. 1984. "Upper Echelons: The Organization as a Reflection of Its Top Managers." *Social Science Electronic Publishing* 9 (2): 193–206.

Inglehart, R. 1997. "Modernization and Postmodernization: Cultural, Economic, and Political Change in 43 Societies." *Foreign Affairs (Council on Foreign Relations)* 76: 3.

Inglehart Ronald, F. 2008. "Changing Values among Western Publics from 1970 to 2006." *West European Politics* 31 (1): 130–146. doi:10.1080/01402380701834747.

Jory, P., and J. Saengthong. 2020. "The Roots of Conservative Radicalism in Southern Thailand's Buddhist Heartland." *Critical Asian Studies* 52 (1): 1–22. doi:10.1080/14672715.2019.1702888.

Lawer, E. T., M. C. Lukas, and S. H. Jørgensen. 2017. "The Neglected Role of Local Institutions in the 'Resource Curse' Debate. Limestone Mining in the Krobo Region of Ghana." *Resources Policy* 54: 43–52. doi:10.1016/j.resourpol.2017.08.005.

Li, Y., X. Bai, and K. Xue. 2020. "Business Modes in the Sharing Economy: How Does the OEM Cooperate with Third-party Sharing Platforms?" *International Journal of Production Economics* 221: 107467.

Lin, N. 2011. "Capitalism in China: A Centrally Managed Capitalism (CMC) and Its Future." *Management and Organization Review* 7 (1): 63–96. doi:10.1111/j.1740-8784.2010.00203.x.

Lorenzo, M., L. Tucci Christopher, and A. Allan. 2017. "A Critical Assessment of Business Model Research." *Academy of Management Annals* 11: 1.

Marquis, C., and Y. Bird. 2018. "The Paradox of Responsive Authoritarianism: Civil Society, Local Governments and Environmental Penalties in China." *Organization Science* 29 (5): 948–968. doi:10.1287/orsc.2018.1212.

Martin, C. J., P. Upham, and L. Budd. 2015. "Commercial Orientation in Grassroots Social Innovation: Insights from the Sharing Economy." *Ecological Economics* 118: 240–251. doi:10.1016/j.ecolecon.2015.08.001.

McLaren, D., and J. Agyeman. 2015. *Sharing Cities: A Case for Truly Smart and Sustainable Cities*. Cambridge, MA: MIT Press.

Micheli, P., M. Schoeman, D. Baxter, and K. Goffin. 2012. "New Business Models for Public-Sector Innovation: Successful Technological Innovation for Government." *Research-Technology Management* 55 (5): 51–57.

Moore, M., and J. Hartley. 2008. "Innovations in Governance." *Public Management Review* 10 (1): 3–20. doi:10.1080/14719030701763161.

Namhoon, K. 2020. "Public Service Motivation and Government Officials' Willingness to Learn in Public Sector Benchmarking Process." *PublicManagementReview*. doi:10.1080/14719037.2019.1708437.

Normann, R., and R. R. Ramirez. 1993. "From Value Chain to Value Constellation: Defining Interactive Strategy." *Harvard Business Review* 71 (4): 65–77.

Olvera, J. G., and C. N. Avellaneda. 2019. "Subnational Government Performance: Testing Multiple Dimensions of Governors' Experience." *Public Administration Review* 79 (3): 383–398. doi:10.1111/puar.13035.

Owyang, J. 2016. "Honeycomb 3.0: The Collaborative Economy Market Expansion Web Strategy by Jeremiah Owyang Digital Business." Accessed 12 April 2018. http://www.web-strategist.com/blog/2016/03/10/honeycomb-3-0-the-collaborative-economy-market-expansion-sxsw

Ranerup, A., H. Z. Henriksen, and J. Hedman. 2016. "An Analysis of Business Models in Public Service Platforms." *Government Information Quarterly* S0740624X16300107.

Rowley, Oh, and Jang. 2019. "New Perspectives on East Asian Leadership in the Age of Globalization: Local Grounding and Historical Comparisons in the Asia Pacific Region." *Asia Pacific Business Review* 25: 2. doi:10.1080/13602381.2018.1557424.

Rowley, C., and I. Oh. 2016. "Business Ethics and the Role of Context: Institutionalism, History and Comparisons in the Asia Pacific Region." *Asia Pacific Business Review* 22 (3): 353–365. doi:10.1080/13602381.2015.1129814.

Seelos, C., and J. Mair. 2007. "Profitable Business Models and Market Creation in the Context of Deep Poverty: A Strategic View." *Academy of Management Perspectives* 21 (4): 49–63. doi:10.5465/amp.2007.27895339.

Sosna, M., R. N. Trevinyo-Rodríguez, and S. R. Velamuri. 2010. "Business Model Innovation through Trial-and-Error Learning: The Naturhouse Case." *Long Range Planning* 43 (2–3): 0–407. doi:10.1016/j.lrp.2010.02.003.

Teece, D. J. 2010. "Business Models, Business Strategy and Innovation." *Long Range Planning* 43 (2–3): 172–194. doi:10.1016/j.lrp.2009.07.003.

Thampi, P. P., A. Jyotishi, and R. Bishu. 2020. "Regional Cultural Diversities Amongst Small Business Entrepreneurs in India." *International Journal of Globalisation and Small Business*, Inderscience Enterprises Ltd 11 (1): 1–17. doi:10.1504/IJGSB.2020.105580.

Thompson, J. D., and I. C. MacMillan. 2010. "Business Models: Creating New Markets and Societal Wealth." *Long Range Planning* 43 (2–3): 0–307.

Tikkanen, H., J. A. Lamberg, P. Parvinen, and J. P. Kallunki. 2005. "Managerial Cognition, Action and the Business Model of the Firm." *Management Decision* 43 (6): 789–809. doi:10.1108/00251740510603565.

Tripsas, M., and G. Gavetti. 2000. "Capabilities, Cognition, and Inertia: Evidence from Digital Imaging." *Strategic Management Journal* 21 (10–11): 1147–1161. doi:10.1002/1097-0266(200010/11)21:10/11<1147::AID-SMJ128>3.0.CO;2-R.

Tsai, H., S. Ren, and A. Eisingerich. 2020. "The Effect of Inter- and Intra-regional Geographic Diversification Strategies on Firm Performance in China." *Management Decision* 58 (1): 16–38. doi:10.1108/MD-01-2018-0104.

Tung, R. L., V. Worm, and T. Fang. 2008. "Sino-Western Business Negotiations Revisited 30 Years after China's Open Door Policy." *Organizational Dynamics* 37 (1): 60–74. doi:10.1016/j.orgdyn.2007.11.005.

Verplanken, B., and H. Aarts. 1999. "Habit, Attitude, and Planned Behaviour: Is Habit an Empty Construct or an Interesting Case of Goal-directed Automaticity?" *European Review of Social Psychology* 10 (1): 101–134. doi:10.1080/14792779943000035.

Waldner, F., M. K. Poetz, C. Grimpe, and M. Eurich. 2015. "Antecedents and Consequences of Business Model Innovation: The Role of Industry Structure." *Business Models and Modelling* (Advances in Strategic Management, Vol. 33), Emerald Group Publishing Limited, pp. 347–386.doi:10.1108/S0742-332220150000033009

Welzel, C., R. Inglehart, and H.-D. Kligemann. 2003. "The Theory of Human Development: A Cross-cultural Analysis." *European Journal of Political Research* 42 (3): 341–379. doi:10.1111/1475-6765.00086.

Xinran, M., R. Xiaopeng, and X. Jiang. 2016. "The Difference of Collectivism between North and South China and Its Cultural Dynamics." *Advances in Psychological Science* 24 (10): 1551–1555. doi:10.3724/SP.J.1042.2016.01551.

Yun, J. J., X. Zhao, J. Wu, K. Park, and W. Y. Jung. 2020. "Business Model, Open Innovation, and Sustainability in Car Sharing Industry—comparing Three Economies." *Sustainability* 12 (1883): 1–27. doi:10.3390/su12051883.

Zhang, Jian, L. X.-N., T. Zhong-Hou, and C. Quan-gong. 2012. "Mapping of the North-south Demarcation Zone in China Based on GIS." *Journal of Lanzhou University(Natural Sciences)* 48 (3): 28–33.

Appendix

Table A1. Descriptive statistics and correlations.

Variables	*Mean*	*SD*	1	2	3	4	5	6	7
1 GDP[a]	17.48	0.66							
2 Population size[a]	6.26	0.59	0.52**						
3 Number of buses	12.67	9.68	0.24**	−0.22*					
4 Number of taxis[a]	8.23	1.03	0.67**	0.23*	0.45**				
5 City classification	0.30	0.46	0.30**	0.02	0.29**	0.69**			
6 Government service quality	37.80	19.10	0.54**	0.04	0.45**	0.54**	0.39**		
7 Region of mayor's birth[b]	0.47	0.50	0.08	−0.06	0.08	−0.13	−0.03	0.25*	
8 Establishment speed of GoFun	348.58	396.65	0.66**	0.18	0.24**	0.61**	0.43**	0.59**	0.09

N = 102; *$p < 0.05$, ** $p < 0.01$.
[a]We used the log of these three variables.
[b]South is coded as 1, and north is coded as 0.

Table A2. Regression results.

	Establishment speed of GoFun		Government service quality	
Variable	Model 1	Model 2	Model 3	Model 4
Constant	−5865.26***	−4771.15***	−198.32**	−177.22***
GDP[a]	0.62***	0.48***	0.52***	0.43***
Population size[a]	−0.20a	−0.15	−0.19+	−0.16+
Number of buses	−0.08	−0.14	0.23a	0.20**
Number of taxis	0.16	0.16	0.01	0.15
City classification	0.16	0.12	0.16	0.11
Government service quality		0.27**		
Region of mayor's birth[b]				0.21a
F	21.09***	20.34***	15.70***	14.98***
R^2	0.52	0.56	0.45	0.49
ΔR^2		0.04a		0.04a

ap < 0.05, **$p < 0.01$, ***$p < 0.001$. [b] South is coded as 1, and north is coded as 0.

The role of business model innovation mix in the transition of contract manufacturers

Tung-Fei Tsai-Lin, Hui-Ru Chi and Yuan-Chieh Chang

ABSTRACT

Many contract manufacturers' successful transition from original equipment manufacturers (OEM), original design manufacturers (ODM) to original brand manufacturers (OBM) is typical for studying latecomers' business model transitions in emerging Asia. This study uses data from two industrial innovation surveys (2004–2006 and 2007–2010) in 14 cities located in the Greater China region to describe the innovation practices followed in different business models and the transitions. The results show that OEM latecomers undergo organizational changes in the transitions. ODM entrants have to enhance product innovation and market promotion, and OBM entrants must tailor their organizational and marketing practices. This paper concludes that the business model transition is the matter of firms making an effort to retool their innovation mix for realizing a new value proposition in a specific business model. Theoretical and managerial implications are suggested.

Introduction

Recently, latecomers' transformations to contract manufacturing have become critical in emerging countries. An increase in contract manufacturing experience has enabled these latecomers to accumulate sufficient technological capabilities to undertake in-house R&D and play catch-up with their customers. This experience has stimulated firms to advance upstream and downstream in the value chain in the pursuit of growth. The original equipment manufacturers–original design manufacturers–original brand manufacturers (OEM–ODM–OBM) transition pathway has become well-travelled for contract manufacturers seeking to renew their business models in emerging Asia (Chu 2009; Hobday 1998: Wan 2015), and it has many success stories. These firms overcome substantial challenges to developing innovative capabilities and reinventing business models in existing markets when they change their value propositions during transitions (Johnson, Christensen, and Kagermann 2008; Teece 2010; Amit and Zott 2012; Guan and Ma 2003; Hobday 2005; Kuo, Lim, and Sonko 2018).

Latecomer firms develop their business activities and create added value in the production work through R&D, manufacturing, and marketing using the value propositions of contract manufacturing business models (Liu, Liu, and Lin 2008; Jacobides,

MacDuffie, and Tae 2016). Furthermore, these firms engage in active organizational management, coordinate internal business activities and establish external relationships with their customers, vendors, and suppliers (Carayannis, Sindakis, and Walter 2015; Wang and Chen 2020; Zott and Amit 2010). Contract manufacturers sustain these advantages by offering new value in existing markets by engaging in different innovation practices, including product, process, marketing, and organizational innovations (Kuo and Minshall 2010; Chu 2009; Hobday 1998; Matthyssens, Vandenbempt, and Weyns 2009).

During a business model transition, a firm adapts its business activities and organizational management to provide more added value in an existing market (Amit and Zott 2001; Chesbrough 2010). Nevertheless, given the firm's repositioning of its value propositions in value chains, reconfiguring its innovation practices is critical to creating value and remaining competitive advantage through the new model (Teece 2010; Wang and Wu 2012; Carayannis, Sindakis, and Walter 2015; Snihur and Wiklund 2019). Therefore, investigating the reconfigurations of innovation practices in a business model transition could provide an understanding of the interconnection between a firm's business model and innovation practices and provide constituents with instructions on how to catch up operating the new business model.

This study uses a large-scale survey of contract manufacturers from 14 cities in the Greater China region to represent the typical manner in which the contract manufacturing business has changed. Many contract manufacturers have developed well-run OEM, ODM, and OBM business models and have transitioned through one or more of these business models (Chu 2009; Kuo and Minshall 2010; Hobday 1998). This study provides detailed observations of the innovation practices followed in the manufacturing sector under the OEM, ODM, and OBM models. Furthermore, the reconfiguration of innovation practices during the transition from one model to another is examined. In the next section, this paper reviews the literature on the interconnection between the business model and innovation and their interactions during a firm's transition. Then, this paper discusses the new manufacturing sector business models and a mix of innovation practices of the OEM, ODM, and OBM models. In the methodology section, more information is provided on this study's data collection, variable compilation, and analytical method. In the results section, this paper presents comprehensive data on business model transitions by contract manufacturers. In the final section, the findings are discussed in light of the results of prior studies to provide an insightful conclusion and to develop implications for the theory and business practices.

Literature review

Business model and innovation

In the last decades, numerous research used different frameworks to describe the concept of the business model for how a firm does business in markets (e.g. Amit and Zott (2001), Osterwalder, Pigneur, and Tucci (2005), Johnson, Christensen, and Kagermann (2008), Chesbrough (2010), and Teece (2010)). These frameworks, which consist of various elements, attempt to depict a firm's value proposition, business activities, and organizational management in the specific market as ways to offer value to customers and receive payoffs (Zott and Amit 2010; Spieth, Schneckenberg, and Ricart 2014). In other words, value creation for customers is a business model's core function, and the production of value creation is a core business activity that relies on using resources and capabilities (Lanzolla and Markides 2020). Before value creation, the value proposition determines a firm's production and describes the value that it will deliver to the customer. Moreover, organizational management plays a coordination role, moderating the firm's business activities and outputs (Wang and Chen 2020; Carayannis, Sindakis, and Walter 2015; Teece 2010). Internally, managerial authority and organizational structures determine organizational efficiency during the implementation of business activities (Taran, Boer, and Lindgren 2015; Teece 2010). Externally, partnerships dominate the interconnections with specific suppliers and partners in the value chain to create aggregate value and promote the customer value (Eng and Spickett-Jones 2009; Sánchez and Ricart 2010).

Both Teece (2010) and Chesbrough (2010) considered that a well-defined business model assures that a firm can efficiently create, deliver, and capture value. However, formulating a competitive strategy and continuously creating innovative value for customers is a critical competitive advantage to a firm (Danarahmanto et al. 2020). In other words, a firm's innovation practices that interconnect with the business model could enhance the implementation of the business strategy by gaining and holding advantages over market competitors. Furthermore, these innovation practices represent the extension of the implementation of the transaction structure, which also needs to employ a firm's resources and capabilities (Teece 2010; Lanzolla and Markides 2020). For example, technological innovation provides new products and better ways to satisfy customer needs (Chesbrough 2010; Pucihar et al. 2019). Marketing innovation implements the novel offerings of product design, placement, promotion, and pricing for existing and potential customers and allows firms to convert customer needs into value creation (Tavassoli and Bengtsson 2018; Sánchez-Gutiérrez et al. 2019). Organizational innovation assures that the firm is adaptive to regenerating many key processes, reorganizing the structure, and improving the effectiveness of decision-making activities that fuel the value creation process (Basile and Faraci 2015). Additionally, organizational innovation in external partnerships helps the firm acquire the necessary resources, capabilities, and complementary assets for use in value creation (Pucihar et al. 2019).

The interconnection of the business model and innovation practices is considered to summarize the operation of a firm's business model as defining a value proposition for the value chain, operating the business activities to create value for customers, and providing new value to sustain a competitive advantage through innovation (Hacklin, Björkdahl, and Wallin 2018; Chesbrough 2010; Teece 2010). In short, a firm must develop an appropriate innovation mix based on its business activities and organizational management during the value creation process to keep the promises that it made to customers.

Business model transition and the change in innovation practices

Profiting from their business models allows incumbent firms to develop well-defined configurations for these models, including innovation practices. Therefore, incumbent firms must transition their configurations when intending to reinvent their business models in existing markets (Johnson, Christensen, and Kagermann 2008; Wirtz and Daiser 2017; Latilla et al. 2020). A transition in the existing market would lead to a reconfiguration of all or part of the elements in a business model regardless of the reasons – in response to environmental changes, the pursuit of growth, to compete with rivals, to reclaim a value proposition for new customers, or a new value offering (Buliga, Scheiner, and Voigt 2016; Massa, Tucci, and Afuah 2017).

However, those firms may face challenges when transitioning their business models. Chesbrough (2010) considered that incumbent firms might encounter conflicts in their resources, capabilities, and assets between their existing business model's configuration and the new business model's reconfiguration. Teece (2010) argued that incumbent firms must recognize business activities in their value chains and implement innovative practices in their business activities to create a new competitive advantage in the existing market when redesigning their business models. Koen, Bertels, and Elsum (2011) believed that incumbent firms must organize a new value network to interconnect the value creation of internal business activities with the work of their upstream and downstream partners when seeking a new business model in an existing market to pursue growth. Euchner and Ganguly (2014) mentioned that incumbent firms should redefine the value proposition to guide them when shifting business activities for new value creation. Carayannis, Sindakis, and Walter (2015) indicated that incumbent firms should cultivate and incorporate active internal organizational management with business activities to sustain innovation practices. Furthermore, the dynamic governance of external partnerships enriches the firm's ability to take full advantage of new business opportunities during transitions to a different business model. Hacklin, Björkdahl, and Wallin (2018) pointed out that incumbent firms often experiment and tweak elements of their existing model in a path-dependent manner when the business may need several pivots to transition to a new business model. Over time, firms need to change and migrate to a new value proposition to stay competitive. In summary, reconfiguration of innovation practices associated with production and organizational innovation may be critical to developing the advantage of new value propositions and enhancing the transition of business activities and organizational management to a new business model. The logic of a business model leads incumbent firms to develop a new mix of innovation practices to aid the business model transition at the root of a new value proposition to stay profitable and competitive.

The new business model in the manufacturing sector: contract manufacturing in OEM, ODM, OBM

Contract manufacturing has become a new opportunity for latecomers in existing markets through the vertical specialization of global production networks (Hummels, Ishii, and Yi 2001; Hummels, Rapoport, and Kei-Mu 1998). This new business opportunity triggers business model innovation in the manufacturing sector, in which the value chain work cuts into the specific but interconnected business models of the involved firms (Matthyssens, Vandenbempt, and Weyns 2009; Hobday 1998). Contract manufacturing encourages and re-assigns the new business models followed in manufacturing production into OEM, ODM, and OBM types. OEM firms are latecomers that produce finished goods to precise specifications under subcontracts with designers or brand companies (Chin, Liu, and Yang 2016; Hobday 1998). ODM firms are latecomers that develop or co-develop for outsourcers and provide finished goods that brand outsourcers sell (Hobday 1998; Bijarboneh 2015). An OBM firm is a latecomer that designs, produces, and sells its own-brand name finished goods as a new entrant in an existing market (Luo 2011; Kuo and Minshall 2010). These business models have defined the general operation of latecomers as specialized manufacturers in the production networks of value chains.

As a value proposition for customers, OEM latecomers posit their value on providing contract manufacturing with cost, speed, and reliability advantages (Chin, Liu, and Yang 2016; Jacobides, MacDuffie, and Tae 2016). ODM latecomers provide customized product development and contract manufacturing and coordinate the marketing strategy with brand subcontractors (Bijarboneh 2015; Lee, Song, and Kwak 2015). OBM latecomers sell innovative products to promote customers' utilization scenarios (Chu 2009; Liu, Liu, and Lin 2008). Regarding business activities, latecomers configure their work through the position of their production work in their value chains, including employing R&D, manufacturing, and marketing (Chu 2009; Manzakoğlu and Er 2018). In addition, to sustain a competitive advantage, latecomers engage in different forms of value creation in their production. In R&D, pursuing product innovation enhances latecomers' ability to introduce a new product (Huang, Chung, and Lin 2009; Wang and Wu 2012). In manufacturing, latecomers invest in process innovation to support the production of new products (Snihur and Wiklund 2019). In marketing, latecomers use innovative marketing strategies to promote sales (Eng and Spickett-Jones 2009; Matthyssens, Vandenbempt, and Weyns 2009). The focus of OEM latecomers is on manufacturing that meets outsourcers' cost, speed, and reliability requests, which they can expect to become incrementally more stable (Chin, Liu, and Yang 2016; Bijarboneh 2015). In other words, innovation in the manufacturing process is at the core of OEM firms' business activities (Forbes and Wield 2008; Hobday, Rush, and Bessant 2004). The primary focus of ODM latecomers is on R&D and manufacturing to provide contract designing and manufacturing work for brand outsourcers. The interconnection between product and process innovation promotes the technological capabilities of ODM firms to assist their customers in providing innovative products (Tiong et al. 2010; Wang and Wu 2012; Hobday, Rush, and Bessant 2004). OBM latecomers, which are new entrants in an existing market, seek to expand their marketing innovation efforts to compete with incumbent firms and strengthen product and process innovation, thus ensuring that their products have technological and manufacturing advantages (Eng 2009; Chu 2009).

Internally, latecomers follow their core businesses when determining the rules of organizational management. OEM latecomers adapt their structures to accommodate manufacturing processes and promote production efficiency (Chen 2016). ODM latecomers combine product and manufacturing lines through organizational management to enhance their contract product development (Ma 2005; Yung and Lai 2012). OBM latecomers restructure to promote product-market organizational management because doing so is beneficial to responding quickly to customer needs (Eng and Spickett-Jones 2009; Eng 2009). Externally, from the aspect of organizational management, outsourcing contract partnerships are at the core of external relationship management in contract manufacturing. OEM latecomers need a stable and long-term relationship with their component suppliers to support their manufacturing activities (Jacobides, MacDuffie, and Tae 2016; Szalkai and Magyar 2017). ODM latecomers may need to manage relationships with module partners, OEM partners, and suppliers and to modify their outsourcing depending on the demands of contract product development (Yung and Lai 2012). OBM

Table 1. Business model and innovation mix in contract manufacturers: OEM, ODM, and OBM.

	OEM	ODM	OBM
1.Value proposition	Contract manufacturing with cost, speed, and reliability advantages	Customized product development and contract manufacturing	Selling innovative products to promote customer value
2.Target customer	Outsourcers	Outsourcers	End-users
3.Core business activities			
R&D	Outsourcer	ODM	Optional
Manufacturing	OEM	ODM	Optional
Marketing	Outsourcer	ODM, Outsourcer	OBM
4. Engagement of innovation practices			
Product innovation	Low	High	High
Process innovation	High	High	Depends on the need for product innovation
Marketing innovation	Low	Dependence on outsourcing business	High
5. Organizational management			
Internal structure	Structuring follows the manufacturing processes	Structuring follows product development	Structuring follows the product -market segments
External partnership	Suppliers, Module partners	Suppliers, OEM partners, and module partners	Suppliers, OEM, ODM partners, module partners, and vendors

latecomers transform their roles from subcontractors to outsourcers and strategically outsource their production to external partners (Chin, Liu, and Yang 2016; Chu 2009).

As can be seen from the summary in Table 1 of contract manufacturing business models, these three models demonstrate differences in the configurations required to conduct business in existing markets. At the same time, when latecomers want to upgrade their business models, they face many common challenges during the transition that are the same as those encountered by most incumbent firms. Therefore, if a contract manufacturer seeks to upgrade its business model, it needs a clear understanding of the model's patterns because its business activities are reconfigured following the repositioning of its value proposition. Additionally, competence building and leveraging by reconfiguring innovation practices enhances a contract manufacturer's organizational sustainability with respect to the speed at which it implements a new business model and competes with other incumbent competitors.

Methodology

Data collection

This study aims to investigate the configuration of innovation practices in firms that follow the OEM, ODM, and OBM models and to examine the reconfiguration of those practices by contract manufacturers undertaking business model transitions. The large-scale Industrial Innovation Survey (IIS) of industries in 14 cities,[1] includes Taipei and its nearby cities located in the Greater China region, and similar to the Community Innovation Survey in Europe, is employed. In those cities, contract manufacturing and export trade are dominated the business model of their manufacturing sector, and there are well-known cases in the transition of OEM-ODM-OBM pathway, such as Acer, Giant, Wistron, Foxconn, and HTC. To collect the data, responses from the second survey of 2004–2006 (IIS2) and the third survey of 2007–2010 (IIS3) were collated (Wu 2009, 2013). 3,944 valid questionnaires remained from IIS2 and 3,838 from IIS3. Moreover, 1,319 firms were listed in both the IIS2 and IIS3 surveys. Firms' business models were also identified, showing 427 OEM firms, 543 ODM firms, and 562 OBM firms in IIS2, and 699 OEM firms, 816 ODM firms, and 1,223 OBM firms in IIS3.

Variable compilation

During the compilation of the variables, values are assigned separately to variables in IIS2 and IIS3. All variables in the study are nominal or dummy variables. To represent engagement in innovation practices, we compile the *Product Innovation* and *Process Innovation* variables, which measure whether a firm is engaged in new product development as a rework of the manufacturing process. To measure marketing innovation, *Product Design, Channel Distribution*, and *Marketing Promotion* represent whether a firm changes its marketing strategies for product design, marketing channels, and promotions in the market in which it sells its products to customers. For organizational innovation, *Authority Realignment* measures the internal changes at a firm, and *Organization Restructuring* assesses the extent to which revisions to a firm's managerial authority and organizational structure occurred. Additionally, *Outsourcing Re-assignment* is used to examine changes in a firm's external outsourcing relationship with its suppliers and customers.

For a contract manufacturer's business model, a sole model is assigned to the firm using the *OEM, ODM*, and *OBM* variables. Regarding business model transitions, data from 1,319 firms listed in both IIS2 and IIS3 are collected. For an OEM firm's upgrade, *OEM transition* from IIS2 is used, which takes the value of 1 to indicate that the firm's business model is OEM in IIS2 but non-OEM in IIS3, and 0 indicates that the firm remains an OEM in both IIS2 and IIS3. All non-OEM firms are skipped. Following the same logic, the *ODM transition* in IIS2 is used to reflect an ODM firm's upgrade. Concomitant with upgrading the business model, *ODM Entrant* in IIS3 was used and took the value of 1 if the firm's business model in IIS3 was ODM but was OEM in IIS2 and 0 to represent other ODM firms in IIS3; all non-ODM firms are skipped. Similarly, *OBM Entrant* in IIS3 is used to reflect upgraded OEM and ODM firms.

The control variables measure a firm's characteristics that may be factoring in the employment of innovation practices. The industrial characteristic of *Hitech* represents a firm's high-tech affiliation using the two-digit codes 20, 26, and 27, with 1 indicating that the firm is a high-tech firm. A firm's size is represented by *SME*, with 1 indicating that a firm has less than 200 people. The geography of a firm's market is coded using *Domestic*, for which 1 indicates that the firm has no sales in other countries. The firm's primary client is represented by *B2C*, which takes the value of 1 to indicate that the firm's primary client is the end-user.

Analytical model

Two critical investigations are in this paper. First, the configuration of innovation practices under the OEM, ODM, and OBM models is investigated using two datasets, IIS2 and IIS3.

An independent sample test is used to examine the differences in innovation practices between IIS2 and IIS3. The results indicate that IIS2 and IIS3 represent two independent samples in *Product Innovation* ($t = 4.381$, $p < 0.001$), *Process Innovation* ($t = -3.025$, $p < 0.01$), *Product Design* ($t = -0.248$), *Channel Distribution* ($t = 5.199$, $p < 0.001$), *Marketing Promotion* ($t = 0.415$), *Authority Realignment* ($t = -9.707$, $p < 0.001$), *Organization Restructuring* ($t = -7.825$, $p < 0.001$), and *Outsourcing Re-assignment* ($t = -6.113$, $p < 0.001$). Therefore, given this study's interest in the business development of contract manufacturing in cities of the sample, IIS3 data are used as the observation dataset. Then, logistic regression is used to investigate the configuration of the innovation practices of firms under the OEM, ODM, and OBM models.

Second, the reconfiguration that occurs during a business model upgrade is examined. To observe the changes during such a transition, 1,319 firms that were in both IIS2 and IIS3 are used. To examine the changes before the transition, the IIS2 data are divided into two sub-datasets of OEM and ODM firms. Logistic regression models are employed, and OEM and ODM transitions are used as independent variables, which may influence firms' innovation practices. The same logic is followed to examine the changes after the transition, the IIS3 data are divided into two sub-datasets of ODM and OBM firms, and logistic regression is employed to analyse the effects of ODM and OBM entrants as the independent variables. For the post hoc analysis, ANOVA is used to validate the results.

Data analysis

Descriptive statistics

As shown in Table 2, The statistics of the general features of the manufacturing sector in the cities of the sample show that high-tech firms represent one-fifth to one-fourth of the total number of firms during 2003–2011. For firm size, SMEs dominate, with 89% in IIS2 and 74% in IIS3. The decrease in the share of domestic market sales from 48% in IIS2 to 31% in IIS3 indicates that manufacturing goods exports continue to gain in significance in the sector. Low business-to-consumer (B2C) rates (25% in IIS2 and 21% inIIS3) show that most manufacturers sell their products to other business customers. Regarding contract manufacturing development, the two surveys show that the combined share of OEM and ODM firms is 25% in IIS2 and 42% in IIS3, indicating that contract manufacturing is the general business model and is increasing in the manufacturing sector. The growth in the number of OBM firms from 14% in IIS2 to 34% in IIS3.

The *Product Innovation* (0.25 in IIS2 and 0.21 in IIS3) and *Process Innovation* (0.22 in IIS2 and 0.25 in IIS3) results for the manufacturing sector show that a high number of manufacturers have yet to engage in innovation practices. In marketing innovation, *Product Design* (0.16 in IIS2 and IIS3) was a significant activity associated with the market for manufacturing firms. In organizational innovation for business development, the frequency of internal changes was more significant than that for modifications to external partnerships. Engagement with organizational changes increased during 2006–2010, as evidenced by an increase in *Authority Realignment* from 0.18 in IIS2 to 0.27 in IIS3, in *Organization Restructuring* from 0.18 in IIS2 to 0.25 in IIS3, and in *Outsourcing Re-assignment* from 0.12 in IIS2 to 0.16 in IIS3. Regarding business model transitions by contract manufacturers, OEM firms (17% of OEM firms in IIS2) seem to have had a stronger motivation to upgrade their

Table 2. Descriptive statistics.

	IIS2		IIS3	
Variables	Frequency	Mean	Frequency	Mean
Hitech	789	.20	1,082	.28
SME	3,046	.89	2,829	.74
Domestic	1,881	.48	1,177	.31
B2C	993	.25	814	.21
OEM	427	.11	753	.20
ODM	543	.14	851	.22
OBM	562	.14	1,313	.34
Product Innovation	977	.25	704	.21
Process Innovation	884	.22	870	.25
Product Design	629	.16	620	.16
Channel Distribution	600	.15	431	.11
Marketing Promotion	385	.10	364	.09
Authority Realignment	707	.18	1,039	.27
Organization Restructuring	715	.18	976	.25
Outsourcing Re-assignment	457	.12	629	.16
OEM Transition	73	.17		
ODM Transition	27	.05		
ODM Entrant			46	.05
OBM Entrant			54	.04

OEM business models than ODM firms (5% of ODM firms in IIS2). Simultaneously, not all of the OEM firms upgraded their business models to OBM, given that only 4% of OBM firms in IIS3 upgraded, and ODM is the first-choice transition of OEM firms – 5% of ODM firms in IIS3 were OEM firms. This result suggests that time as an ODM on the OEM–ODM–OBM path may be an essential step in upgrading contract manufacturers' business models.

Configuration of innovation practices in OEM, ODM, and OEM models

This study investigates the effect of the configuration of innovation practices in contract manufacturing, adopts the three specific OEM, ODM and OBM models, and employs logistic regression to examine the influence of these business models on the practices of the surveyed firms (Table 3). For OEM contract manufacturers, no significant engagement in product ($\beta = -.233$), process ($\beta = -.049$), and marketing (*Product Design*, $\beta = .322$; *Channel Distribution*, $\beta = .099$; *Marketing Promotion*, $\beta = -.128$, $p < 0.001$) innovation is indicated. Regarding changes in organizational management, OEM firms may engage significantly in corporate restructurings ($\beta = .318$, $p < 0.05$). A post hoc ANOVA analysis (Table 4) also confirms that OEM firms have low engagement in all innovation practices in their business activities. Meanwhile, ODM contract manufacturers aggressively engage in product ($\beta = .351$, $p < 0.01$) and process ($\beta = .553$, $p < 0.001$) innovation and significantly in marketing innovation (*Product Design*, $\beta = 1.030$, $p < 0.001$; *Channel Distribution*, $\beta = .693$, $p < 0.001$; *Marketing Promotion*, $\beta = .829$, $p < 0.001$). ODM firms face a high degree of engagement in innovation practices for production and show a significant change in organizational management in the areas of managerial authority ($\beta = .219$, $p < 0.10$), organizational structure ($\beta = .649$, $p < 0.001$), and outsourcing partnership ($\beta = .819$, $p < 0.001$).

Table 3. Engagement of innovation practices by OEM, ODM, and OBM firms.

	Product Innovation	Process Innovation	Product Design	Channel Distribution	Marketing Promotion	Authority Realignment	Organization Restructuring	Outsourcing Re-assignment
Hitech	.271***	−.131	−.151	.029	−.273*	−.014	.640***	−.428***
	(.094)	(.091)	(.103)	(.116)	(.133)	(.084)	(.083)	(.106)
SME	−.598***	−.385***	.022	.164	−.621***	−.502***	−.603***	−.310**
	(.094)	(.090)	(.104)	(.120)	(.121)	(.084)	(.085)	(.099)
Domestic	−1.168***	−1.234***	−.646***	−.804***	−.939***	−1.046***	−1.184***	−1.469***
	(.135)	(.119)	(.115)	(.139)	(.138)	(.100)	(.107)	(.143)
B2C	.086	.134	.648***	.017	.715***	−.058	.181+	.252*
	(.113)	(.104)	(.106)	(.133)	(.133)	(.097)	(.098)	(.113)
OEM	−.233	−.049	.322	.099	−.128***	−.077	.318*	−.020
	(.155)	(.137)	(.179)	(.191)	(.372)	(.128)	(.127)	(.169)
ODM	.351**	.553***	1.030***	.693***	.829***	.219+	.649***	.819***
	(.135)	(.122)	(.158)	(.167)	(.199)	(.117)	(.118)	(.141)
OBM	.447***	.249*	1.423***	.771***	1.430***	.699***	.291**	.708***
	(.124)	(.116)	(.143)	(.154)	(.176)	(.103)	(.110)	(.132)
Pseudo R^2	.069	.057	.066	.034	.125	.069	.087	.080
LR chi^2	238.56***	221.65***	224.46***	90.53***	300.69	309.60***	376.41***	275.11***
Freedom	7	7	7	7	7	7	7	7
Log- likelihood	−1,622.221	−1,828.664	−1,583.005	−1,302.760	−1,053.042	−2,085.836	−1,987.391	−1,572.439
N	3,432	3,420	3,836	3,836	3,836	3,836	3,836	3,836

Note: Computed in IIS3 by logistic regression, coefficient and S.E. are shown, and significance level at +p < 0.10, *p < 0.05, **p,0.01, and ***,p < 0.001

Table 4. ANOVA table for variation in the engagement of innovation practices for OEM, ODM, and OBM firms.

B.M.	N	Product Innovation	Process Innovation	Product Design	Channel Distribution	Marketing Promotion	Authority Realignment	Organization Restructuring	Outsourcing Re-assignment
OEM	699	.130	.190	.094	.077	.012	.189	.234	.097
ODM	816	.234	.328	.179	.139	.100	.269	.328	.223
OBM	1,223	.249	.265	.251	.147	.173	.367	.264	.208
F		20.188***	18.688***	39.537***	11.483***	66.773***	39.434***	9.673***	26.343***

Note: Computed in IIS3, *$p < 0.05$, **p,0.01, and ***, $p < 0.001$

OBM manufacturers also have significant positive engagement in innovation practices in all aspects of production work, including product innovation ($\beta = .447$, $p < 0.001$), process innovation ($\beta = .249$, $p < 0.05$), and marketing innovation (*Product Design*, $\beta = 1.423$, $p < 0.001$; *Channel Distribution*, $\beta = .771$, $p < 0.001$; *Marketing Promotion*, $\beta = 1.430$, $p < 0.001$). Moreover, at a high frequency, they make adjustments to their organizational management in the areas of managerial authority ($\beta = .699$, $p < 0.001$), organizational structure ($\beta = .291$, $p < 0.01$), and management of outsourcing partnership ($\beta = .708$, $p < 0.001$).

As indicated in Table 4, the ANOVA test of the relationship between innovation practices and business models also confirms that ODM and OBM firms engage significantly in all innovation practices. However, the configuration of innovation practices followed by ODM and OBM manufacturers differ. On the one hand, ODM firms are more engaged in process innovation and organization restructuring and are equivalently involved in product innovation, marketing channels, and outsourcing management. On the other hand, OBM firms engage more actively in marketing strategies and make aggressive modifications to managerial authority to support their business activities.

Contract manufacturers' configuration of innovation practices before business model upgrades

As is known, a contract manufacturer's model upgrade redefines its way of doing business. As a result, the contract manufacturer faces the task of reconfiguring many different aspects of its organizational configurations and business activities. When a firm plans to reinvent its business model, it must properly prepare before the transition to ensure success. Therefore, this section examines the degree to which firms work their innovation practices before upgrading. First, the differences in preparing to upgrade and the status quo of OEM firms are considered. Table 5 shows that no significant changes are made to OEM firms' innovation practices in production before they make upgrades in product innovation ($\beta = -.120$), process innovation ($\beta = .445$), and marketing innovation (*Product Design*, $\beta = .020$; *Channel Distribution*, $\beta = .251$; *Marketing Promotion*, $\beta = -.272$) – the same as the ANOVA test results in Table 6. Although only a significant engagement in managerial authority change ($\beta = .893$, $p < 0.01$) is indicated in Table 5, the ANOVA test in Table 6 shows that OEM firms are more able to change all aspects of their organizational management (*Authority Realignment*, $F = 10.208$, $p < 0.01$; *Organization Restructuring*, $F = 0.524$, $p < 0.05$; *Outsourcing Re-assignment*, $F = 5.581$, $p < 0.05$) before upgrading.

Second, the differences in the configuration of ODM firms are considered before upgrading. Table 7 shows that ODM firms have many non-significant differences in the configurations of innovation before upgrading, including in *Product Innovation* ($\beta = .213$), *Product Design* ($\beta = -.157$), *Marketing Promotion* ($\beta = -.137$), *Authority Realignment* ($\beta = .583$), *Organization Restructuring* ($\beta = -.038$), and *Outsourcing Re-assignment* ($\beta = -.767$). However, other results from the same table indicate that ODM firms reduce their engagement during process innovation ($\beta = -.918$, $p < 0.05$) and the exploration of marketing channels ($\beta = -1.070$, $p < 0.10$). Furthermore, the ANOVA test in Table 6 confirms these findings and finds a visible increase in *Authority Realignment* ($\mu = .556 > .388$) and decreases in *Outsourcing Re-assignment* ($\mu = .185 < .290$).

Table 5. The configuration of innovation practices by OEM firms before the transition.

	Product Innovation	Process Innovation	Product Design	Channel Distribution	Marketing Promotion	Authority Realignment	Organization Restructuring	Outsourcing Re-assignment
Hitech	−.041	.284	.670*	.349	.437	.534+	.691*	.254
	(.308)	(.300)	(.313)	(.326)	(.371)	(.309)	(.303)	(.389)
SME	−.077	−.409	−.445	−.391	−.299	−.147	−.529+	.059
	(.308)	(.297)	(.315)	(.326)	(.376)	(.310)	(.303)	(.395)
Domestic	−.139	−.343	−.183	−.121	−.178	.347	−.613	.138
	(.323)	(.323)	(.348)	(.362)	(.416)	(.335)	(.344)	(.428)
B2C	−.370	.830	.712*	.392	.337	.042	.298	.064
	(.342)	(.352)	(.354)	(.371)	(.422)	(.362)	(.352)	(.458)
OEM	−.120	.445	.020	.251	−.272	.893**	−.047	.863
Transition	(.315)	(.306)	(.328)	(.334)	(.400)	(.314)	(.314)	(.390)
Pseudo R^2	.006	.043	.041	.021	.015	.050	.047	.030
LR chi^2	1.70	12.99*	11.28	5.4	3.00	14.10*	13.7*	5.79
Freedom	5	5	5	5	5	5	5	5
Log- likelihood	−140.961	−145.990	−131.195	−124.203	−101.294	−135.386	−138.947	−95.151
N	220	220	220	220	220	220	220	220

Note: Computed in IIS2 by logistic regression, coefficient and S.E. are shown, and significance level at +p < 0.10, *p < 0.05, **p,0.01, and ***,p < 0.001

Table 6. ANOVA table for variation in the engagement of innovation practices in the transition for OEM, ODM, OBM firms.

	Product Innovation	Process Innovation	Product Design	Channel Distribution	Marketing Promotion	Authority Realignment	Organization Restructuring	Outsourcing Re-assignment
Before the transition (IIS2)								
OEM								
Continuing (N = 147)	.660	.449	.299	.238	.184	.279	.361	.122
Transition (N = 73)	.644	.589	.342	.315	.164	.493	.411	.247
F	.055	3.86	.419	1.485	0.123	10.208**	.524*	5.581*
ODM								
Continuing (N = 247)	.580	.612	.294	.302	.171	.388	.412	.290
Transition (N = 27)	.630	.407	.259	.148	.148	.556	.444	.185
F	.249	4.260*	.140	2.825	.093	2.852	.103	1.319
After the transition (IIS3)								
ODM								
Incumbent (N = 215)	.265	.395	.239	.162	.126	.329	.441	.252
Entrant (N = 43)	.163	.372	.130	.109	.022	.326	.413	.326
F	2.012	.081	2.609	.837	4.340*	.001	.124	1.063
OBM								
Incumbent (N = 345)	.264	.365	.221	.067	.131	.363	.248	.216
Entrant (N = 50)	.440	.449	.370	.111	.296	.537	.389	.370
F	6.720**	1.271	5.795*	1.389	10.267**	6.122*	4.834**	6.312*

Note: *p < 0.05, **p,0.01, and ***, p < 0.001

Table 7. The configuration of innovation practices by ODM firms before the transition.

	Product Innovation	Process Innovation	Product Design	Channel Distribution	Marketing Promotion	Authority Realignment	Organization Restructuring	Outsourcing Re-assignment
Hitech	.295	.048	.171	.220	.189	.071	.258	.355
	(.277)	(.277)	(.292)	(.297)	(.349)	(.281)	(.277)	(.298)
SME	−.149	−.314	.054	−.026	−.044	−.606*	−.768**	−.514+
	(.270)	(.273)	(.289)	(.295)	(.347)	(.271)	(.268)	(.290)
Domestic	.-.708	.568+	−.654+	−.273	.334	−1.111**	−.676*	−.949**
	(.287)	(.301)	(.338)	(.326)	(.363)	(.326)	(.308)	(.366)
B2C	.119	.172	.104	1.013**	−.037	.195	.462	.737*
	(.318)	(.325)	(.346)	(.332)	(.410)	(.332)	(.323)	(.348)
ODM	.213	−.918*	−.157	−1.070+	−.137	.583	−.038	−.767
Transition	(.433)	(.428)	(.474)	(.580)	(.579)	(.433)	(.430)	(.539)
Pseudo R^2	.023	.027	.014	.039	.005	.060	.046	.052
LR chi^2	8.47	9.94+	4.56	12.77*	1.23	22.06***	16.86**	16.77**
Freedom	5	5	5	5	5	5	5	5
Log-likelihood	−180.394	−178.944	−161.611	−156.606	−123.005	−172.5048	−176.199	−152.745
N	272	272	272	272	272	272	272	272

Note: Computed in IIS2 by logistic regression, coefficient and S.E. are shown, and significant level at +p < 0.10, *p < 0.05, **p,0.01, and ***,p < 0.001

Reconfiguration of innovation practices after contract manufacturers' business model upgrades

After transitioning to the new business model, the new entrant makes an effort to develop new business activities and reconfigure its production in its value chains to compete with incumbent firms. Examining the differences in the innovation practices of new entrants and incumbent firms provides an opportunity to understand the apparent efforts of new entrants to catch up with the established practices of the new business and to manage new challenges. However, new entrants into the ODM business and ranks may have significantly insufficient engagement in product innovation ($\beta = -.856$, $p < 0.10$) and marketing promotion ($\beta = -1.890$, $p < 0.10$) relative to incumbent firms (Table 8).

The means of engagement in innovation practices are tabulated in Table 6, indicating that new ODM entrants have distinctly low average activity in *Product Innovation* ($\mu = .163 < .265$), *Product Design* ($\mu = .130 < .239$), *Channel Distribution* ($\mu = .109 < .162$), and *Marketing Promotion* ($\mu = .022 < .126$) relative to incumbents. OEM contract manufacturers face challenges in developing new competencies in R&D and marketing when they transition to the ODM model.

New OBM entrants exhibit comprehensive production enhancements (Table 9), including in product innovation ($\beta = .728$, $p < 0.05$), process innovation ($\beta = .277$), and marketing innovation (*Product Design*, $\beta = .631$, $p < 0.05$; *Channel Distribution*, $\beta = .504$; *Marketing Promotion*, $\beta = .893$, $p < 0.05$). Moreover, these entrants typically rework organizational management internally (*Authority Realignment*, $\beta = .650$, $p < 0.05$; *Organization Restructuring*, $\beta = .647$, $p < 0.05$) and externally (*Outsourcing Re-assignment*, $\beta = .599$, $p < 0.10$). The ANOVA results in Table 6 confirm these results, indicating that engagement means showing that new OBM entrants make considerably greater efforts to establish their new business practices to compete.

Discussion

This paper uses data on contract manufacturers from 14 cities in the Greater China region to study their efforts in reconfiguring their innovation mix through business model transitions. A review of business model innovation in contract manufacturing as carried out by latecomer firms reveals that OEM, ODM, and OBM firms employ different business models to achieve value creation and implement value propositions in an existing market. In detail, the interconnection between the mix of innovation practices and business models explains contract manufacturers' attempts to create new value and reconfigure their organizations to sustain their competitive advantages.

Entry-level OEM firms in contract manufacturing have lower engagement in production innovation work. Simultaneously, they make fewer changes in organizational management. In the OEM model, the core goal of the firm is to sustain excellent manufacturing efficiency, and avoiding changes that risk the firm's cost advantages is critical to firm performance. Wang and Wu (2012) examined the contract manufacturing model's moderation of the relationship between R&D investment and operating performance and found a negative effect from the OEM model, with R&D investments possibly reducing OEM firms' performance. Liu, Liu, and Lin (2008) argued that OEM contract manufacturers leverage existing manufacturing competence, which involves low risk.

Table 8. Reconfiguration of innovation practices by ODM new entrants.

	Product Innovation	Process Innovation	Product Design	Channel Distribution	Marketing Promotion	Authority Realignment	Organization Restructuring	Outsourcing Re-assignment
Hitech	.109	.219	−.245	−.750+	−.939+	−.134	−.275	−.623+
	(.312)	(.277)	(.325)	(.408)	(.503)	(.289)	(.296)	(.321)
SME	−.584+	−.315	−.291	−.262	−1.555***	−.903***	−1.411***	−.729*
	(.300)	(.269)	(.307)	(.355)	(.440)	(.274)	(.282)	(.292)
Domestic	−.577	−.788*	.298	.160	.916+	−.293	−1.456***	−.591
	(.426)	(.370)	(.359)	(.422)	(.473)	(.352)	(.394)	(.404)
B2C	−.263	−.541+	.100	.219	−.121	.195	−.216	−.256
	(.361)	(.323)	(.346)	(.395)	(.491)	(.314)	(.324)	(.349)
ODM	−.856+	−.241	−.721	−.282	−1.890+	−.156	−.328	.357
Entrant	(.482)	(.370)	(.475)	(.520)	(1.051)	(.367)	(.362)	(.365)
IIS2	.195	−.086	.128	−.630	−.213	.387	.284	.432
	(.352)	(.308)	(.356)	(.511)	(.669)	(.294)	(.317)	(.356)
Pseudo R^2	.033	.029	.018	.030	.132	.045	.129	.048
LR chi^2	9.44	9.98	4.94	6.97	24.19	15.31*	47.20***	14.85*
Freedom	6	6	6	6	6	6	6	6
Log-likelihood	−139.812	−167.718	−138.793	−111.181	−79.764	−161.993	−160.002	−147.520
N	258	258	268	268	268	268	268	268

Note: Computed in IIS3 by logistic regression, coefficient and S.E. are shown, and significance level at +p < 0.10, *p < 0.05, **p,0.01, and ***,p < 0.001

Table 9. Reconfiguration of innovation practices by OBM new entrants.

	Product Innovation	Process Innovation	Product Design	Channel Distribution	Marketing Promotion	Authority Realignment	Organization Restructuring	Outsourcing Re-assignment
Hitech	.234	−.145	−.317	.484	−.873*	−.555*	.380	−.724*
	(.249)	(.239)	(.264)	(.394)	(.376)	(.231)	(.236)	(.286)
SME	−.327	.323	−.066	.261	−.930**	−.353+	.033	−.160
	(.236)	(.226)	(.237)	(.389)	(.293)	(.214)	(.233)	(.240)
Domestic	−.946*	−1.156***	−.776*	−1.451+	−2.469*	−.723*	−.074	−1.240**
	(.375)	(.330)	(.358)	(.757)	(1.027)	(.295)	(.292)	(.425)
B2C	.018	−.252	.229	.170	.430	.229	.068	.213
	(.272)	(.259)	(.266)	(.437)	(.321)	(.241)	(.260)	(.272)
OBM	.728*	.277	.631*	.504	.839*	.650*	.647*	.599+
Entry	(.316)	(.315)	(.314)	(.488)	(.356)	(.304)	(.309)	(.318)
IIS2	−.040	−.019	.215	.056	.158	−.369	.377+	−.103
	(.230)	(.215)	(.248)	(.403)	(.364)	(.212)	(.225)	(.264)
Pseudo R^2	.040	.034	.032	.035	.136	.051	.021	.062
LR chi^2	18.71**	17.34**	15.15*	7.71	49.50***	29.17***	10.59	29.15***
Freedom	6	6	6	6	6	6	6	6
Log- likelihood	−227.092	−250.190	−228.884	−107.451	−157.718	−271.251	−243.085	−219.552
N	395	391	429	429	429	429	429	429

Note: Computed in IIS3 by logistic regression, coefficient and S.E. are shown, and significance level at +p < 0.10, *p < 0.05, **p,0.01, and ***, p < 0.001

Moreover, the success of the OEM model depends on the effectiveness of current organizational efforts to sustain incremental improvements in the ability to fulfill customer needs (Kittilaksanawong 2015).

Meanwhile, for ODM firms, product innovation, process innovation, product design, and organizational change configurations play significant and positive engagement roles in innovation practices and how a business is managed. Contract manufacturers use the ODM model to extend their valuable work to upstream outsourcing in new product development, product innovation and process innovation synergies in the firm's technological capabilities, as demonstrated in the primary product design process (Lee, Song, and Kwak 2015; Wang and Wu 2012). Furthermore, the ODM model connects the firm's value work to downstream marketing innovation practices, demonstrating the ability of latecomers to react to the changing needs of end-users and to sell market flexibility to customers (Chu 2009; Manzakoğlu and Er 2018). Additionally, ODM firms' organizational management needs to be responsive to dynamic markets and ready to renew internal organizational practices to adapt quickly to changes as it rebuilds external partnership to foster new product development and manufacturing processes (Yung and Lai 2012; Christensen, Bartman, and Van Bever 2016). In contrast to OEM firms, ODM contract manufacturers must embrace the evolution of how their business activities are carried out to capture more production work in their value chains and engage in innovative practices to ensure the success of their business model and develop competitive advantages.

For latecomer firms, the OBM model represents a radical change from supplier to second-mover in an existing market (Chu 2009). Regarding the configuration of innovation practices, the results indicate that OBM firms actively engage in all production and sustainable organizational management. As latecomers in an existing market, OBM firms must improve their technological innovation capacity and develop high value-added products. They also need to strengthen their marketing capabilities to ensure more skilled operations and value-added marketing activities in their competitive markets (Eng and Spickett-Jones 2009; Liu, Liu, and Lin 2008; Wan 2015). Moreover, OBM firms also need sustainable organizational management to ensure that specific business activities run smoothly and to align with dynamic market changes (Day 2006; Carayannis, Sindakis, and Walter 2015; Foss and Saebi 2016).

After confirming the existence of a differentiated structure of innovation practices under the OEM, ODM, and OBM models, this study also finds that the configuration before and after a transition is a critical threshold for upgrading business models. In short, this study observes the interaction between changes in the innovation mix and business model transitions. In OEM firms about to undergo an upgrade, organizational management changes positively, but these firms' business activities do not significantly change relative to other OEM firms with no intention to change their business models. Many prior scholars indicated that organizational changes influence the development of new capabilities and partnership in business model transitions, and OEM firms that upgrade represent a radical change requiring the promotion of innovation practices to capture more valued contract manufacturing work. In other words, OEM firms need to overcome the organizational inertia barriers associated with the old business model when preparing to move to the new business model (Carayannis, Sindakis, and Walter 2015; Jacobides, MacDuffie, and Tae 2016; Bijarboneh 2015). However, ODM firms preparing to upgrade to the OBM model do not exhibit an apparent change except for a significant reduction in manufacturing process innovation. In other words, ODM firms may move on from concentrating on the necessary process innovation for core products to concentrating on branding development.

Furthermore, this paper compares the innovation practice configurations of new entrants and incumbent firms after the business model transition to ODM or OBM. During the early stage, after the transition from OEM to ODM, new entrants into the ODM business undertake limited new product development and have weak marketing capabilities relative to existing ODM firms. For a new ODM firm, promoting R&D and marketing is a determinant of success through the business model transition to develop its competence and business practices. Therefore, long-term vision and investments are needed to develop a new competitive advantage (Liu, Liu, and Lin 2008; Eng and Spickett-Jones 2009; Matthyssens, Vandenbempt, and Weyns 2009). During the transition to the OBM model, new entrants demonstrate strategic changes and comprehensive enhancements of production and organizational management. This finding indicates that new entrants into the OBM business need to make more considerable effort to overcome the challenges that competitive markets pose for second movers (Chu 2009; Lee, Song, and Kwak 2015; Yan 2012).

From this observation of the OEM, ODM, and OBM models of contract manufacturers in the sample, the differentiated innovation mix configurations under these models measure a firm's ability to fit its business activities to its value chain requirements. Moreover, the OEM–ODM–OBM path of reinventing a business model is associated with the reconfiguration of a firm's business activities, as determined by its value proposition. During the business model transition, radical upgrading creates the necessity to promote the engagement of innovation practices that allow adaption to the new value proposition.

Theoretical contribution

In this study, the identified interconnection between business model and innovation provides several theoretical contributions. First, prior research indicated that the business model is the description of the value creation that firms promise to deliver to satisfy customer needs (Amit and Zott 2012). Additionally, firms' innovation practices illustrate the engagement in creating new value for customers to sustain a competitive advantage (Snihur and Wiklund 2019; Baden-Fuller and Haefliger 2013). The innovation configuration is compared between the OEM, ODM, and OBM models, which have different but interconnecting settings of value creation for a specific value proposition. By defining value creation using firms' business models, different innovation mixes under the three models confirm their alignment, and innovation is the critical mechanism through which firms posit their unique value to the market. Moreover, innovation reveals an interdependency among business models and provides a lens through which to explain the implementation of a business strategy for firms' growth and competition.

Second, in this paper, organizational management and innovation are partial elements of the business model to bridge value creation and capture (Teece 2010; Zott and Amit 2010; Lanzolla and Markides 2020). Prior literature indicated that internal organizational management determines the resource allocation efficiency and leverage of competence to operate the business (Teece 2010; Taran, Boer, and Lindgren 2015). Furthermore, organizational management of the external partnership with stakeholders in a value chain makes firms acquire and utilize the external resources, capabilities, and complementary assets that contribute to production (Eng 2009; Sánchez and Ricart 2010). In other words, firms' organizational management is considered to be a critical business activity for collaborating with production in value creation. Consistently, organizational innovation makes firms modify their practices to fit with the implementation of business activities. For the three models, ongoing external and internal organizational innovation is found more frequently than is engaging in production practices. Although organizational innovation is a necessity when migrating business activities and innovation practices in the business model, it suggests that organizational management and its innovations should be embedded into the value creation aspect of the business model that makes firms bridge value works by spanning their internal and external organizational practices. Moreover, organizational innovation also indicates that an adaptive organization is an influential factor in enhancing value creation in the business model and firm performance.

Third, prior research indicated that business model transitions in incumbent firms are generated as a result of repositioning a value proposition in an existing market (Zott and Amit 2010; Amit and Zott 2012; Johnson, Christensen, and Kagermann 2008). Firms realign their business activities and reposition themselves to renew value creation for their customers and to compete with rivals (Bucherer, Eisert, and Gassmann 2012; Teece 2010). In our case, when OEM and ODM firms intend to change their business models, they purchase the transitional innovation mix in production to reconfigure their business operations and position their new value propositions in an existing market (Sánchez and Ricart 2010; Carayannis, Sindakis, and Walter 2015). Moreover, ODM entrants' engagement in product innovation, product design, and marketing practices is insufficient during the early stage when OEM firms are transiting their business models to upgrade their value propositions. OBM entrants overinvest in all innovation practices in the early stage when firms reinvent their value propositions to become new players in an existing market. Therefore, firms may face a fluid reconfiguration of business activities and innovation practices in prior business model transitions because their value propositions were extensions of or breakthroughs in the original business model. In other words, a business model transition has the risk of value migration in search of an appropriate reconfiguration in firms' business activities and innovation practices.

Managerial implications

Given the rise of globalization, vertical specialization has encouraged business model innovation in the manufacturing sector through contract manufacturing in existing markets, providing latecomers in emerging economies with business opportunities to participate in global value chains. This paper confirms that OEM, ODM, and OBM latecomers have differential innovation mixes to sustain growth and a competitive advantage depending on their value propositions (Hobday 2005; Forbes and Wield 2008; Kuo, Lim, and Sonko 2018).

Challenges are identified that latecomers face when upgrading their business models. First, although the aim of the transition to the ODM or OBM model is to expand R&D and marketing efforts, a firm's innovation practices fail to focus on this aim. New entrants need to be encouraged to develop a new configuration of innovation practices that help them appropriately reposition their value propositions (Teece 2010; Euchner and Ganguly 2014). Second, the tension from the radical change from OEM to ODM tests a firm's capability to undertake new product R&D and marketing capabilities, and long-term investments and accumulating expertise may be needed (Chesbrough 2010; Yan,

Chiang, and Chien 2014). Third, organizational management is the core mechanism sustaining the operation of a business and its activities as well as fostering the transition of the business model. For ODM and OBM models, adaptive organizational management may give firms the excellent ability to react flexibly to dynamic market changes by linking those changes to other business activities (Carayannis, Sindakis, and Walter 2015; Koen, Bertels, and Elsum 2011). Fourth, insufficiency or overinvestments in innovation practices suggests that firms must take time to tailor their innovation practices to their business model transitions (Hacklin, Björkdahl, and Wallin 2018).

Conclusions

The rise of contract manufacturing in emerging Asia enables the new business model and its transition to provide many insightful clues when observing the business model's operation. Given an increase in successful stories, the case in the Great China region as a typical latecomer allows for the relationship between the business model and a firm's innovation practices to be figured out. A firm's business model should interconnect with its innovation in promoting value creation for customers and gaining an advantage to run a business and stay competitive. The business strategy perspective indicates that a firm defines its business model with the value chain proposition, and innovation practices are critical strategical mechanisms to promote value creation to the market competition. To transition its business and gain new advantages, an incumbent firm should incrementally tailor its innovation practices by following the business model for new value propositions and change its value creation pattern through innovation to compete as a new entrant. The business strategy perspective leads to the conclusion that an innovation mix transition would assist an incumbent firm in transitioning its business model and helping it fulfill a new strategic direction in creating the posited value. In other words, the business model concerns the operation of value creation, and innovation involves creating new value. Interconnecting the business model with innovation is viewed as mutually complimentary for the firm's growth, competition, and transition in meeting customer needs. The manufacturing industry must transform specific assets to differentiate the concept of these assets from its business-to-business engagements to maintain long-term relationships.

This study has two limitations that create opportunities for future research. This study details the different innovation focuses that have resulted from different contract manufacturing business models. Although this study follows the changes in these focuses over the business model transitions, with IIS2 and IIS3 data across two periods with time on the horizontal axis, a time series analysis of observations at consecutive one-year intervals would provide a more dynamic view of contract manufacturers' business model transitions. Additionally, although the case from 14 cities in the Great China region offers good evidence of the relationship between business model transitions and innovation practices, different industrial contexts in different Asian regions (e.g. south Asia and south-east Aisa) may still make it necessary to modify the conclusions reached about this relationship. Thus, a comparison of this relationship across different regions is encouraged.

Note

1. The list of cities includes Taipei, New Taipei, Keelung, Taoyuan, Hsinchu, Yilan, Taichung, Changhua, Yunlin, Nantou, Chiayi, Tainan, Kaohsiung, and Pingtung.

Acknowledgements

The authors wish to thank the anonymous reviewers for their valuable suggestions. This research is supported by the financial support from Ministry of Science and Technology, Taiwan (Project No.: MOST 106-2410-H-468-024; MOST 108-2745-8-239-001 and MOST 109-2410-H-239-013).

Disclosure statement

No potential conflict of interest was reported by the authors.

References

Amit, R., and C. Zott. 2001. "Value Creation in E-business." *Strategic Management Journal* 22 (6-7): 493–520. doi:10.1002/smj.187.

Amit, R., and C. Zott. 2012. "Creating Value Through Business Model Innovation." *MIT Sloan Management Review* 53 (3): 41–49.

Baden-Fuller, C., and S. Haefliger. 2013. "Business Models and Technological Innovation." *Long Range Planning* 46 (6): 419–426. doi:10.1016/j.lrp.2013.08.023.

Basile, A., and R. Faraci. 2015. "Aligning Management Model and Business Model in the Management Innovation Perspective: The Role of Managerial Dynamic Capabilities in the Organizational Change." *Journal of Organizational Change Management* 28 (1): 43–58. doi:10.1108/JOCM-10-2013-0199.

Bijarboneh, B. Y. 2015. "Research on the Risks of Strategy Transformation from Original Equipment Manufacturing (OEM) to Original Design Manufacturing (ODM)." *Journal of Applied Sciences Research* 11 (10): 29–34.

Bucherer, E., U. Eisert, and O. Gassmann. 2012. "Towards Systematic Business Model Innovation: Lessons from Product Innovation Management." *Creativity and Innovation Management* 21 (2): 183–198. doi:10.1111/j.1467-8691.2012.00637.x.

Buliga, O., C. W. Scheiner, and K.-I. Voigt. 2016. "Business Model Innovation and Organizational Resilience: Towards an Integrated Conceptual Framework." *Journal of Business Economics* 86 (6): 647–670. doi:10.1007/s11573-015-0796-y.

Carayannis, E. G., S. Sindakis, and C. Walter. 2015. "Business Model Innovation as Lever of Organizational Sustainability." *The Journal of Technology Transfer* 40 (1): 85–104. doi:10.1007/s10961-013-9330-y.

Chen, D. 2016. "Survival Strategy of OEM Companies: A Case Study of the Chinese Toy Industry." *International Journal of Operations & Production Management* 36 (9): 1065–1088. doi:10.1108/IJOPM-04-2015-0212.

Chesbrough, H. 2010. "Business Model Innovation: Opportunities and Barriers." *Long Range Planning* 43 (2–3): 354–363. doi:10.1016/j.lrp.2009.07.010.

Chin, T., R.-H. Liu, and X. Yang. 2016. "'Reverse Internationalization'in Chinese Firms: A Study of How Global Startup OEMs Seek to Compete Domestically." *Asia Pacific Business Review* 22 (2): 201–219. doi:10.1080/13602381.2015.1055087.

Christensen, C. M., T. Bartman, and D. Van Bever. 2016. "The hard truth about business model innovation." *MIT Sloan Management Review*, 58 (1): 30–40.

Chu, W.-W. 2009. "Can Taiwan's Second Movers Upgrade via Branding?" *Research Policy* 38 (6): 1054–1065. doi:10.1016/j.respol.2008.12.014.

Danarahmanto, P. A., I. Primiana, Y. Azis, and U. Kaltum. 2020. "The Sustainable Performance of the Digital Start-up Company Based on Customer Participation, Innovation, and Business Model." *Business: Theory and Practice* 21 (1): 115–124. doi:10.3846/btp.2020.11053.

Day, George S. 2006. "Aligning the Organization with the Market". MIT Sloan Management Review 48 (1):41–49.

Eng, T.-Y. 2009. "Manufacture Upgrade and Interfirm Relationship Development: The Case of Electronics Firms in the Pearl River Delta." *Asia Pacific Business Review* 15 (4): 507–525. doi:10.1080/13602380802461419.

Eng, T.-Y., and J. G. Spickett-Jones. 2009. "An Investigation of Marketing Capabilities and Upgrading Performance of Manufacturers in Mainland China and Hong Kong." *Journal of World Business* 44 (4): 463–475. doi:10.1016/j.jwb.2009.01.002.

Euchner, J., and A. Ganguly. 2014. "Business Model Innovation in Practice." *Research-Technology Management* 57 (6): 33–39. doi:10.5437/08956308X5706013.

Foss, Nicolai J., and Tina Saebi. 2016. "Fifteen Years of Research on Business Model Innovation: How Far Have We Come, and Where Should We Go?" Journal of Management 43 (1):200–227. doi: 10.1177/0149206316675927.

Forbes, N., and D. Wield. 2008. "Innovation Dynamics in Catch-Up Firms: Process, Product and Proprietary Capabilities for Development." *Industry and Innovation* 15 (1): 69–92. doi:10.1080/13662710701850741.

Guan, J., and N. Ma. 2003. "Innovative Capability and Export Performance of Chinese Firms." *Technovation* 23 (9): 737–747. doi:10.1016/S0166-4972(02)00013-5.

Hacklin, F., J. Björkdahl, and M. W. Wallin. 2018. "Strategies for Business Model Innovation: How Firms Reel in Migrating Value." *Long Range Planning* 51 (1): 82–110. doi:10.1016/j.lrp.2017.06.009.

Hobday, M. 1998. "Latecomer Catch-up Strategies in Electronics: Samsung of Korea and ACER of Taiwan." *Asia Pacific Business Review* 4 (2–3): 48–83. doi:10.1080/13602389812331288364.

Hobday, M. 2005. "Firm-level Innovation Models: Perspectives on Research in Developed and Developing Countries." *Technology Analysis & Strategic Management* 17 (2): 121–146. doi:10.1080/09537320500088666.

Hobday, M., H. Rush, and J. Bessant. 2004. "Approaching the Innovation Frontier in Korea: The Transition Phase to Leadership." *Research Policy* 33 (10): 1433–1457. doi:10.1016/j.respol.2004.05.005.

Huang, Y.-A., H.-J. Chung, and C. Lin. 2009. "R&D Sourcing Strategies: Determinants and Consequences." *Technovation* 29 (3): 155–169. doi:10.1016/j.technovation.2008.08.002.

Hummels, D., J. Ishii, and K.-M. Yi. 2001. "The Nature and Growth of Vertical Specialization in World Trade." *Journal of International Economics* 54 (1): 75–96. doi:10.1016/S0022-1996(00)00093-3.

Hummels, D. L., D. Rapoport, and Y. Kei-Mu. 1998. "Vertical Specialization and the Changing Nature of World Trade." *Economic Policy Review* 4: 2.

Jacobides, M. G., J. P. MacDuffie, and C. J. Tae. 2016. "Agency, Structure, and the Dominance of OEMs: Change and Stability in the Automotive Sector." *Strategic Management Journal* 37 (9): 1942–1967. doi:10.1002/smj.2426.

Johnson, M. W., C. M. Christensen, and H. Kagermann. 2008. "Reinventing Your Business Model." *Harvard Business Review* 86 (12): 50–59.

Koen, P. A., H. M. J. Bertels, and I. R. Elsum. 2011. "The Three Faces of Business Model Innovation: Challenges for Established Firms." *Research-Technology Management* 54 (3): 52–59. doi:10.5437/08953608X5403009.

Kittilaksanawong, Wiboon. 2015. "How Do Emerging Economy Firms Learn to Evolve from Contract Manufacturing to Own Brand Management?" In Global Enterprise Management: New Perspectives on Challenges and Future Developments Volume II, edited by Angelo A. Camillo, 1–17. New York: Palgrave Macmillan US.

Kuo, T.-K., and T. Minshall. 2010. "Innovation Capability Reconfiguration In Business Transition: A Case Study On Taiwanese PC Firm." In *Creating and Managing a Technology Economy*, edited by F. Betz, T. Khalil, Y. Hosni, and H. E. Mostafa, 33–55. Singapore: World Scientific Publishing.

Kuo, T.-K., S. S. Lim, and L. K. Sonko. 2018. "Catch-up Strategy of Latecomer Firms in Asia: A Case Study of Innovation Ambidexterity in PC Industry." *Technology Analysis & Strategic Management* 30 (12): 1483–1497. doi:10.1080/09537325.2018.1475642.

Lanzolla, G., and C. Markides. 2020. "A Business Model View of Strategy." *Journal of Management Studies*. doi:10.1111/joms.12580.

Latilla, V. M., F. Frattini, S. Franzo, and V. Chiesa. 2020. "Organizational Change and Business Model Innovation: An Exploratory Study of an Energy Utility." *International Journal of Innovation Management* 24 (4): 2050036. doi:10.1142/s136391962050036x.

Lee, K., J. Song, and J. Kwak. 2015. "An Exploratory Study on the Transition from OEM to OBM: Case Studies of SMEs in Korea." *Industry and Innovation* 22 (5): 423–442. doi:10.1080/13662716.2015.1064257.

Liu, F.-H., H.-Y. Liu, and T.-L. Lin. 2008. "The Competence and Constraints of Brand Building for Contract Manufacturers." *Journal of Brand Management* 15 (6): 412–432. doi:10.1057/bm.2008.8.

Luo, C. 2011. "SME Competitive Strategy: Learning from Taiwan's ODM Industry." *Business Strategy Series* 12 (3): 107–114. doi:10.1108/17515631111130077.

Ma, Y. 2005. "A Case Study on Non-parametric Design Method in ODM Collaborative Product Development." *International Journal of Product Development* 2 (4): 411–434. doi:10.1504/IJPD.2005.008228.

Manzakoğlu, B. T., and Ö. Er. 2018. "Design Management Capability Framework in Global Value Chains: Integrating the Functional Upgrading Theory from OEM to ODM and OBM." *The Design Journal* 21 (1): 139–161. doi:10.1080/14606925.2018.1395577.

Massa, L., C. L. Tucci, and A. Afuah. 2017. "A Critical Assessment of Business Model Research." *Academy of Management Annals* 11 (1): 73–104. doi:10.5465/annals.2014.0072.

Matthyssens, P., K. Vandenbempt, and S. Weyns. 2009. "Transitioning and Co-evolving to Upgrade Value Offerings: A Competence-based Marketing View." *Industrial Marketing Management* 38 (5): 504–512. doi:10.1016/j.indmarman.2008.08.008.

Osterwalder, A., Y. Pigneur, and C. L. Tucci. 2005. "Clarifying Business Models: Origins, Present, and Future of the Concept." *Communications of the Association for Information Systems* 15: 1–40.

Pucihar, A., G. Lenart, M. K. Borštnar, D. Vidmar, and M. Marolt. 2019. "Drivers and Outcomes of Business Model Innovation—Micro, Small and Medium-Sized Enterprises Perspective." *Sustainability* 11 (2): 344. doi:10.3390/su11020344.

Sánchez, P., and J. E. Ricart. 2010. "Business Model Innovation and Sources of Value Creation in Low-income Markets." *European Management Review* 7 (3): 138–154. doi:10.1057/emr.2010.16.

Sánchez-Gutiérrez, J., F. Pablo Cabanelas, L. Jesús, and E. González-Alvarado Tania. 2019. "The Impact on Competitiveness of Customer Value Creation through Relationship Capabilities and Marketing Innovation." *Journal of Business & Industrial Marketing* 34 (3): 618–627. doi:10.1108/JBIM-03-2017-0081.

Snihur, Y., and J. Wiklund. 2019. "Searching for Innovation: Product, Process, and Business Model Innovations and Search Behavior in Established Firms." *Long Range Planning* 52 (3): 305–325. doi 10.1016/j.lrp.2018.05.003.

Spieth, P., D. Schneckenberg, and J. E. Ricart. 2014. "Business Model Innovation – State of the Art and Future Challenges for the Field." *R&D Management* 44 (3): 237–247. doi:10.1111/radm.12071.

Szalkai, Z., and M. Magyar. 2017. "Strategy from the Perspective of Contract Manufacturers." *IMP Journal* 11 (1): 150–172. doi:10.1108/IMP-06-2015-0028.

Taran, Y., H. Boer, and P. Lindgren. 2015. "A Business Model Innovation Typology." *Decision Sciences* 46 (2): 301–331. doi:10.1111/deci.12128.

Tavassoli, S., and L. Bengtsson. 2018. "The Role of Business Model Innovation for Product Innovation Performance." *International Journal of Innovation Management* 22 (7): 1850061. doi:10.1142/s1363919618500615.

Teece, D. J. 2010. "Business Models, Business Strategy and Innovation." *Long Range Planning* 43 (2–3): 172–194. doi:10.1016/j.lrp.2009.07.003.

Tiong, R., S. L. Sun, H. Chen, and E. G. Pleggenkuhle-Miles. 2010. "Moving Upward in Global Value Chains: The Innovations of Mobile Phone Developers in China." *Chinese Management Studies* 4 (4): 305–321. doi:10.1108/17506141011094118.

Wan, M. 2015. "Strategic Transformation in the Value-added Wood Products Companies: Case Study Evidence from China." *International Journal of Emerging Markets* 10 (2): 224–242. doi:10.1108/IJOEM-09-2012-0107.

Wang, F., and K. Chen. 2020. "Do Product Imitation and Innovation Require Different Patterns of Organizational Innovation? Evidence from Chinese Firms." *Journal of Business Research* 106: 60–74. doi:10.1016/j.jbusres.2019.08.046.

Wang, H.-W., and M.-C. Wu. 2012. "Business Type, Industry Value Chain, and R&D Performance: Evidence from High-tech Firms in an Emerging Market." *Technological Forecasting and Social Change* 79 (2): 326–340. doi:10.1016/j.techfore.2011.05.008.

Wirtz, B., and P. Daiser. 2017. "Business Model Innovation: An Integrative Conceptual Framework." *Journal of Business Models* 5 (1): 14–34.

Wu, S.-H. 2009. "The Analysis of the Second Industrial Innovation Survey." In Survey Research Data Archive. Taipei: Academia Sinica.

Wu, S.-H. 2013. "The Third Industrial Innovation Survey." In Survey Research Data Archive. Taipei: Academia Sinica.

Yan, Ho-don, Charlie Chiang, and Charles S. Chien. 2014. "From original equipment manufacturing to branding: entrepreneurship, strategic leadership, and Taiwan's firm transformation". International Entrepreneurship and Management Journal 10 (1):81–102. doi: 10.1007/s11365-011-0213-0.

Yan, H.-D. 2012. "Entrepreneurship, Competitive Strategies, and Transforming Firms from OEM to OBM in Taiwan." *Journal of Asia-Pacific Business* 13 (1): 16–36. doi:10.1080/10599231.2012.629877.

Yung, I.-S., and M.-H. Lai. 2012. "Dynamic Capabilities in New Product Development: The Case of Asus in Motherboard Production." *Total Quality Management & Business Excellence* 23 (9–10): 1125–1134. doi:10.1080/14783363.2012.669542.

Zhu, H., M. Y. Zhang, and W. Lin. 2017. "The Fit between Business Model Innovation and Demand-side Dynamics: Catch-up of China's Latecomer Mobile Handset Manufacturers." *Innovation* 19 (2): 146–166. doi:10.1080/14479338.2016.1275979.

Zott, C., and R. Amit. 2010. "Business Model Design: An Activity System Perspective." *Long Range Planning* 43 (2–3): 216–226. doi:10.1016/j.lrp.2009.07.004.

Business model innovation as mediator for the strategic flexibility-performance relationship

Hongjun Xiao, Zhen Yang and Yelin Hu

ABSTRACT

This paper explores the internal mechanism of corporate strategic flexibility on corporate performance. Through the empirical test of 197 Chinese enterprises, the empirical test is performed on the statistical hypothesis using the statistical method of SEM and linear regression. We find that the corporate strategic flexibility has a significant positive impact on its financial performance and market performance, and business model innovation has a significant positive impact on corporate financial performance and market performance, and efficiency-centred business model innovation plays a partial mediating role between strategic flexibility (resource flexibility and coordination flexibility) and corporate financial concentration; novelty-centred business model innovation plays a fully mediating role between resource flexibility and corporate market performance, and a partial mediating role between coordination flexibility and corporate market performance.

Introduction

Since the 21st century, the rapid development of digital and intelligent technology makes the competitive environment of organizations highly dynamic and complex, and the competition paradigm between enterprises has gradually shifted from competition among individual enterprises to the competition based on the value network and business ecosystem at the micro-enterprise level. Against this background, enterprises need to adjust the organizational strategy and corresponding innovation orientation in a timely and effective manner to cope with the increasingly complex and dynamic competitive environment. Objectively, it requires organizations to have the dynamic capability to adapt to environmental changes (Teece, Pisano, and Shuen 1997). Strategic flexibility is a dynamic capability of enterprises to respond to environmental changes (Brozovic 2016; Teece, Pisano, and Shuen 1997; Teece 2018). Strategic flexibility can effectively maintain a high degree of environmental sensitivity in the complex and ever-changing external competitive environment and overcome the resource inertia or competence rigidity of organizations, which can achieve resources reallocation and recombination of organizations and is beneficial for enterprises to explore and develop new business or innovation opportunities (Sanchez 1995; Zhou and Wu 2010; Bock et al. 2012). Scholars have defined strategic flexibility as the defence capability of organizations to adapt to environmental changes, and these environmental changes are continuous, uncertain and rapid. Undoubtedly, this capability is beneficial for organizational performance (Aaker and Mascarenhas 1984. However, from existing empirical research results, it is difficult to reach an agreed conclusion on the relationship between strategic flexibility and corporate performance in academic circles, including positive correlations, negative correlations, and inverted U-shaped correlations (Grewal et al., 2001; Nadkarni and Herrmann 2010; Nadkarni and Narayanan 2007).

In the digital era, a series of new digital technologies, such as big data, artificial intelligence, mobile Internet and blockchain, promote the enterprise strategy to be more flexible and innovative (Nylén and Holmström 2015). Business model innovation has become a feasible means for enterprises to maintain strategic flexibility in the digital era. Enterprises are eager to realize the dynamic response of enterprises to the digital environment through business model innovation (BMI) (Chin et al. 2020). BMI is mainly defined as the change of organizational value creation structure (Foss and Saebi 2017). A systematic literature review covering more than 20 years on business model innovation emphasizes that existing research largely ignores the internal driving factors of business models (Foss and Saebi 2017). Specifically, the research on whether and how strategic flexibility affects business model innovation and ultimately maintains the competitiveness of enterprises is very limited. Therefore, this study aims to explore the impact of strategic flexibility on corporate performance through business model innovation using unique survey data of Chinese enterprises in the process of digital transformation. The second level is that existing studies ignore the internal mechanism between strategic flexibility and enterprise performance. Some studies often explain the mechanism of strategic flexibility on enterprise performance from the perspective of organizational dual innovation and organizational learning ability (Brozovic 2018; Zhou and Wu 2010), which ignored that under the background of a new round of digital information revolution, business model innovation, as a key way for enterprises to acquire market competitiveness, can play an important role in transforming enterprise capabilities into corresponding financial value or market value. Thus, this paper attempts to explain the internal mechanism of strategic flexibility on corporate performance from the perspective of business model innovation and clarify the role of strategic flexibility on corporate performance against the digital context, thus having better understand the theoretical connotation of strategic flexibility in digital age.

Literature review

From existing studies, in terms of contextual factors of strategic flexibility, one perspective is to study the impact of the external environment of organizations on corporate strategic flexibility from the perspective of external environment dynamics of organizations, holding that the intensity of market competition is a direct reflection of environmental dynamics and uncertainty where the enterprise is located. Complex and dynamic environmental information will distract their attention so that they will be less sensitive to external changes, thereby affecting the relationship between corporate strategic flexibility and corporate performance (Grewal and Tansuhaj 2001). Another perspective is to focus on strategic decision-makers, namely executive factors, including the impact of the strategic orientation and entrepreneurial orientation of entrepreneurs and the heterogeneity of the executive team on the relationship between strategic flexibility and corporate performance, which will ultimately help enterprises better cultivate and give play to the value effect of corporate strategic flexibility (Hambrick and Mason 1984).

From the perspective of the competitive advantage acquisition process of enterprises, Amit and Zott (2001) pointed out that competitive advantage not only came from the competitive strategy of product (service) market, but also from the business model of enterprises. Existing studies have found that the business model is an important explanatory factor for the performance difference between different enterprises (Guo et al. 2017). The research carried out by Zott and Amit (2008) suggested that the efficient and novelty-centred business model innovation of enterprises had a significant promoting effect on the performance of entrepreneurial enterprises. Although academic circles have multiple perspectives on the business model in the current stage, they mainly focus on the technical perspective (Chesbrough and Rosenbloom 2002), transaction structure perspective (Amit and Zott 2001) and value creation perspective (Tukker 2004). Schlegelmilch, Diamantopoulos, and Kreuz (2003) regarded the business model innovation as a type of strategic innovation. Richardson (2008) argued that the business model is a series of strategic combinations, which helped enterprises to link their strategies and competition theories with their concrete activities or implementation. Therefore, from the perspective of organizational strategy, enterprises need to reorganize organizational resources based on different strategic orientations in the process of designing their own business models (Demil et al. 2015; Chin et al. 2019; Nair and Blomquist 2020). However, the business model innovation of organizations is not isolated, but needs to be supported by a series of corresponding modules and activities covering the transaction interaction of organizations (Nair and Blomquist 2020), including the entire organizational structure, organization operation management mode and business process, that is, the prerequisite of business model innovation lies in the corresponding resource base and dynamic capability of organizations (Wei et al. 2014; Teece 2010, 2018). Therefore, this paper believes that in a complex and dynamic competitive environment, strategic flexibility can help enterprises effectively adjust their internal and external resources and capabilities in the business model innovation process, and achieve the effective matching between organizational resource capability and business model innovation. Therefore, an 'isolation mechanism' that is difficult to imitate can be formed and ultimately promotes corporate performance (Zott and Amit 2008).

Theoretical analysis and hypothesis development

Strategic flexibility and corporate performance

Sanchez (1997) believed that strategic flexibility included resource flexibility and coordination flexibility, and the mechanism of different types of flexibility on corporate performance is completely different. Resource flexibility can be divided into product development flexibility and product manufacturing flexibility. From the perspective of resource flexibility and based on the resource-based view, the competitive advantage of organizations comes from their possession of valuable, and scarce resources that cannot be imitated and are difficult to replace. Also, organizational resources include internal and external resources and strategic flexibility shows a strong flexible integration capability in the process of acquiring and integrating resources. Therefore, on the basis of resource-based view, strategic flexibility can effectively reduce the coordination cost in the resource conversion process, improve the resource flexibility of enterprises in the strategic reform process and enhance the capability of enterprises to integrate and allocate existing resources, and reuse and recombine idle resources, thus obtaining a greater cost advantage for enterprises in the market competition process.

From the perspective of coordination flexibility, coordination flexibility is mainly explained based on the theory of dynamic capabilities (Miroshnychenko et al., 2020). It is argued in the theory of dynamic capabilities that coordination flexibility is the ability of enterprises to quickly coordinate, integrate, and allocate various resources inside and outside the organization in response to the complex and ever-changing environment, which improves the organization's ability to identify and adapt to the environment, and cope with the dynamic complexity of the environment (Teece, Pisano, and Shuen 1997). The coordination flexibility of enterprises is the capability to reorganize and allocate organizational resources in the process of adapting to the environment. Among enterprises with a high degree of coordination flexibility, on the one hand, organizations can quickly identify, recombine, and allocate resources inside and outside the organization based on changes in the environment. The active seeking of the recombination and allocation of resources can reduce the risk and uncertainty of corporate strategic reform, reduce the cost and time consumed by the corporate strategic reform, and give full play to the resource advantage of enterprises quickly. Therefore, organizations with coordination flexibility can quickly identify and develop market opportunities in the ever-changing market environment, quickly respond to market changes based on the reorganization and allocation capability of resources, seize opportunities in the market competition, and finally achieve the strategic reform and obtain new competitive advantages for enterprises. On this basis, the following research hypotheses are proposed:

H1a: Resource flexibility exerts a positive impact on corporate financial performance.

H1b: Resource flexibility exerts a positive impact on corporate market performance.

H2a: Coordination flexibility exerts a positive impact on corporate financial performance.

H2b: Coordination flexibility exerts a positive impact on corporate market performance.

Business model innovation and corporate performance

The business model is the logic that describes how an organization creates value. Under different business models, enterprises have different value propositions, value creation networks, and value acquisition methods, thereby further forming differentiated market competitive advantages. The business model proposed by Amit and Zott (2001) described the design of transaction content, structure, and governance so as to create value by capitalizing on business opportunities. Teece (2010) believed that the business model clarified the logic of the enterprise's support for customer value propositions and a feasible transaction structure of the revenue and cost if the enterprise provided that value. Zott and Amit (2007) believes that there are generally two main types of business model innovation in enterprises. The first type is to improve existing business models based on imitation orientation to improve the efficiency of existing business models, which is the efficiency-centred business model, and the second type is the development of new business models to form new operation and management models based on new value proposition and value creation network, which is the novelty-centred business model (Spieth, Laudien, and Meer 2020).

The type of business model innovation adopted by enterprises will determine how they use internal and external resources and capabilities to improve the corporate performance. The efficiency-centred business model innovation enables enterprises to focus more on utilizing and transforming resources within enterprises, promoting information sharing, reducing information isolated islands between enterprises, improving information transparency, reducing uncertainty in transactions, reducing transaction costs and enhancing corporate competitive advantages (Loon and Chik 2019). As a result, corporate financial performance can be improved. For example, enterprises can lower the cost and improve the profit by simplifying the transaction process, reducing transaction complexity, improving transaction relationship, increasing transaction frequency, and increasing transaction speed. In addition, efficiency-centred business model innovation can use internal and external resources and capabilities to improve corporate financial performance, speed up the response to the market (Shimizu and Hitt 2004), and improve corporate market performance by improving customer satisfaction. Brettel et al. (2012) studied the impact of novelty-centred and efficiency-centred business models on corporate performance, and found that the design of efficiency-centred business model was more conducive to improving corporate performance in the later period of corporate life cycle. Based on the above analysis, the following hypotheses are made:

H3a: Efficiency-centred business model innovation exerts a positive impact on corporate financial performance.

H3b: Efficiency-centred business model innovation exerts positive impact on corporate market performance.

Novelty-centred business model innovation enables enterprises to focus more on discovering and utilizing external resources, adopting new cooperation methods or transaction structures, adding new partners, new connection methods and transaction mechanisms, new ways to meet users' needs, new market space and new resource combination methods. Enterprises can upgrade existing production methods or resource values through 'disruptive innovation', thereby creating new sources of profit (Berends 2016). Therefore, novelty-centred BMI can improve the level of corporate market performance and financial performance. Based on the above analysis, the following hypotheses are made:

H4a: Novelty-centred business model innovation exerts a positive impact on corporate financial performance.

H4c: Novelty-centred business model innovation exerts a positive impact on corporate market performance.

Strategic flexibility, business model innovation and corporate performance

Although the positive impact of strategic flexibility on corporate performance has been confirmed by many studies (Guo and Cao 2014), from the perspective of resource-based view and theory of dynamic capabilities, strategic flexibility is essentially a resource base and dynamic capability of enterprises, whose corresponding positive impact on organizational performance still needs to be achieved through the implementation of corresponding innovation activities (Brozovic 2016). This paper believes that the positive impact of organizational strategic flexibility on corporate performance can be achieved through the innovative activity of business model innovation. Specifically, it is based on the resource integration and organizational reorganization of organizations to improve the usage efficiency of existing resources and Identify market opportunities to achieve the business model innovation of enterprises, which will further promote corporate performance. In essence, business model innovation involves the operational management process of the entire organization and needs to be supported by various resources and capabilities of enterprises. Demil et al. (2015) believed that the basis of business model innovation was still organizational resources, and the basic principle of business models was the broad cooperation of value creation subjects on the basis of resources and capacities to provide certain product or service (Tukker 2004; Tukker and Tischner 2006). Therefore, business model innovation is also essentially an innovation activity of organizations. When the organization is improving existing business models or developing new business models of enterprises, corresponding organizational resources or capabilities are required, so as to build a new value network and create new values for new stakeholders.

At the same time, the business model is interpreted from the strategic perspective. The business model not only describes the profit model and transaction structure of enterprises, but also considers the strategy and customer market of enterprises. Therefore, the business model is regarded as the main reflection of corporate strategies (Demil and Lecocq 2010). Therefore, based on strategic flexibility, enterprises can combine, allocate and coordinate the resources and capabilities of internal and external stakeholders, and promote enterprises to satisfy new demands in the market through business model innovation in the dynamic environment (Majid et al. 2020). We hold that the strategic flexibility, as the dynamic capability and basic resources of an organization, can provide corresponding enabling mechanism in the business model innovation process for the organization, achieve the strategic reform and improve the value creation efficiency of enterprises through the implementation of business model innovation. Based on the theory of dynamic capabilities, the strategic flexibility of an organization essentially, form new value propositions, seek the recombination and efficient usage of internal and external resources of organizations based on the variability of internal resource of enterprises and provide enterprises with a new window of opportunities in the business model innovation process(Herhausen et al. 2020).Thirdly, the organization can effectively integrate existing resources and potential resources according to the external environment. Therefore, strategic flexibility (resource flexibility and coordination flexibility) can promote enterprises to use exploratory methods to improve the use efficiency of resources in the current stage, and maximize the value of organizational resources, which is conducive to the efficiency-centred business model innovation of enterprises, and then improves the corporate performance.

On the other hand, under the role of strategic flexibility, business model innovation can create more value for customers based on coordination flexibility. The reason is that high degree of coordination flexibility indicates that enterprises have dynamic capabilities and can quickly identify opportunities and needs in the market, which can help enterprises obtain the most urgent and direct demand information of consumers in the market and then lay the foundation for forming new value propositions (Li et al. 2018). Therefore, strategic flexibility, as an important dynamic capability of the organization, can promote enterprises to develop new business models, which is the novelty-centred business model. The novelty-centred business model innovation needs to be realized through the reorganization and allocation of resources within the organization, which also calls for the substantial restructuration of internal and external resources. Therefore, enterprises with higher coordination flexibility usually have greater resource reorganization and allocation capability. Therefore, strategic flexibility can directly promote the novelty-centred business model innovation of enterprises and ultimately promote corporate performance. Based on the above analysis, the following hypotheses are proposed:

H5a: Efficiency-centred business model innovation plays a mediating role between resource flexibility and corporate financial performance.

H5b: Efficiency-centred business model innovation plays a mediating role between coordination flexibility and corporate financial performance.

H6a: Efficiency-centred business model innovation plays a mediating role between resource flexibility and corporate market performance.

H6b: Efficiency-centred business model innovation plays a mediating role between coordination flexibility and corporate market performance.

H7a: Novelty-centred business model innovation plays a mediating role between resource flexibility and corporate financial performance.

H7b: Novelty-centred business model innovation plays a mediating role between coordination flexibility and corporate financial performance.

H8a: Novelty-centred business model innovation plays a mediating role between resource flexibility and corporate market performance.

H8b: Novelty-centred business model innovation plays a mediating role between coordination flexibility and corporate financial performance.

On this basis, this paper further draws the following research conceptual model (Figure 1):

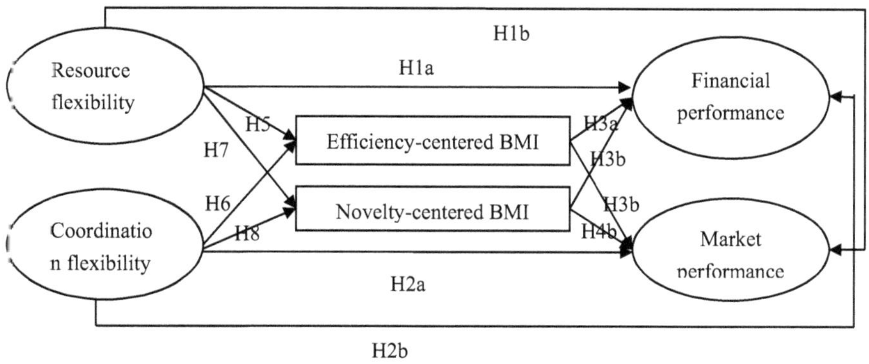

Figure 1. Research model.

Methods

Questionnaire design and data collection

This research uses the questionnaire to collect sample data from Chinese enterprises for empirical research. In this survey, middle and senior management personnel and technical personnel are selected as the survey object. This research combines on-site distribution, commissioned distribution and online (WeChat) questionnaires to collect data. This questionnaire survey covers 11 provinces and municipalities in China and obtains a total of 226 questionnaires. After excluding invalid questionnaires, a total of 197 valid questionnaires are obtained (as shown in Table 1). It can be seen from Table 1 that the enterprise age of the majority of sample enterprises is over 3 years; the distribution of enterprise size is relatively even and the number of employees stays between 19% and 21% in each section; from the nature of the property rights of sample enterprises, the sample includes the state-owned

Table 1. Descriptive statistics of sample enterprises (N = 197).

Attribute	Characteristics	Frequency	Percentage %	Attribute	Characteristics	Frequency	Percentage %
Enterprise age	Less than 3 years	11	5.6	Income scale	Less than 5 million	18	9.1
	3–5 years	20	10.2		5–10 million	2	1.0
	6–10 years	53	26.9		10–50 million	40	20.3
	10–15 years	35	17.8		50–300 million	50	25.4
	More than 15 years	78	39.6		More than 300 million	87	44.2
Number of employees	Less than 100	40	20.3	Industry	Manufacturing	21	10.7
	101–500	39	19.8		Construction	6	3.0
	501–1000	38	19.3		Wholesale and retail	8	4.1
	1000–5000	38	19.3		Transportation, warehousing and post	8	4.1
	More than 5000	42	21.3				
Nature of property rights	State-owned	66	33.5		Information, computer and software	33	16.8
	Private	103	52.3				
	Overseas-funded	12	6.1		Insurance, banking and securities	69	35.0
	Joint venture	6	3.0				
	Others	10	5.1		Others	52	26.4

and private firms and overseas-funded firms, but the state-owned and private enterprises account for the majority of the total (33.3 and 52.3%), and these sample enterprises involved financial industry, information service industry, manufacturing, wholesale and retail industry, transportation and other industries, and the sales revenue of the sample enterprises is mainly over 10 million (89.9%).

Variable measurement

Variable measurement uses the five-point Likert scale, from 1 to 5 representing different degrees of identification, among which 1 represents totally disagree and 5 indicates totally agree. The main variables are as follows:

Strategic flexibility

We referred to Sanchez (1997) study on the dimension about strategic flexibility, in his research of strategic flexibility, strategic flexibility is divided into resource flexibility and coordination flexibility and five indexes are used to measure resource flexibility, which are: the degree to which we use the same resource to develop different products or services is high. We use the same resource to develop different products or services at a lower cost. Our product R&D department often finds new application of existing resources. We have been committed to creating more value with existing resources. We can make full use of existing resources to produce new products or services. Also, five indexes are used to measure coordination flexibility, which are: we are good at discovering new opportunities in unknown territory and making response before opponents. We can innovate products and develop new markets faster than competitors. We can effectively organize innovation resources to respond to changes in external market. We are good at responding quickly to customer needs, and we can quickly respond to new market trends through the cooperation with partners.

Type of business model innovation

Based on the research carried out by Zott and Amit (2007) and Clauss (2016), this paper classifies business model innovation into efficiency-centred business model innovation and novelty-centred business model innovation. Among them, 5 items are used to measure the efficiency-centred BMI: we are committed to improving the efficiency of existing resources, we are committed to communicating with partners to reduce various costs; we can understand the information of products, services and partners in a timely manner, we have been dedicated to reducing communication costs, transaction processes, and improving efficiency, and we try to use existing resources for multiple purposes as much as possible. Five items are designed to measure the novelty-centred business model innovation based on the research of Zott and Amit (2007), which are: the new method can bring us new partners, we use new transaction methods to create values for our partners, we are good at working with partners to satisfy customer demands in new ways, we improve the transaction volume through the continuous innovation of business models, and new cooperation methods enable us to provide customers with new products or services.

Corporate performance

Scholars generally use multiple dimensions to study the corporate performance. Brush and Vanderwerf (1992) believed that the evaluation of corporate performance should include two aspects of financial performance and market performance. This paper draws on the classification method of Brush and Vanderwerf (1992), and classifies corporate performance into two dimensions, namely financial performance and market performance. Market performance represents whether the business model innovation method can bring value to users and be recognized by users, while financial performance reflects the level at which value is converted into profit. These two aspects reflect the overall performance level of enterprises in terms of value creation and value conversion.

We select control variables including enterprise age, number of employees, nature of property rights, industry and income scale, among which the enterprise age is represented by the number of years between the establishment of enterprises and the income scale is measured by sales revenue.

Empirical analysis

Common method bias analyses

In this paper, the self-evaluation of managers and technicians in enterprises is used to answer the questionnaire, which may have the same source method bias effect. In order to avoid the influence on the accuracy of the research conclusion, the following methods were adopted. The first is that questionnaire measurement programme control, mainly including group discussion and revision of the questionnaire to avoid the ambiguity and ambiguity of the content of the scale items, the second is that we use the principle of information hiding of the respondents to avoid the psychological guessing of the measurement purpose; designing reverse scoring and approving items and random and the order of the items in the discharge table can reduce the error of the order effect. Furthermore, Harman single factor test was used to test the severity of the common method variance of sample data. All items of research variables were included in SPSS 21.0, 11 factors with characteristic roots greater than I were extracted, and no single factor was isolated; the total variance of 11 factors was more than 60%, and there was no serious homologous method deviation problem that one factor explained most variances of all variables, indicating that the homology bias of the data in this paper has been well controlled, and the Harman single factor test was used to test the severity of the common method variance of the sample data, and the results showed that the common method deviation in the sample data was not an issue.

Reliability and validity analysis

The Cronbach's α coefficient and the CITC coefficient is used for internal consistency test, as shown in Table 2. It can be seen from Table 2 that the Cronbach's α coefficient of two dimensions of the strategic flexibility measurement scale (resource flexible RF and coordinated flexible CF) is 0.811 and 0.866, respectively; the Cronbach's α coefficient of two dimensions (Efficiency-centred BMI and Novelty-centred BMI) in the measurement scale of the type of business model innovation is 0.816 and 0.868, respectively; the Cronbach's α coefficient of two dimensions in the measurement scale of corporate performance (financial

Table 2. Reliability test of research variables (N = 197).

Items	CITC value	Cronbach's α with deleted items	Cronbach's α
RF1 The degree to which we use the same resource to develop different products or services is high.	.655	.756	0.811
RF2 We use the same resource to develop different products or services at a lower cost.	.566	.783	
RF3 our product R&D department often finds new application of existing resources.	.619	.769	
RF4 We have been committed to creating more value with existing resources.	.583	.780	
RF5 We can make full use of existing resources to produce new products or services.	.578	.780	
CF1 We are good at discovering new opportunities in unknown territory and making response before opponents.	.653	.849	0.866
CF2 We can innovate products and develop markets faster than competitors.	.731	.827	
CF3 We can effectively organize innovation resources to respond to changes in external market.	.744	.826	
CF4 We are good at responding quickly to customer needs.	.669	.843	
CF5 We can quickly respond to new market trends through the cooperation with partners.	.657	.846	
EBMI1 We are committed to improving the efficiency of existing resources.	.583	.786	0.816
EBMI2 We are committed to communicating with partners to reduce various costs.	.649	.766	
EBMI3 We can understand the information of products, services and partners in a timely manner.	.594	.784	
EBMI4 We have been dedicated to reducing communication costs, transaction processes, and improving efficiency.	.630	.774	
EBMI5 We try to use existing resources for multiple purposes as much as possible.	.580	.787	
NBMI1 The new method can bring us new partners.	.673	.845	0.868
NBMI2 We use new transaction methods to create values for our partners.	.697	.840	
NBMI3 We are good at working with partners to satisfy customer demands in new ways.	.674	.845	
NBMI4 We can improve the transaction volume through the continuous innovation of business models.	.700	.839	
NBMI5 New cooperation methods enable us to provide customers with new products or services.	.719	.834	
FP1 Compared with the same industry, the sales revenue of our enterprise is better than the past two years.	.665	.819	0.850
FP2 Compared with the same industry, the rate of return on investment of our enterprise is better than the past two years.	.698	.811	
FP3 Compared with the same industry, the profit margin of our enterprise has maintained at a higher level in the past two years.	.623	.831	
FP4 Compared with the same industry, the average production cost of our enterprise has decreased.	.669	.820	
FP5 The operational capability of our enterprise has improved in the past two years.	.668	.818	
MP1 The market share of our enterprise has increased rapidly in the past two years.	.667	.874	0.886
MP2 The market share of new products and services launched in the past two years has increased rapidly.	.797	.845	
MP3 The market share of new products and services of our enterprise has increased significantly.	.798	.843	
MP4 Compared with the same industry, the new product and service of our enterprise is highly competitive.	.719	.862	
MP5 Our enterprise has continued to launch new products and services in the market over the past two years.	.647	.879	

performance FP and market performance MP) is 0.850 and 0.886, respectively, which is much higher than the minimum standard of internal consistency test at 0.70. Also, the CITC value of all related items covered in the scale is higher than the minimum standard requirement at

0.50. At the same time, the deletion of any related items will lead to the decrease of Cronbach's α coefficient. Therefore, the measurement scale of the type of business model innovation type is of good internal consistency and all items in the scale should be retained.

Validity analysis

In order to test the validity of the questionnaire for the research question, the content validity and structure validity of the scale need to be further examined. In this paper, the maximum likelihood value is used in this paper to extract factors, and the maximum variance is used to perform factor analysis after rotation. The KMO value and Bartlett spherical test value of all items in the measurement scale of each variable in this paper are significantly different from 0, and thus it is suitable for factor analysis (as shown in Table 3). It is discovered in the factor analysis that all characteristic roots are greater than 1; the factor loading of all items is greater than the minimum requirement at 0.5 and two factors are identified in each case, indicating that there is no cross load. Therefore, the questionnaire is of high convergence validity and discriminant validity, so that all the items should be kept. At the same time, this paper refers to the method of Boyer and Verma (2000) avoid the systematic error caused by homology in the survey process. In this research, two executives in each enterprise are invited to answer the questionnaire A and B. Questionnaire A contains the design of variables of novelty-centred and efficiency-centred business model innovation while questionnaire B contains the design of variables of resource flexibility, coordination flexibility and corporate performance to avoid the risk caused by systematic errors as much as possible.

Correlation analysis

The correlation between various variables is shown in Table 4. There is a significant correlation between segmentation variables of strategic flexibility, business model

Table 3. Factor analysis of items in the scale of strategic flexibility, business model innovation, and corporate performance scale items (N = 197).

	Factor loading			Factor loading			Factor loading	
Items of strategic flexibility	Factor 1	Factor 2	Items of business model innovation	Factor 1	Factor 2	Items of corporate performance	Factor 1	Factor 2
RF1	.150	.806	EBMI1	.168	.719	FP1	.409	.672
RF2	−.102	.816	EBMI2	.146	.778	FP2	.241	.768
RF3	.118	.764	EBMI3	.096	.744	FP3	.167	.771
RF4	.452	.612	EBMI4	.138	.763	FP4	.245	.770
RF5	.428	.618	EBMI5	−.115	.765	FP5	.260	.749
CF1	.750	.258	NBMI1	.762	.252	MP1	.797	.187
CF2	.817	.057	NBMI2	.813	.042	MP2	.862	.234
CF3	.849	.044	NBMI3	.798	.058	MP3	.837	.275
CF4	.787	.127	NBMI4	.815	.070	MP4	.761	.277
CF5	.757	.183	NBMI5	.826	.065	MP5	.640	.409
KMO	0.811		KMO	0.839		KMO	0.874	
Bartlett	974.139		Bartlett	792.763		Bartlett	1122.906	
Cumulative variance change of explanatory variables	63.534%		Cumulative variance change of explanatory variables	62.389%		Cumulative variance change of explanatory variables	66.455%	

Table 4. Correlation between variables (N = 197).

Variables	1	2	3	4	5	6	7	8	9	10
1 Enterprise age	1									
2 Number of employees	.575***	1								
3 Nature of property rights	−.163*	−.093	1							
4 Industry	−.183**	−.050	.019	1						
5 Income scale	.492***	.679***	−.011	−.005	1					
6.Efficiency-centred BMI	−.082	−.175*	−.103	.048	−.242***	1				
7Novelty-centred BMI	−.141*	−.089	.085	.115	−.093	.232**	1			
8 Financial performance FP	−.122	−.003	.061	.177*	.080	.419***	.311***	1		
9 Market performance MP	−.198**	−.074	.248***	.117	.019	.189**	.657***	.621***	1	
10 Resource flexibility RF	−.151*	−.127	.052	.200**	−.070	.596***	.243***	.431***	.206**	1
11 Coordination flexibility CF	−.237***	−.131	.347***	.135	−.026	.207**	.732***	.367***	.681***	.426***

Note: ***$p < 0.001$, **$p < 0.01$, *$p < 0.05$ (two-tailed)

innovation and corporate performance. Specifically, there is significant positive correlation between resource flexibility in the strategic flexibility and efficiency-centred business model innovation ($R = 0.596$, $p < 0.01$) and there is significant positive correlation between coordination flexibility and novelty-centred business model innovation ($R = 0.732$, $p < 0.01$); there is significant positive correlation between resource flexibility in strategic flexibility and financial performance ($R = 0.431$, $p < 0.01$) and there is significant positive correlation between coordination flexibility and market performance ($R = 0.681$, $p < 0.01$); there is significant positive correlation between efficiency-centred business model innovation and corporate financial performance ($R = 0.419$, $p < 0.01$) and there is significant positive correlation between novelty-centred business model innovation and corporate market performance ($R = 0.657$, $p < 0.01$). This shows that the preliminary hypotheses in this paper have been initially verified, and the hierarchical regression analysis is used for further verification.

Hypothesis testing

Test results of the relationship between strategic flexibility and business model innovation on enterprise performance (H1-H4)

On the basis of correlation analysis, that is, there is a significant positive correlation between strategic flexibility (resource flexibility and coordination flexibility) and enterprise performance (market performance and financial performance), the main research hypothesis H1a-H2b proposed in this paper is further analysed based on structural equation model. In this paper, stata15.0 software is used to test the above hypotheses by constructing structural equation model. Firstly, in order to test whether resource flexibility and coordination flexibility have a significant positive impact on financial performance and market performance of enterprises (H1a-H1b), it can be seen from the results in Table 5 that resource flexibility has significant positive impact on financial performance ($\gamma = 0.558$, $P < 0.01$) and market performance ($\gamma = 0.319$, $P < 0.01$), Coordination flexibility has significant positive effects on financial performance ($\gamma = 0.510$, $P < 0.01$) and market performance ($\gamma = 0.809$, $P < 0.01$), Therefore, from the regression results of independent variable (strategic flexibility) to dependent variable (enterprise performance), the research hypotheses H1a, H1b, H2a, H2b proposed in this paper are initially supported by empirical results, which shows that strategic flexibility, as a resource base of an organization, can obtain and integrate resources with high flexibility. On the other hand, coordination flexibility in strategic flexibility, as a kind of

Table 5. Results of hypothesis test.

Path	Estimate (γ)	P vaule	Research hypothesis	Test results
Resource flexibility → Financial performance	0.558	0.000	H1a	Supported
Resource flexibility → Market performance	0.319	0.000	H1b	Supported
Coordination flexibility → Financial performance	0.510	0.000	H2a	Supported
Coordination flexibility →market performance	0.809	0.000	H2b	Supported
Efficiency-centred BMI → Financial performance	0.546	0.000	H3a	Supported
Efficiency-centred BMI → Financial performance	0.292	0.000	H3b	Supported
Novelty-centred BMI → Financial performance	0.455	0.000	H4a	Supported
Novelty-centred BMI→ Market performance	0.786	0.000	H4b	Supported

***p < 0.001 (two-tailed), **p < 0.01(two-tailed), *p < 0.05 (two-tailed)

dynamic ability of organization, can quickly identify and develop market opportunities in the rapidly changing market environment and improve the market competitive advantage of enterprises.

Furthermore, this paper further tests the relationship between business model innovation and enterprise performance. Based on the path coefficient analysis results of structural equation model, that is, in the two dimensions of BMI, whether efficiency-centred BMI and Novelty-centred BMI affect enterprise financial performance and market performance. From the results of Table 3, it can be seen that efficiency-centred BMI innovation has significant positive impact on financial performance ($\gamma = 0.546$, $P < 0.01$) and market performance ($\gamma = 0.292$, $P < 0.01$). Novelty-centred BMI has significant positive impact on financial performance ($\gamma = 0.455$, $P < 0.01$) and market performance ($\gamma = 0.786$, $P < 0.01$), Therefore, from the regression results of mediating variable (business model innovation) to dependent variable (enterprise performance), the research hypotheses of H3a, H3b, H4a, H4b proposed in this paper are initially supported by empirical results.

Mediating effect test (H5-H8)

Existing studies have shown that SEM is a suitable method to test the mediating effect (Cheung and Lau 2008). Thus, this study uses bootstrap method to analyse the mediating role of entrepreneurial self-efficacy in the model. The bootstrap method can effectively reduce the first kind of errors in the process of use, especially suitable for the mediating effect test of empirical research with small sample size. In this study, bootstrap was used to randomly select 5000 samples and 95% confidence interval. The maximum likelihood method was used for calculation. The calculation results are shown in Table 4.

It can be found from Table 4 that in the path of 'resource flexibility→efficiency-centred BMI→enterprise financial performance', the 95% confidence interval of indirect effect does not include 0, and the indirect effect is 0.329, which is significant ($P < 0.05$). Therefore, the intermediary effect exists in the path, indicating that at the same time, in the path of 'coordination flexibility→'efficiency-centred BMI→enterprise financial performance", the 95% confidence interval of indirect effect does not include 0, the indirect effect is – 0.087, and the 90% confidence interval of indirect effect does not contain 0, which is significant ($P < 0.10$), which indicates that the efficiency-centred BMI plays a partial mediating role between the coordination flexibility and financial performance. Furthermore, the paper studies the mediating role of efficiency-centred BMI between the strategy flexibility and enterprise market innovation. In the path of 'resource flexibility→efficiency-centered BMI→enterprise market performance', the 95% confidence interval of indirect effect does not include 0, and the indirect effect is 0.39, which is significant ($P < 0.05$). In the path of 'coordination flexibility → efficiency-centered BMI → enterprise market performance', the 95% confidence interval of indirect effect contains 0, and the indirect effect is 0.39, and it is not significant ($P > 0.05$). Therefore, the mediating effect t does not exist in the path, that is, the efficiency-centred BMI fails to produce mediating effect between the coordination flexibility and the enterprise market performance. Based on this, the mediating effect of efficiency-centred BMI shows that efficiency-centred BMI partially mediates the relationship between resource flexibility and financial performance, and hypothesis of H5a, H5b and H6a are supported by empirical results, while H6b is not supported by empirical results (As showed in Table 6).

Table 5. The mediating effect of business model innovation between strategic flexibility and firm performance.

Path	Indirect effect	95% confidence interval		P value	Research hypothesis	Test results
		Lower	Upper			
Resource flexibility →Efficiency-centred BMI → Financial performance	0.329	0.049	0.608	0.021	H5a	supported
Coordination flexibility →Efficiency-centred BMI → Financial performance	−0.087	−1.875	0.012	0.087	H5b	supported
Resource flexibility →Efficiency-centred BMI → Market performance	0.379	0.079	0.679	0.013	H6a	Supported
Coordination flexibility →Efficiency-centred BMI → Market performance	−0.102	−0.224	0.196	0.100	H6b	Unsupported
Resource flexibility →Novelty-centred BMI → Financial performance	−0.038	−0.114	0.038	0.326	H7a	Unsupported
Coordination flexibility →Novelty-centred BMI → Financial performance	0.207	−0.150	0.563	0.256	H7b	Unsupported
Resource flexibility →Novelty-centred BMI → Market performance	−0.045	−0.104	0.013	0.127	H8a	Unsupported
Coordination flexibility →Novelty-centred BMI → Market performance	0.249	−0.020	0.517	0.070	H8b	Supported

In the results of testing the mediating effect of Novelty-centred BMI between enterprise strategic flexibility and enterprise financial performance, the 95% confidence interval of indirect effect includes 0 in the path of 'resource flexibility→novelty-centred BMI→ enterprise financial performance', which fails to pass the significance test ($P > 0.1$). Therefore, there is no intermediary effect in the path, which indicates that Novelty-centred BMI has no intermediary effect. At the same time, in the path of 'coordination flexibility→novelty-centred BMI→enterprise financial performance', the 95% confidence interval of indirect effect contains 0, which fails to pass the significance test ($P > 0.1$), which indicates that Novelty-centred BMI fails to play an mediating role between coordination flexibility and financial performance. Furthermore, the mediating effect of Novelty-centred BMI on the relationship between strategic flexibility and enterprise market performance is investigated. In the path of 'resource flexibility →novelty-centred BMI→enterprise market performance', the 95% confidence interval of indirect effect contains 0, which fails to pass the significant test ($P > 0.1$). Therefore, the intermediary effect in the path does not exist, indicating that the Novelty-centred BMI fails to play a mediating role between resource flexibility and enterprise market performance. In the path of 'coordination flexibility→novelty-centred BMI→enterprise market performance', the 95% confidence interval of indirect effect does not include 0, and the indirect effect is – 0.087, which is significant ($P < 0.05$) . Based on these results, the mediating effect results of Novelty-centred BMIs show that the research hypothesis of H8b is supported, while the hypotheses of H7a, H7b and H8a are not supported by the empirical results.

Robustness test

In order to further ensure the robustness of this study, this paper uses two methods to analyse the robustness of this paper. Firstly, the items of resource flexibility and coordination flexibility are merged to form strategic flexibility, the items of efficient business

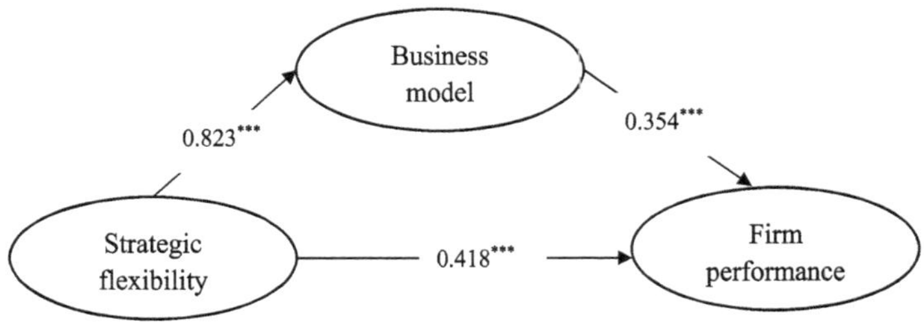

Figure 2. The mediating effect of business model innovation on the relationship between strategic flexibility and firm performance.

model innovation and novel business model innovation are merged to form business model innovation, and the items of enterprise financial performance and enterprise market performance are merged into enterprise performance, and further based on structural equation model. The mediating effect of business model innovation on the relationship between strategic flexibility and enterprise performance is examined, as shown in Figure 2. The test results show that strategic flexibility has a significant positive impact on business model innovation ($\beta = 0.823$, $P < 0.001$), and strategic flexibility has a significant positive impact on enterprise performance ($\beta = 0.418$, $P < 0.001$). In the path of 'resource flexibility → efficient business model innovation → enterprise market performance', the 95% confidence interval of indirect effect does not include 0, and the indirect effect is 0.291, which is significant ($P < 0.05$). Therefore, the intermediary effect exists in the path, indicating that business model innovation has an mediating effect between strategic flexibility and enterprise performance. In the global dynamic competition environment based on digitalization, business model innovation, as an internal mechanism of enterprise strategic flexibility affecting enterprise performance, has become an effective mechanism of enterprise capability acting on enterprise performance in the digital era.

The second robust method is that we further follow the research steps of hierarchical regression analysis proposed by Baron and Kenny (1986), the research hypotheses of H1a, H1b, H2a and H2b are initially supported by the empirical results. And from the regression results of mediating variable (BMI) to dependent variable (Enterprise performance), the research hypotheses of H3a, H3b, H4a, H4b proposed in this paper are initially supported by empirical results. Finally, this paper constructs four models to test empirically the mediating role of efficiency-centred BMI and novelty-centred BMI innovation between strategic flexibility and enterprise performance, and the research hypothesis of H5a-H5b proposed in this paper is relatively stable. Based on these, the above conclusions further ensure the robustness of the research conclusions in this paper.

Discussion

Theoretical implication

This study makes an important contribution to the literature of dynamic capability and business model innovation. First of all, our research contributes to the theoretical mechanism of dynamic capabilities on enterprise performance. Since Teece, Pisano, and Shuen (1997) put forward the theory of dynamic capabilities, dynamic capabilities emphasize the reallocation and recombination of resources to realize the value creation of enterprises, and strategic flexibility is regarded as an important dynamic capability of enterprises. However, the internal mechanism of strategic flexibility on enterprise performance is still unclear, especially in the digital era, facing the rapid development of digital information technology, the frequency of business model innovation is accelerating, and the ability basis of driving enterprises to continuously carry out business model innovation is still the dynamic ability of enterprises. Therefore, one of our important theoretical contributions is to open the 'black box' of strategic flexibility on enterprise performance in the digital era from the perspective of business model innovation, and find a new theoretical mechanism of strategic flexibility acting on enterprise performance.

Secondly, our research contributes to the study of strategic flexibility. Sanchez (1997) divides strategic flexibility into resource flexibility and coordination flexibility. According to the theory of strategic flexibility, the dynamic reconfiguration of resources depends on the flexibility of resources and the coordination flexibility of organizational processes. Resource flexibility depends on the use scope of existing resources, the cost of resource use conversion and the time required for resource use conversion, and coordination flexibility is the ability of an enterprise to reorganize internal and external resources and establish a new resource chain to adapt to environmental uncertainty. Therefore, in the digital era, the traditional organizational operation process and organizational resource allocation mode are constantly changing, and the two different types of strategic flexibility have different effects on enterprises facing the uncertainty in the digital era. Based on this, the second important theoretical contribution of this paper is to find the collaborative matching between strategic flexibility type and the type of business model innovation, that is, resource flexibility can promote financial performance and market performance through novelty-centred business model innovation and efficiency-centred business model innovation, but coordination flexibility can only promote enterprise market performance through novelty-centred business model innovation. The matching conduction model of 'strategic flexibility-business model innovation -enterprise performance' is established.

Finally, our research contributes to the literature of business model innovation in the digital age. On the Internet environment based on digital information technology, business model design and innovation can realize the change of enterprise resources, process, cost and income through value proposition, value capture, value creation, value distribution and value sharing (Amit and Zott 2001; Zott and Amit 2015). However, the types of performance pursued by different enterprises are heterogeneous(Chin et al. 2020),both efficiency-centred business model innovation and novelty-centred business model innovation exert a significant positive impact on corporate financial performance and market performance. Specifically, the impact of efficiency-centred business model innovation on corporate financial performance is more prominent while the impact of novelty-centred business model innovation on market performance is more prominent, which indicates that the design of efficiency-centred business model promotes corporate financial performance and market performance by reducing the information asymmetry, complexity and uncertainty between trading partners; and the design of novelty-centred business model realizes new value creation and value acquisition through establishing new value creation networks or business systems based on new value propositions, thus promoting corporate financial performance and market performance.

Based on this, this study enriches the value effect of business model innovation types in digital age.

Practical implications

Our findings provide important practical implications for enterprises in the Asia Pacific region, where the digital process is accelerating (Rowley and Oh, 2020). Based on the empirical conclusions in this paper, for enterprises in transition economies in the Asia-Pacific region, there are three aspects of management enlightenment. Firstly, corporate strategic flexibility is a dynamic capability of organizations to cope with the complex and dynamic environment. Enterprises need to effectively recognize their strategic flexibility level enterprise in the strategic innovation process to avoid the negative impact brought by capacity rigidity in the strategic reform process. What's more, the impact of resource flexibility on corporate financial performance is more prominent while the impact of coordination flexibility on corporate market performance is more prominent. Therefore, enterprises should attach great significance to the heterogeneous impact of strategic flexibility on corporate financial performance and market performance (Wang et al., 2020).

Secondly, when confronting the highly dynamic business environment, especially in the digital context, the business model innovation process has become highly dynamic and diverse. In the digital era, the strategic competitive advantage of enterprises is not limited to the strategic innovation of products or service markets, but also the innovation of their business models, which is considered to be an innovative tool for enterprises to improve their performance and gain the competitive advantage in the digital era. However, there are many types of business model innovation and different types of business model innovation can have a heterogeneous impact on corporate performance. Finally, business model innovation is an effective and feasible way in the context of global competition, which can be used as an intermediate link between corporate capability and performance.

Limitations and future research

This paper has the following limitations. The first is the number and coverage of samples, the second is that this research uses the questionnaire as the main method for data acquisition and only one questionnaire is distributed for each enterprise, and the dimension of main variables such as business model innovation should be further refined so the scope of business model innovation should be expanded to all participants in subsequent studies, including other type of business model innovation. The second is that the business model innovation is a network transaction structure that crosses the boundary of enterprises or industries, which not only affects dominant enterprises, but all stakeholders as well, so the social performance should be future test in future study. Finally, the impact of different business models and innovation types on corporate performance varies in time cycle, intensity and velocity, the conclusion of this paper needs to verify through the acquisition and application of time series or panel data.

Conclusions

In the digital era, business model innovation is an important innovation way for enterprises to obtain financial performance and market performance by establishing a new activity system to achieve value creation and value acquisition. This study shows that the corporate strategic flexibility has a significant positive impact on its financial performance and market performance. The more significant the corporate resource flexibility and coordination flexibility, the stronger its business model innovation ability, and business model innovation has a significant positive impact on corporate financial performance and market performance. Also, the impact of efficiency-centred business model innovation on corporate financial performance is more prominent, and the impact of novelty-centred business model innovation on corporate market performance is more prominent. And efficiency-centred business model innovation plays a partial mediating role between strategic flexibility (resource flexibility and coordination flexibility) and corporate financial performance, but novelty-centred business model innovation plays a fully mediating role between resource flexibility and corporate market performance, and a partial mediating role between coordination flexibility and corporate market performance.

Disclosure statement

No potential conflict of interest was reported by the authors.

Funding

The present study was Sponsored by Key projects of National Social Science Foundation (18AGL011) to the first author.

References

Aaker, D. A., and B. Mascarenhas. 1984. "The Need for Strategic Flexibility." *The Journal of Business Strategy* 5 (2): 74. doi:10.1108/eb039060.

Amit, R., and C. Zott. 2001. "Value Creation in E-Business". *Strategic Management Journal* 22 (6–7): 493–520. doi:10.1002/smj.187.

Baron, R. M., and D. A. Kenny. 1986. "The Moderator-Mediator Variable Distinction in Social Psychological Research: Conceptual, Strategic and Statistical Considerations." *Journal of Personality and Social Psychology* 51: 1177–1182. doi:10.1037/0022–3514.51.6.1173.

Berends, H., A. Smits, I. Reymen, and K. Podoynitsyna. 2016. "Learning while (Re)configuring: Business Model Innovation Processes in Established Firms." *Strategic Organization* 14 (3): 181–219. doi:10.1177/1476127016632758.

Bock, A. J., T. Opsahl, G. George, and D. M. Gann. 2012. "The Effects of Culture and Structure on Strategic Flexibility during Business Model Innovation." *Journal of Management Studies* 49 (2): 279–305. doi:10.1111/j.1467-6486.2011.01030.x.

Boyer, K. K., and R. Verma. 2000. "Multiple Raters in Survey-based Operations Management Research: A Review and Tutorial." *Production and Operations Management* 9 (2): 128–140. doi:10.1111/j.1937-5956.2000.tb00329.x.

Brettel, M., S. Strese, and T. C. Flatten. 2012. "Improving the Performance of Business Models with Relationship Marketing Efforts–An Entrepreneurial Perspective." *European Management Journal* 30(2): 85–98. doi:10.1016/j.emj.2011.11.003.

Brozovic, D. 2016. "Strategic Flexibility: A Review of the Literature." *International Journal of Management Reviews* 20 (1): 3–31. doi:10.1111/ijmr.12111.

Brush, C. G., P. A. Vanderwerf. 1992. "A Comparison of Methods and Sources for Obtaining Estimates of New Venture Performance." *Journal of Business Venturing* 17 (2): 157-170. doi:10.1016/0883-9026(92)90010–O.

Chesbrough, H., and R. S. Rosenbloom. 2002. "The Role of the Business Model in Capturing Value from Innovation: Evidence from Xerox Corporation's Technology Spin-off Companies." *Industrial and Corporate Change* 11 (3): 529–555. doi:10.1093/icc/11.3.529.

Cheung, G. W., and R. S. Lau. 2008. "Testing Mediation and Suppression Effects of Latent Variables: Bootstrapping with Structural Equation Models." *Organizational Research Methods* 11 (2): 296–325. doi:10.1177/1094428107300343.

Chin, T., Y. Shi, C. Rowley, and J. Meng. 2020. "Confucian Business Model Canvas in the Asia Pacific: A Yin-yang Harmony Cognition to Value Creation and Innovation." *Asia Pacific Business Review* 3: 1–17. doi:10.1080/13602381.2020.1795481.

Chin, T., Y. Yang, P. Zhang, X. Yu, and L. Cao. 2019. "Co-creation of Social Innovation: Corporate Universities as Innovative Strategies for Chinese Firms to Engage with Society." *Sustainability* 11: 1438. doi:10.3390/su11051438.

Clauss, T. 2016. "Measuring Business Model Innovation: Conceptualization, Scale Development, and Proof of Performance." *R&D Management* 47 (3): 385–403. doi:10.1111/radm.12186.

Demil, B., and X. Lecocq. 2010. "Business Model Evolution: In Search of Dynamic Consistency." *Long Range Planning* 43 (2–3): 227–246. doi:10.1016/j.lrp.2010.02.004.

Demil, B., X. Lecocq, J. E. Ricart, and C. Zott. 2015. "Introduction to the SEJ Special Issue on Business Models: Business Models within the Domain of Strategic Entrepreneurship." *Strategic Entrepreneurship Journal* 9 (1): 1–11. doi:10.1002/sej.1194.

Foss, N. J., and T. Saebi. 2017. "Fifteen Years of Research on Business Model Innovation." *Journal of Management* 43 (1): 200–227. doi:10.1177/0149206316675927.

Grewal, R., J. M. Comer,and R. Mehta. 2001. "An Investigation into the Antecedents of Organizational Participation in Business-to-Business Electronic Markets." *Journal of Marketing* 65(3): 17–33. doi:10.1509/jmkg.65.3.17.18331.

Grewal, R., and P. Tansuhaj. 2001. "Building Organizational Capabilities for Managing Economic Crisis: The Role of Market Orientation and Strategic Flexibility." *Journal of Marketing* 65 (2): 67–80. doi:10.1509/jmkg.65.2.67.18259.

Guo, H., J. Tang, Z. Su, and J. A. Katz. 2017. "Opportunity Recognition and SME Performance: The Mediating Effect of Business Model Innovation." *R&D Management* 47 (3): 431–442. doi:10.1111/radm.12219.

Guo, H., and Z. Cao. 2014. "Strategic Flexibility and SME Performance in an Emerging Economy." *Journal of Organizational Change Management* 27: 273–298. doi:10.1108/JOCM-11-2012-0177.

Hambrick, D. C., and P. A. Mason. 1984. "Upper Echelons: The Organization as a Reflection of Its Top Managers." *Academy of Management Review* 9 (2): 193–206. doi:10.5465/amr.1984.4277628.

Herhausen, D., R. E. Morgan, D. Brozović, and H. W. Volberda. 2020. "Re-examining Strategic Flexibility: A Meta-Analysis of Its Antecedents, Consequences and Contingencies." *British Journal of Management*. in press. doi:10.1111/1467-8551.12413.

Li, J., L. Zhou, X. Zhang, Z. Chen, and F. Tian. 2018. "Technological Configuration Capability, Strategic Flexibility, and Organizational Performance in Chinese High-Tech Organizations." *Sustainability* 10 (5): 1665. doi:10.3390/su10051665.

Loon, M., and R. Chik. 2019. "Efficiency-centered, Innovation-enabling Business Models of High Tech SMEs: Evidence from Hong Kong." *Asia Pacific Journal of Management* 36 (1): 87–111. doi:10.1007/s10490-017-9558-4.

Majid, A., M. Yasir, M. Yasir, and Z. Yousaf. 2020. "Network Capability and Strategic Performance in SMEs: The Role of Strategic Flexibility and Organizational Ambidexterity." *Eurasian Business Review*. in press. doi:10.1007/s40821-020-00165-7.

Miroshnychenko, I., A. Strobl, K. Matzler, and A. De Massis. 2020. "Absorptive Capacity, Strategic Flexibility, and Business Model Innovation: Empirical Evidence from Italian SMEs." *Journal of Business Research*. in press. doi:10.1016/j.jbusres.2020.02.015.

Nadkarni, S., and P. O. L. Herrmann. 2010. "CEO Personality, Strategic Flexibility, and Firm Performance: The Case of the Indian Business Process Outsourcing Industry." *Academy of Management Journal* 53 (5): 1050–1073. doi:10.5465/amj.2010.54533196.

Nadkarni, S., and V. K. Narayanan. 2007. "Strategic Schemas, Strategic Flexibility, and Firm Performance: The Moderating Role of Industry Clockspeed." *Strategic Management Journal* 28 (3): 243–270. doi:10.1002/smj.576.

Nair, S., and T. Blomquist. 2020. "Business Model Design in the Case of Complex Innovations: A Conceptual Model." *Technology Analysis and Strategic Management* 1–12. in press. doi:10.1080/09537325.2020.1805103.

Nylén, D., and J. Holmström. 2015. "Digital Innovation Strategy: A Framework for Diagnosing and Improving Digital Product and Service Innovation." *Business Horizons* 58 (1): 57–67. doi:10.1016/j.bushor.2014.09.001.

Richardson J .2008. "The Business Model: an Integrative FrameWork for Strategy Execution." *Strategic Change* 17 (5-6): 133–144. doi:10.1002/jsc.821.

Rowley, C., and I. Oh. 2020. "Trends in Chinese Management and Business: Change, Confucianism, Leadership, Knowledge & Innovation." *Asia Pacific Business Review* 26 (1): 1–8. doi:10.1080/13602381.2019.1698707.

Sanchez, R. 1995. "Strategic Flexibility in Product Competition." *Strategic Management Journal* 16 (S1): 135–159. doi:10.1002/smj.4250160921.

Sanchez, R. 1997. "Preparing for an Uncertain Future : Managing Organizations for Strategic Flexibility." *International Studies of Management Organization* 27(2): 71–94. doi:10.1080/00208825.1997.11656708

Schlegelmilch, B. B., A. Diamantopoulos, and P. Kreuz. 2003. "Strategic Innovation: The Construct, Its Drivers and Its Strategic Outcomes." *Journal of Strategic Marketing* 11 (2): 117–132. doi:10.1080/0965254032000102948.

Shimizu, K., and M. A. Hitt. 2004. "Strategic Flexibility: Organizational preparedness to reverse ineffective strategic decisions". *Academy of Management Executive* 18 (4): 44–58. doi:10.5465/ame.2004.15268683.

Spieth, P., S. M. Laudien, and S. Meer. 2020. "Business Model Innovation in Strategic Alliances: A Multi-layer Perspective." *R&D Management* 1–16. in press. doi:10.1111/radm.12410.

Teece, D. J. 2010. "Business Models, Business Strategy and Innovation." *Long Range Planning* 43 (2–3): 172–194. doi:10.1016/j.lrp.2009.07.003.

Teece, D. J. 2018. "Business Models and Dynamic Capabilities." *Long Range Planning* 51 (1): 40–49. doi:10.1016/j.lrp.2017.06.007.

Teece, D. J., G. Pisano, and A. Shuen. 1997. "Dynamic Capabilities and Strategic Management." *Strategic Management Journal* 18 (7): 509–533. doi:10.1002/(SICI)1097-0266(199708)18.

Tukker, A. 2004. "Eight Types of Product–service System: Eight Ways to Sustainability? Experiences from SusProNet." *Business Strategy and the Environment* 13 (4): 246–260. doi:10.1002/bse.414.

Tukker, A., and U. Tischner. 2006. *New Business for Old Europe. Product Services, Sustainability and Competitiveness*. Sheffield, UK: Greenleaf Publishing .

Wang, C. H., T. Chin, and J. H. Lin. 2020. "Openness and Firm Innovation Performance: The Moderating Effect of Ambidextrous Knowledge Search Strategy." *Journal of Knowledge Management* 24 (2): 301–323. doi:10.1108/JKM-04-2019-0198.

Wei, Z., D. Yang, B. Sun, and M. Gu. 2014. "The Fit between Technological Innovation and Business Model Design for Firm Growth: Evidence from China." *R&D Management* 44 (3): 288–305. doi:10.1111/radm.12069.

Zhou, K. Z., and F. Wu. 2010. "Technological Capability, Strategic Flexibility, and Product Innovation." *Strategic Management Journal* 31 (5): 547–561. doi:10.1002/smj.830.

Zott, C. and R. Amit. 2015. Business Model Innovation: Toward a Process Perspective. In *The Oxford Handbook of Creativity, Innovation, and Entrepreneurship*, edited by C. E. Shalley, M. A. Hitt, & J. Zhou, 395–406. Oxford University Press.

Zott, C., and R. Amit. 2007. "Business Model Design and the Performance of Entrepreneurial Firms." *Organization Science* 18 (2): 181–199. doi:10.1287/orsc.1060.0232.

Zott, C., and R. Amit. 2008. "The Fit between Product Market Strategy and Business Model: Implications for Firm Performance." *Strategic Management Journal* 29 (1): 1–26. doi:10.1002/smj.642.

Index

For Product Safety Concerns and Information please contact our EU
representative GPSR@taylorandfrancis.com
Taylor & Francis Verlag GmbH, Kaufingerstraße 24, 80331 München, Germany

www.ingramcontent.com/pod-product-compliance
Ingram Content Group UK Ltd.
Pitfield, Milton Keynes, MK11 3LW, UK
UKHW052211190926
475702UK00006B/971

* 9 7 8 1 0 3 2 4 1 6 3 3 5 *